A History of
Glasgow's
Byres Road

Barclay Price

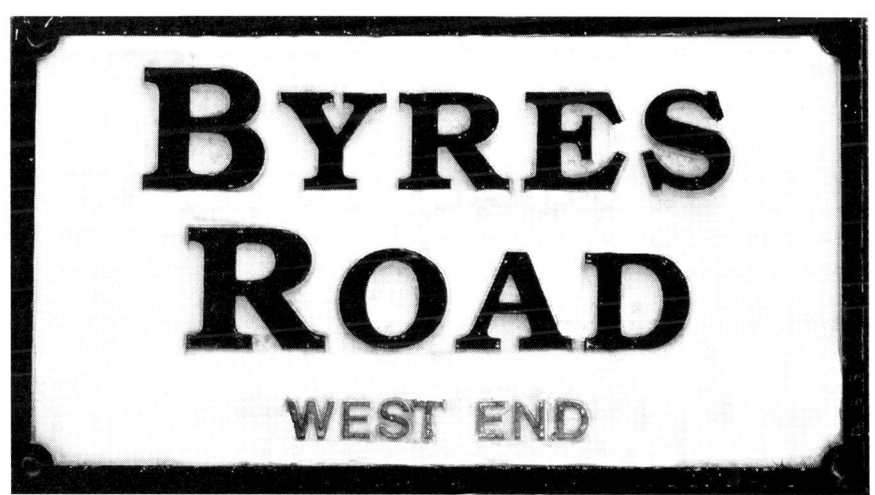

Stenlake Publishing Ltd

© 2024 Barclay Price
First Published in the United Kingdom, 2024
Stenlake Publishing Limited
54-58 Mill Square, Catrine, KA5 6RD
www.stenlake.co.uk

ISBN 978-1-84033-979-6

Printed by
Blissetts, Unit E1-E8 Shield Drive,
West Cross Ind Pk, Brentford, TW8 9EX

> With Byres Road at its spine and the University and the BBC like pit bings at either end, the old W2 remains imprinted on my memory, part grimy sepia and part autumnal; umber and ochre.
>
> *Distances: A Personal Evocation of People and Places (2001)*
> by Stewart Conn

Dowanhill Observatory around 1900. This was Glasgow University's third observatory and was established on the summit of Horslethill in 1836, at the time far from the edge of Glasgow. Agreement was reached with the owners of the surrounding land that no tall buildings or smoke emiting furnaces would be erected. However, by the end of the 19th century the site was surrounded by villas and terraces. After the First World War the observatory was allowed to decline. By the time Ludwig Becker, Regius Professor of Astronomy, retired in 1935 it was mostly used for teaching and little observation was carried out. A few years later the University sold the site and much of the equipment, leaving only the street name as an indication of its existence.

Lewis Hutton collection

Front cover: Looking south along Byres Road from the junction with Great George Street in the late 1960s.

Guthrie Hutton

Contents

Looking south along Byres Road from the junction with Creswell Street in the late 1960s.   *Guthrie Hutton*

The mansion house at the Byres of Partick thought to be of similar age to the 1680 house beside it. In the late 1700s the mansion was owned by Glasgow banker Broady Wylie. On the opposite, east, side of Byres Road there was the Colquhoun Well. This engraving was included in the *Notes and Reminiscences Relating to Partick* by James Napier, 1874 and sketched by D. Mackinlay.
Lewis Hutton collection

Introduction

In his 1854 book, *Rambles round Glasgow*, Hugh MacDonald, a journalist and poet, wrote:

> Leaving Partick by what is called the Byres Road, we now proceed, in a northerly direction, for a distance of about a mile, during which nothing calling for special remark comes within our observation, until we arrive at the Great Western Road, immediately in front of the entrance to the Botanic Gardens.

It is impossible to think that anyone enjoying the equivalent ramble today could make a similar observation, and this book explores Byres Road's development from unremarkable byway to today's notable thoroughfare.

There are those who claim that everything which happens in Glasgow happens first in Byres Road, though others are more restrained, merely contending that the people who make things happen in the city tend to start talking about it in a Byres Road pub or café. This conceit the poet and dramatist, Liz Lochhead jocularly pokes fun at in her 1991 book, *Bagpipe Muzak*:

> And it's all go (again) the Devolution debate and pro… pro… proportional representation.
> Over pasta and pesto in a Byres Road bistro, Scotland Declares hersel' a nation.

While not everything may happen in Byres Road, this account shows that Byres Road has been home to many significant events, and countless plans have indeed been hatched in its cafes and pubs.

Henry Brougham Morton, 1971

Henry Brougham Morton collection

Aspects of Byres Road's history have been included in two richly illustrated books – *A Hillhead Album* by Henry Brougham Morton published in 1973 by The Hepburn Trust (sadly out of print) and *Along the Great Western Road* by Gordon Urquhart, published in 2000 by Stenlake Publishing (which is in print). Also out of print is a small book, *Byres Road* by John Robertson and Rachel Pateman published by The Glasgow File in 1987. However, there is a great deal more to recount.

Thousands of people have lived in Byres Road over the decades and this book can only include a few. To provide a flavour of the changing nature of residents, I chose to trace the occupants of flats in two closes: Nos. 85 and 313. These addresses were chosen at random, although one was selected from the Partick end and one from the Hillhead end, as the differing sizes of flats were more likely to portray the road's diversity of residents. It is an unfortunate fact that historical information on women is often much harder to come by. In records many are only designated as 'wife' or 'widow'; clearly failing to do justice to their significant role in caring for their families, often on limited resources, or other unrecorded achievements.

Thanks to the many people that have assisted with my research – directly and indirectly. Special thanks to

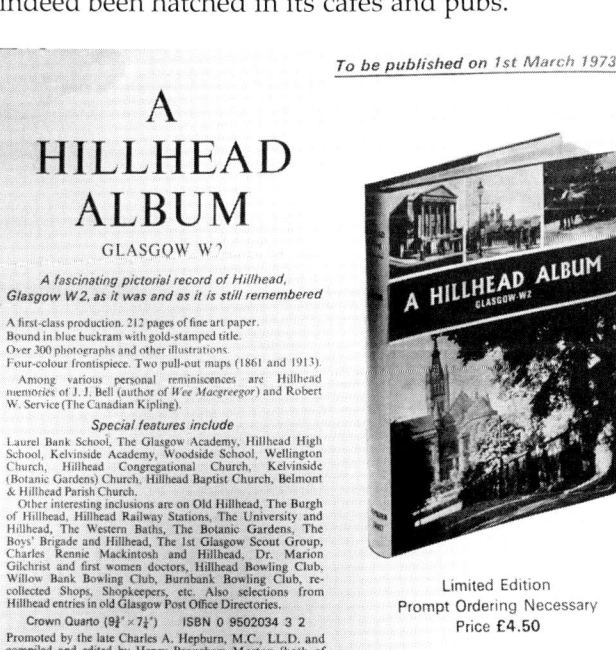

Flyer for *The Hillhead Album* by Henry Brougham Morton

Henry Brougham Morton collection

Joseph Price, c.1860. *Author's collection*

Roberta Doyle, Stewart Conn, Michael Dale, Fiona Dick, Alan Dimmick, Alasdair Gray's estate, Avril Paton, Richard Stenlake, Lewis Hutton, Gordon Urquhart, and Renato and Giuliana Zanotti. Also the staff at Glasgow City and University of Glasgow archives. I have trawled widely for images to illustrate Byres Road's history and in a few cases been unable to trace ownership of photographs. I apologise if I have inadvertently failed to give appropriate credit or breached a copyright. If so I hope the oversight will be forgiven for having been in good faith. For any such instances, to correct any mistakes, please get in touch with Stenlake Publishing.

I decided to write this book as for my first twenty-two years I lived in Ruthven Lane, in the house that was part of the livery stables that my great-grandfather, Joseph Price, built in 1870. His was one of the first businesses to open in the area and he chose well, for the business became a notable part of the history of Glasgow's West End. Growing up in Byres Road I trudged thousands of times up Great George Street on my way to Hillhead High School, bought gobstoppers and my weekly *Wizard for Boys* magazine at Murray's newsagent, saw the last tram rattle down the road, winched in the back row of the Grosvenor cinema, and so much more. However, this is Byres Road's history, not mine, so time to crack on, and begin at the beginning.

Barclay Price 2024

An engraving of an old house at Byres on the Castle Hill of Partick, which was not named after Partick Castle but for a large square house called The Castle at the north end of Byres.
Lewis Hutton collection

Chapter One

The Making of Byres Road

The old Byres Road, probably little more than a dirt track, left Partick village and bent away, roughly from where Byres Road and Church Street meet today, and proceeded to the snuff and paper mills on the River Kelvin at Gairbraid. Although sometimes referred to as 'The Roman Road', there is no evidence that it dated back to Roman times. A military map from the mid-18th century shows that it travelled through open land, passing Hyndland Farm and Balgray hamlet. On its right, as it left Partick village, roughly where Torness Street is today, was a small ancient hamlet, Byres of Partick, or Bishop's Byres; thus named as the cows belonging to the Bishops were kept there. The hamlet may also have been used by Highland drovers, as the area round Partick village was their final stopping off point as they walked their cattle to Glasgow's slaughterhouses. By the early 1800s the hamlet consisted of just a small row of buildings, sited on a path known as Byres Lane connecting Byres Road to Church Street. Two of the hamlet's buildings

Byres of Partick, engraving showing the buildings that were still in place around 1870.   *Lewis Hutton collection*

survived into the 1880s: a thatched cottage that had the date, 1680 incised into its lintel, and a two-storey house that once had been the country mansion of a Glasgow banker, Broady Wylie. Both were demolished to extend the Church Street school.

Partick village grew up around Dumbarton Road, an ancient route into Glasgow that crossed the River Kelvin by the Old Bridge, and was part of the lands of the Bishops of Glasgow, who summered at Partick Castle. There were flour mills at Partick since at least the 16th century, and by the 18th century weaving had been introduced, although in 1800 the population was still only about 1,500.

Around 1820, buildings began to be erected at the Partick Cross end of the old Byres Road. These were built by the Partick Building Society and consisted of two-storey tenements on the north east corner of Byres Road and Dumbarton Road, and similar tenements on the north-west side, off which ran two groups of small houses, Church Place and Wallace Place. These were collectively known as the Society Buildings and in 1867 were advertised for sale: 'These substantial tenements of shops, dwelling houses fronting Dumbarton Road, Wallace Place, Church Place and Byres Road, and known as the Society Buildings, Rental £463 yielding a large return. Reduced upset price £4,000.'

Partick East United Presbyterian Church was built in 1824, north of Church Place, with entrances from Church Place and Byres Road. Next to the church was Dowanvale House, which was entered from Byres Road. No building date has been found but it may be from around 1810. James Napier in his book *Notes and Reminiscences Relating to Partick* published in 1873 mentions a well at the house:

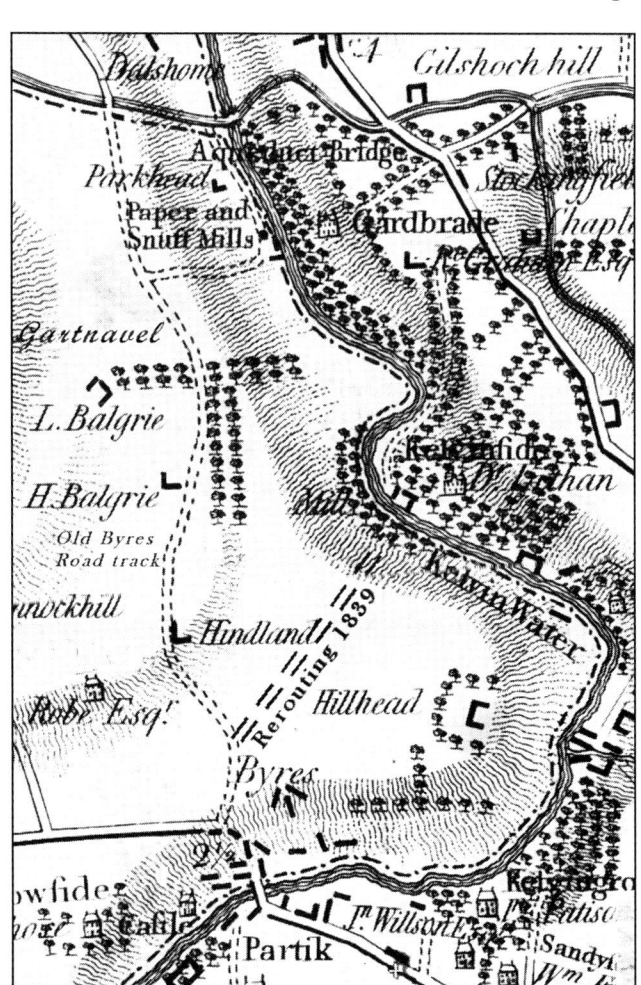

Military map of 1760 showing the original road and the rerouted road in 1839.

National Library of Scotland

At Dowanvale House is a dipping well, not very deep. This well was common and the water was of good

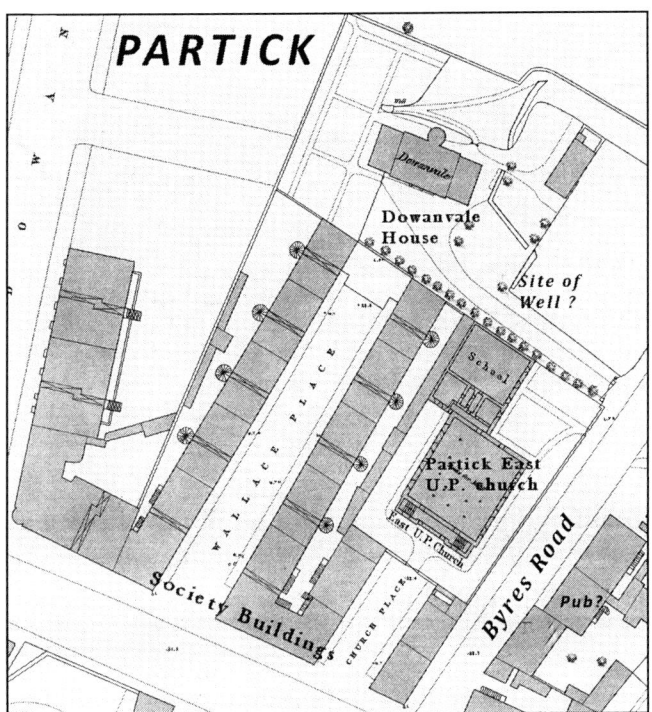

Top right: Partick East United Presbyterian Church, 1902.
Lewis Hutton collection

Right: Advert for sale of property at the Partick Cross end of Byres Road, 1833

Map of 1840 showing the buildings at the Partick Cross end of Byres Road. *National Library of Scotland*

BY ADJOURNMENT.
UPSET PRICES GREATLY REDUCED.
ELIGIBLE PROPERTY AT PARTICK FOR SALE.
To be sold, by public roup, within William Stuart's Sale-Rooms, No. 90, Argyll Street, Glasgow, on Wednesday the 21st day of August 1833, at One o'Clock Afternoon, under the powers of Sale contained in an Heritable bond,

THESE valuable SUBJECTS at PARTICK, belonging to the Partick Building Society, lying upon the north side of the Dumbarton Road, immediately to the west of the Road leading to the Byres of Partick, and adjoining to the United Secession Church there. These Subjects consist of various Tenements of Land, of Two Stories in height, which have been substantially built within these seven years, and are all occupied by good tenants.

The Subjects will be exposed either in whole, or in eight different lots, which will be pointed out to intending purchasers.

Apply to Mr. William Waddell, writer, 11, Miller Street; or to Dow & Couper, Writers, 49, Ingram Street, Glasgow, in the hands of the latter of whom the Title Deeds and Articles of Roup may be seen.

Glasgow, 1st August, 1833.

Dowanvale House, *c*.1890. *R. Ferguson*

quality. We understand that the well and the passage to it from the Byres Road is public property; at all events, all the old feuars of Hillhead ground have a right to the well. It is one of the few public rights not yet seized upon.

The first traced record of Dowanvale House is the marriage of Janet, daughter of James and Marion Stewart, to James Wilson, an ironmonger, that took place in the house in 1847. James Stewart was a retired tavern keeper, having previously run the Cossack Commercial Inn in Jamaica Street. The Stewarts also had three sons whose fate was less happy then their sister's. The eldest, Gabriel left home to become a sailor and the family lost contact with him. Andrew died in 1853 at Dowanvale House when only aged twenty-two and James, who a few years earlier had inherited Dowanvale when his father died, accidentally drowned in Loch Lomond in 1860, aged just twenty-five. Following his death, Marion moved away; the house was put on the market for £600, and sold for £800. It was bought by Thomas and Mary McWalter. He was a builder and erected stables and a workshop in the grounds. After his death in 1866 his wife and family lived on in the house, but the workshops and stable were leased to James Leggatt, a dairyman, who converted the workshop into a byre where he housed 35 cows. In 1871, one of the Dowanvale residents advertised: 'Goose found. By proving ownership and defraying expenses within three days will be given up, otherwise it will be sold.' Perhaps this was the pet goose that around this time was kept by Mr Petrie, a baker and confectioner. It was recounted that the goose wandered at will in and out his shop at No. 120 Dumbarton Road, just a few doors along from Byres Road. A few years later it went missing and Petrie hired a private detective to track it down, but the pet goose was never traced.

On the hill to the east of the old Byres Road stood Hillhead House, the residence of the Gibson family, who owned much of the neighbouring land. Part of the family's wealth came from extracting coal, stone

James Gibson of Hillhead by William Wallace.
University of Glasgow Archives

and clay for brick-making, and the area between the old Byres Road and Hillhead was littered with old workings. In 1828 an advert offered: 'all the bricks on the brickfield to the west of the Mansion House of Hillhead amounting to about 250,000 and the clay in the field, extending to about five acres for the purpose of making bricks.'

From the late 18th century, a number of wealthy Glaswegian merchants, most having made their fortunes from sugar and tobacco grown on Caribbean plantations worked by enslaved labour, began to buy land in the area and built country mansions and estates. One was James Buchanan who, in the early 1800s, built Dowanhill House on land through which the old Byres Road passed.

In 1802, James Gibson became the Laird of Hillhead when just two-years-old. In the early 1820s he began to develop and sell off portions of his estate for new housing: 'Various lots of Villa ground for sale, part of the lands of Hillhead, opposite Woodside, and beautifully situated on the banks of the river Kelvin.' This showed the potential for development of spacious suburbs to the west of the city, and to enable expansion an Act of Parliament in 1836 authorised the construction of the Great Western Road from St George's Cross to Anniesland.

VILLA GROUND FOR SALE.

To be sold, by public roup, within the Lyceum Rooms, Glasgow, upon Wednesday the 19th day of September next, at one o'clock P. M., if not previously disposed of by private bargain,

VARIOUS LOTS of VILLA GROUND, part of the LANDS of HILLHEAD, opposite Woodside, and beautifully situated upon the Banks of the river Kelvin.

For farther particulars apply to Mr. Gibson at Hillhead; to Mr. Reid, St. Andrew's Square; or to James Grieve, writer, Brunswick Place, in the latter of whose hands is a plan of the lands intended to be sold.

Advert for ground for sale, 1826

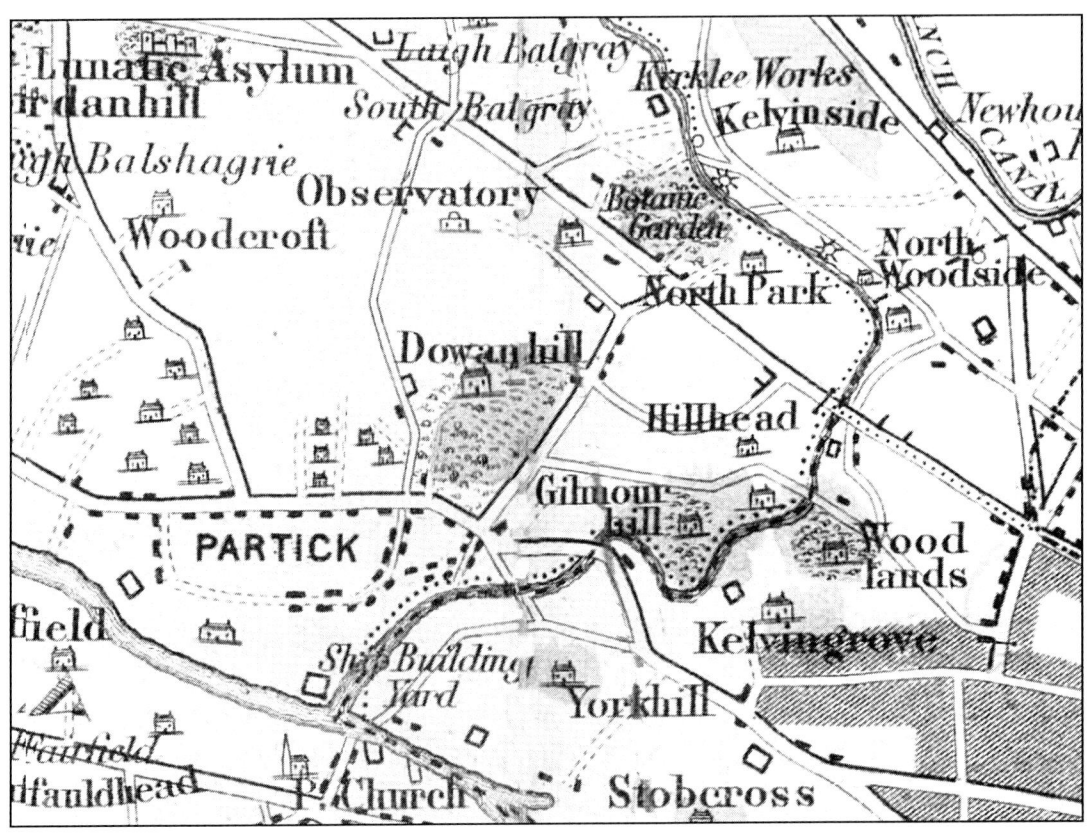

Map *c.* 1840s showing mansions and estates in the locality and new Byres Road.

National Library of Scotland

In 1839 land on Great Western Road was purchased to create the new Botanic Gardens. To encourage more people to move to the houses being built in the West End, a one-horse omnibus was introduced in 1847, running along Great Western Road from the city centre to the Botanic Gardens.

As Buchanan had closed off the section of the old road that passed through his new estate to general traffic, in spite of it having been a right of way in the past, it was decided to reroute Byres Road to connect with the new Great Western Road. In 1839, the section of the old road from Partick to the bend was retained, but widened and improved, and a new road constructed from there that ran in almost a straight line to meet Great Western Road across from the Botanic Gardens: the Byres Road that exists today. It was constructed as a turnpike with a toll chain at the Partick end, and those travelling up and down had to pay to travel it until the toll was discontinued in 1883. Part of the new road was named Victoria Street in honour of Queen Victoria but the name did not take: 'Attempts have been made to have this street called after Her Majesty, but the disloyal suburb rebels against "Victoria Street" and insists on keeping the old name, Byres Road, or Byres Road of Partick.' Up to 1900 it was mainly written as 'Byar's Road' – possibly due to the way people heard 'Byres' pronounced.

The first buildings erected on the new section of Byres Road were the Curlers Tavern and an adjoining house. The notion that the pub dates back to the 17th century is mistaken, as before 1839 the site would have been in the middle of fields. That it was built in the 1840s is evidenced by there being records of the Partick Curling Club meeting in the premises of Mr Sinclair, spirit dealer in Partick in 1842, and by 1849, after the club had created a rink in Hillhead, meeting in 'Mrs Sinclair's Curlers Tavern.' Thus, it seems certain that the Sinclairs built the Curlers in the mid-1840s and moved their business from Partick. The new site was doubly perfect: the curlers could celebrate victories or bemoan losses, while carters travelling up and down the new turnpike road could stop for refreshment.

The new Byres Road acted as a spine for further building in the locality. In 1844 advertised for sale was:

> That lot of ground lying on the east side of Hillhead Street, and containing 8,944 square yards bounded on the west by said street, the road leading from Partick on the south, a contemplated street on the east, and on the north the plot of ground sold to Andrew Kerr. The water company and gas company have laid pipes in the neighbourhood.

In 1851 Partick village elected to become a Police Burgh. The Burgh Police (Scotland) Acts of 1833 and 1850 enabled local areas to decide to become a Police Burgh and manage many of their affairs through the election of Burgh Commissioners; a distinctive

Scottish version of municipality. Areas had to have in excess of 3,000 inhabitants and more than 21 householders had to sign the petition. The term 'police' in this context had a much wider meaning than its contemporary sense as, in addition to managing crime and punishment, Police Burghs oversaw water supplies, paving, lighting and maintenance of streets, sewers, drainage, cleansing, and general public health. A body of commissioners was elected to administer the burgh. Partick Burgh's boundary included the upper section of Byres Road. The northern boundary ran along part of Ashton Lane, across Byres Road and along Downside Lane. An article from 1851 in the *Glasgow Gazette* described the new Burgh before the impact of the later industrial expansion:

> Among the various suburban villages scattered around this city, none has risen into more deserved importance than the delightfully situated village of Partick. On all sides comfortable villas and elegant mansions have either of late been built or are at this moment in progress of erection. Situated at the confluence of the rivers Kelvin and Clyde at the favourite West end of the city, with a pure atmosphere, and all the rural advantages of hill and dale, wood and water, and abundant means of rapid transport to and from the city,

this village cannot fail at no distant day to become by far the most important in the neighbourhood of our city.

In 1856 each of four houses in Sardinia Place, Cecil Street were advertised for sale at an upset price of £1,250. Also advertised were feus as part of the development of Dowanhill estate: 'The area is suitable for various classes of houses. It is proposed to lay out the lands for villas, and partly in streets, crescents and terrace with the advantage of a large park or square in the centre.' Stone was still being quarried locally to build houses; in 1858 one was opened where Vinicombe Street is today: 'An extensive bed of freestone rock of excellent quality had been found and a quarry opened, and the rock is available for local building at a moderate price, and the cartage will be trifling and all tolls saved.'

Although the new road was in place by 1840 and the Curlers Tavern built a few years later, no other buildings were erected in the new section of Byres Road until the 1860s. The first was Kelvinside Free Church on the corner of Great Western Road and Byres Road, which opened in 1862. Five years later the first block of tenements in Byres Road (Nos. 174 – 190) was completed. Originally named Ashton

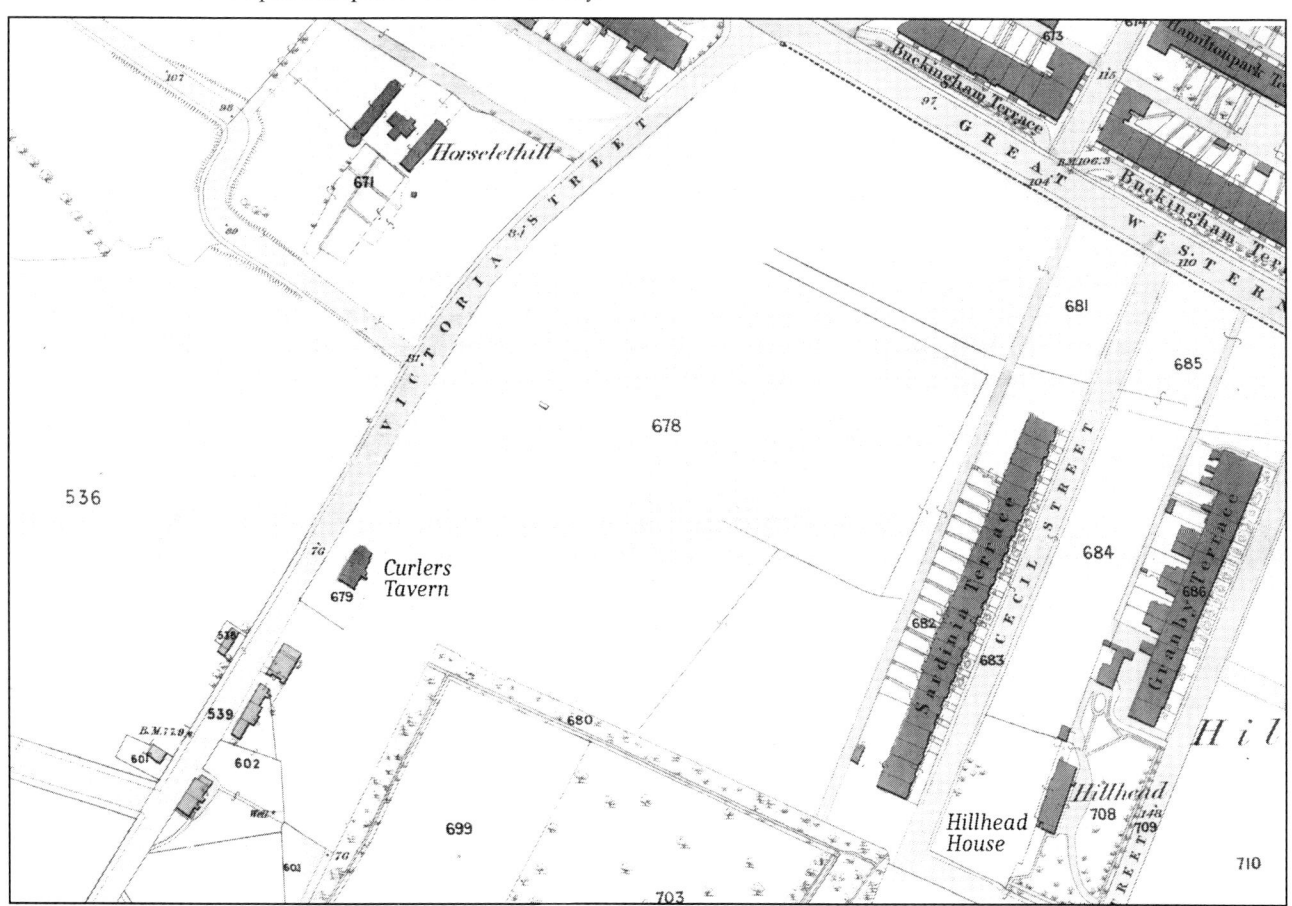

Map *c.*1850 showing first buildings erected in Hillhead, the Curlers Tavern and the north end of Byres Road.

National Library of Scotland

Place, the block was built for John Swan, an iron merchant as an investment. In November 1867 the first Byres Road shops were advertised: 'To let, at Ashton Place, three very superior shops suitable for a grocer and wine merchant, a baker and butcher. These afford an excellent opening for the establishment of a respectable family business in each.' They were rented by William Frame, grocer and wine merchant; A & A Colquhoun, baker and confectioner; and William Forbes, cab hirer. Both Colquhoun and Forbes also rented stables behind in Ashton Lane. The other shops in the row were completed during 1868 and were taken by James Purdie, chemist; John Orr, painter and decorator; Matthew Williamson, butcher; Rattray & Logie, plumbers & gasfitters; and John Bell, ironmonger. The flats above these first shops were advertised in February 1868: 'To let, flats of five and eight rooms.'

In 1869, Hillhead in turn successfully applied for Burgh status and its area included the upper end of Byres Road from Great Western Road to the Partick Burgh boundary, but only the east side as the boundary with Kelvinside ran up the middle of the road. Hillhead Burgh Hall (on the current site of the library) was opened in 1873 and included a Public Hall, the Burgh Court Hall, the Fiscal's Office, and, behind, a Police Office, including cells, a fire station, cleansing department, plus housing for the police and fire employees. The police were under the jurisdiction of Lanark County and the County also opened a small police office behind the Curler's Tavern. Alongside the new Burgh Hall were a few ramshackle huts:

> One was used by Mr McDougall, the local veterinary surgeon. Above his door was a model of a dog's head; a schipperke, a popular breed. Another was briefly used by a German barber with one leg but his tendency to drink did not reassure customers and he moved on.

Also in 1873, a pre-fabricated 'tin church' of a type that was common in the second half of the 19th century was built directly across from the Burgh Hall. Constructed of galvanised iron and lined inside with wood, it was in the Gothic style and had a fifty-foot-high belfry. It was moved around 1880 to Hyndland Road.

In 1868 Horselethill Farm in Kelvinside was advertised for sale:

> That part of the land of Horselethill, consisting of twenty acres or thereby, situated on the West side of the Byres Road, and bounded on the North by Grosvenor, Kew, and Belhaven Terraces, and on the South and West by the lands of Dowanhill, and having a frontage to the Byres Road of 1,445 feet or thereby. These lands are the most suitable at the West End of Glasgow for the erection of first-class dwelling houses, the surrounding property being restricted against nuisances and the erection of any sort of public work.

The Gilmorehill Estate to the east had been purchased in 1845 by the Glasgow Western Cemetery Company to build a cemetery, but the project never materialised. So in 1865 the company sold the land to the University of Glasgow. Expansion of the University had been constrained by its site in the High Street and by selling its existing site to enable railway development, the University was able to move to a new building at Gilmorehill. It opened in 1870. The University's teaching hospital, the Royal Infirmary, also moved from its High Street site to the east of the University on a site known as

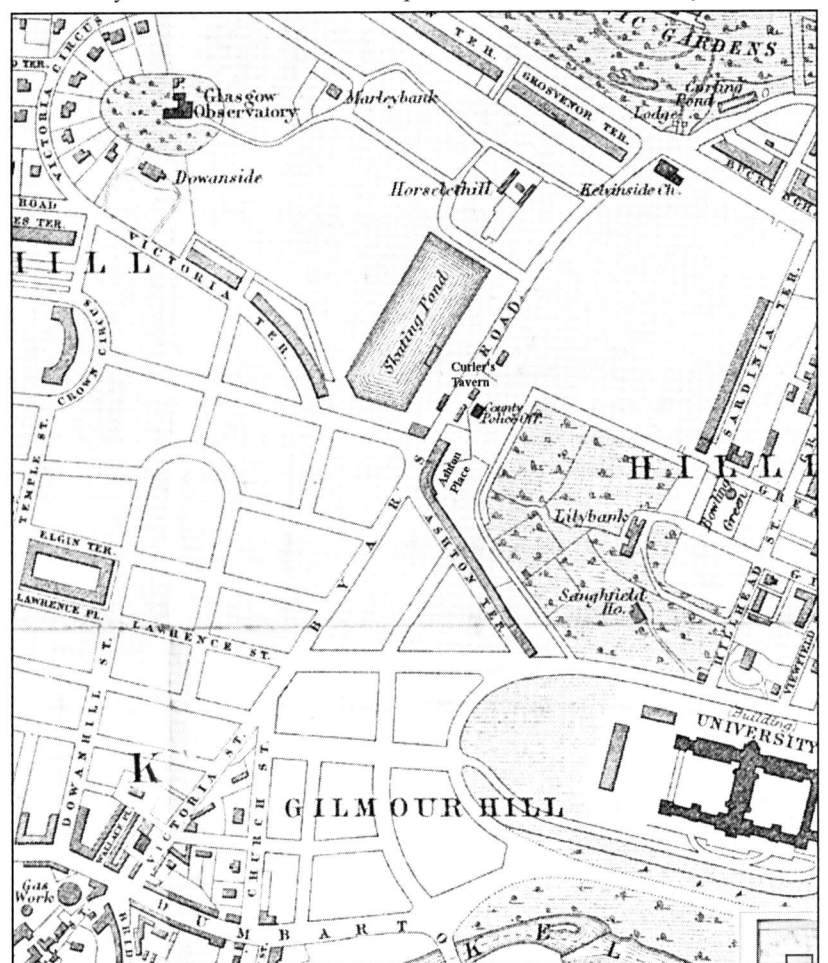

Map c.1870 showing first block (Ashton Place) erected in Byres Road. Also the Glasgow Skating Club rink.

National Library of Scotland

Kelvinside Free Church, *c.*1870.

The prefabricated building of St. Bride's Episcopal Church in Beaconsfield Road in the early 1890s. This church was originally in the grounds of Douglas Castle before it was offered to the Bishop of Glasgow by the Earl of Home. The congregation later moved to the site in Hyndland Road where the present day St. Bride's stands.

Lewis Hutton collection

Hillhead Burgh Hall *c.*1900.
Gordon Urquhart collection

The new buildings of the University shortly after opening in 1870. The familiar spire was constructed between 1887 and 1891.
Lewis Hutton collection

Donaldshill, with an entrance lodge in Church Street. Although still a teaching hospital for the University, it was expanded to become a second general infirmary for the city. Renamed the Westen Infirmary, it opened in 1874. Although the lands on which the University and hospital were built originally came within Partick Burgh, on the completion of the new buildings Glasgow negotiated for its boundary to be extended to encompass both.

While building around Byres Road was well under way by the mid-1870s, much of the area was still open countryside:

> Partickhill had no buildings on it from Hyndland Street to Hamilton Crescent, save Muirpark House and Stewartville House, and to the top of the hill nothing could be seen but luxuriant pasture land, with the summit crowned with beautiful trees. Hyndland Road, was a favourite walk on a summer evening to see the sun setting over Goatfell and enjoy the breeze from the Kilpatrick Hills.

An article of 1878 in the *North British Daily Mail* described the pace of development.

> During the past two years the property built in Byars Road alone, including the unbroken line of handsome blocks from the University Avenue to Kelvinside Free Church, must amount in value to several hundred thousand pounds. The two burghs, Partick and Hillhead, are now completely joined at Victoria Cross (the junction at Highburgh Road), and round University Avenue itself large homes have appeared in all directions. Messrs Gilchrist and Gardner from the Ashton Terrace and Messrs Miller & Wallace from the avenue side, have now completed Sutherland Terrace, both of which blocks have since been sold. Mr William McDonald is busy finishing a block of flatted houses, affording accommodation to the extent of from five to nine rooms and kitchen on Albion Crescent Road, and the ground is about to be broken by the same builder to make room for the foundations of other four self-contained lodgings in the same locality. The ground on the left-hand side of Byars Road, on entering it from the Partick end, extending up to Lawrence Place, has been feued and perhaps before the year closes the old Dowanhill quarry, which supplied some capital stone towards the erection of many a good block on the Dowanhill Estate, will be replaced by a square of commodious houses. Near this locality a couple of new streets will soon be formed. In fact, going from Partick on the left-hand side of Byars Road, all the ground is now feued.

The quality of the roads did not match that of the properties as a tongue-in-cheek letter to the press in 1878 pointed out:

> I reside in Partick but attend church in Hillhead, and occasionally, on a Saturday evening, visit the Kibble Palace. Might I respectfully suggest to the officials in charge of the Byars Road or 'canal', the propriety of putting in a punt or raft on that line of communication, especially on the Sabbath mornings and Saturday evenings? I have heard a sailing boat suggested, but I fear the depth of liquid is scarcely sufficient; besides, its being thicker than the boat's average native element it would tend to retard the progress of the craft, so that mere sails might not be powerful enough to impel it. Gibson Street, too, immediately west of the Kelvin, is just now in very fine order for anyone who has a taste for wading. Might I ask, in all innocence and in real ignorance what we pay road-rates for?

The poor state of the road was no doubt in part due to the heavy traffic bringing in stone and other building materials, and the Curlers' Tavern offered the carters a place to stop for refreshment: 'The turnpike road is frequently blocked at the Curlers' Tavern with cabs, carts and lorries, all standing without carters.'

The quarrying and excavation of stone and clay for brick-making left a number of disused quarry workings and clay pits, some of which filled with water and in the winter were used for skating. A letter in 1878 published in the *Glasgow Herald* bemoaned the danger of the quarry workings that still littered the area:

> About a stone-throw from the Byars Road, immediately behind the small iron church, and some thirty or forty yards from Ruthven Street, there is a disused quarry. The field around it is entirely unfenced, and so is the quarry which is filled with water from six to ten feet deep. On Saturday it was frozen over, and about ten-o'clock a little milk boy ventured upon it; the ice gave way and he perished before help could reach him. The other quarry near Roxburgh Street that I formerly wrote about was fenced a few days ago, but in an utterly inefficient manner. I should like to know who are responsible for the existence of such perils in the very centre of a populous locality.

In 1882 the first block of new tenements at the Partick end was erected between the north edge of Dowanvale House and Chancellor Street (then called Clarendon Street) (Nos. 53 to 67). The flats in the tenements built towards the Partick end had fewer rooms and the shops also tended to be smaller.

While a few Byres Road tenements were constructed for clients, the majority were built speculatively by local builders, such as Lindsay & Benzie who opened a base at No. 162 in 1873. William Benzie was born around 1846, the son of a crofter in Banffshire, and by the 1870s was working as a joiner in Glasgow. In 1873 he married Catherine Auld and they moved into No. 61 Gibson Street, where Catherine bore the first of eight children. John Lindsay was born in Fife in 1846 and trained as a mason. He married Helen Stirling in 1872 and they moved into No. 25 Ruthven Street, where the first of their five children was born. One of the partnership's earliest projects, completed in 1873, was four 'very superior houses' on the corner of Downhill Street and Lawrence Street that they named Lindsay Terrace (sadly William did not get a place named after him). By 1881 they were employing 60 men and nine boys. In 1884 the firm advertised:

FOR SALE.
HIGH-CLASS SELF-CONTAINED LODGINGS in Athole Gardens, Lilybank Gardens, Westbourne Gardens and Terrace, and Dundonald Road, &c. Prices from £1650 to £2700.
Also,
VERY HANDSOME VILLA in Kelvinside, overlooking Great Western Road.
These Houses are carefully constructed, of superior finish, every convenience and improvement introduced, and cannot fail to give satisfaction, and prove a safe investment at the price.
Apply to Lindsay & Benzie, 162 Byars Road, Hillhead.

Advert, 1884.

Lindsay Terrace, built by Lindsay & Benzie in the 1870s.
Author

Like other building firms they had problems with non-payment. In 1875 they were contracted to carry out joinery work in new buildings in Byres Road by another building firm, but halfway through the job the first instalment of payment failed to materialise. So, Lindsay & Benzie, 'removed mason's sheds, ceiling joists and every shape of wood that could be lifted.' In 1877 the firm had an unusual worker issue. One of the firm's apprentices was a 'Yankee', William Hamilton. Although all the other firm's workers were union members, Hamilton was an anti-unionist, and his refusal to join eventually ended with him coming to blows with another of the apprentices. Both ended up in court and were fined.

Lindsay & Benzie retained some of the flats they built and rented those for income, including two of seven houses they built in Ashton Road. The firm also began to act as property agents on behalf of others. In 1888 Catherine Benzie died giving birth to her eighth child, leaving William a widower with a new baby and seven other children under the age of twelve. Often men and women widowed with young children married again, as did William, marrying Rachel Bain in 1889. They moved into No. 4 Bute Gardens and employed a cook, a housemaid and a nurse to help Rachel care for the family. John and his family moved to Westbourne Gardens. Around 1896 William decided to focus on managing properties and as John continued as a builder, they ended their partnership. William moved his office to Cresswell Street while John opened a works yard in Beaumont Gardens. In 1895 William suffered a second tragic loss when Rachel died of pneumonia.

View down Byres Road. The tenements on each side were the first built, c.1890.
Crown Copyright, RCAHMS

She had not borne him any children but when he married for a third time in 1897, his new wife Margaret Cherry gave birth to two. William continued in business through to his retirement around 1915 and died in 1925. Unfortunately, in 1910 John's finances became overstretched, as happened to a number of speculative builders, and he was declared bankrupt. He died the following year.

Byres Road's expansion was supported by new forms of transport. Horse-drawn trams served the road by the 1880s and these were electrified in the 1890s. The subway system opened in 1896 with Hillhead Station in Byres Road and Partick (now Kelvinhall)

Original Hillhead Subway entrance, c.1910. *Courtesy of David Thomson*

Station at Partick Cross. The opening of Partick Station led to redevelopment in the area and by 1910 all the properties that had been built in the 1820s, including Dowanvale House and the church, had been demolished to make way for the building of Dalcross Street. These, and other tenement blocks completed after 1890, are built from red sandstone, rather than the yellowish sandstone of the earlier tenements. This is common throughout Glasgow; supplies of local sandstone began to be more expensive to extract, and less expensive red sandstone from Dumfriesshire, much favoured by architects, began to be brought in by rail.

Glasgow City annexed Hillhead Burgh in 1891 but Partick held out until 1912. In 1910 the successful Glasgow furniture and furnishings store, Wylie & Lochhead built a large garage on the one undeveloped plot that lay opposite Vinicombe Street. First used for its funeral vehicles, in the 1920s it became the firm's car showroom. In 1931 the plumbing and electrical firm, Mackinlays,

Tram passing Hillhead Underground station, c.1950s.

which had been based in a row of one-storey properties between Observatory Road and the garage, bought out the other owners and demolished the old buildings, replacing them with the elegant Grosvenor Mansions.

In the 1950s a block of flats to house police was built between the Burgh Hall and Cresswell Street where previously there had been old wooden buildings. That block was superseded by a modern block of flats with shops below in the late 1990s. The 1970s saw a rash of major changes to the road. Wylie & Lochhead's garage and showroom was demolished and replaced by a modern block of maisonettes with a supermarket below. One-storey shops between Grosvenor Lane and Grosvenor Terrace were destroyed in the 1978 fire that swept through the Grosvenor Hotel and the area incorporated into the redeveloped hotel. Hillhead Burgh Halls and its associated properties were demolished to build Hillhead Library. As part of the expansion of Glasgow University, the properties Nos. 146 to 172 were pulled down to enable University Avenue to be rerouted to meet the Highburgh Road, creating the triangular car park that exists today. The original end of University Avenue running alongside the Western Infirmary was renamed University Place. In 1977 modernisation of the underground system included enlarging Hillhead Station, when the properties between Ashton Lane and the Curlers were demolished and redeveloped.

Over the years the 18th century coal workings have led to subsidence, particularly at the top of the road. In 1893 the tenement on the corner of Vinicombe Street had 'several fissures' and a large

Grosvenor Mansions, built 1931.
Author

Redirected University Avenue on top of map showing original roadscape.
National Library of Scotland

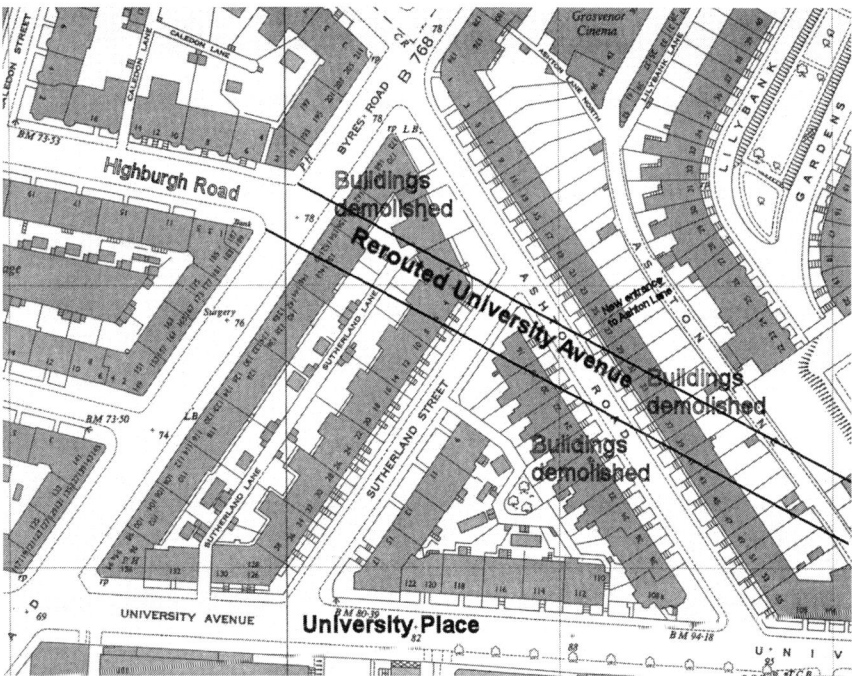

View of Byres Road with tenements on the right those that were demolished to reroute University Avenue.
A. C. Stirling

Tenement on corner of Vinicombe Street and Byres Road under scaffolding due to subsidence damage. All but ground floors demolished soon after, *c.*1970s.
Henry Morton collection

Shops, Nos. 374 to 388, after tenement on corner of Vinicombe Street demolished, 1999.

Heavy traffic flow on Great Western Road, c.1960s.   *Scottish Roads Archive*

glass window in one of the ground floor shops, 'cracked from top to bottom.' The Vinicombe Street tenements were repaired but the problem reappeared in the 1970s and the tenement was declared unsafe. The Coal Board refused to accept liability and although the council provided support for buildings at risk elsewhere, this was not made available to the owners of these properties. To save their businesses the shop owners on the ground level formed a consortium and bought out the flats above (then No. 386). The upper floors were then carefully demolished and the saved shops – Nos. 374 to 388 – reroofed. Hence, today's unusual row of one-storey shops and the flat gable end facing on to Vinicombe Street.

In the early 1960s Glasgow embarked on a major road building programme to create an urban ring road. Swathes of the city were demolished to make way for motorways. Concern at increasing traffic

flow along Great Western Road led to the proposal that the road become a dual-carriageway express-way, with no access for traffic from any of the existing side streets. Only a few crossing points for pedestrians were to exist, and these by tunnel beneath the new carriageway. However, the existence of the railway tunnel at the top of Byres Road made a pedestrian tunnel impractical so instead it was planned that the new dual-carriageway would rise up and over the existing junction. Fortunately, this was one part of Glasgow's disastrous new road system that did not progress, not because of the many protests against the Great Western Road plan, but because of an economic downturn.

While Byres Road escaped the planning blight that such a road development would have brought, another of the City's policies did negatively affect businesses in the road. In 1966, there was a major revision to the rateable values of commercial properties and Byres Road shops, as elsewhere in Glasgow, were faced with massive rises. The *Glasgow Herald* reported on some of the revised rates for businesses in Byres Road: 'confectioner, from £377 to £1,272, Aragon Bar, £330 to £1,138, chemist, £355 to £1,188, and restaurant, £197 to £1,397'. For Elizabeth Lattimer who had a tobacconist and confectionery shop at No. 142 this was the last straw. Her rates were increased from £44 to £284. Mrs Lattimer showed a journalist a letter from her solicitor showing her net profit for the last year as just £173.

When I took over the shop I paid £2,170 for the goodwill. It is due to come down under the

---

**S I X   W E L L - L O C A T E D   S H O P S   I N
BYRES ROAD, GLASGOW, W.2.**

Street No.	Present Use	Approximate Area	Price
374	GROCER	1,000 Square Feet	£17,500
382	LADIES' WEAR	490 Square Feet	£7,500
384	TOBACCONIST	750 Square Feet	£12,500
388	TV RENTALS	640 Square Feet	£12,000
396	FISHMONGER	900 Square Feet	£15,000
404	HOUSE FURNISHER	2,200 Square Feet	£25,000

380 and 396 SOLD.

Further particulars and viewing arrangements may be had from and Offers should be sent to

KEITH S. BOVEY, Solicitor, 313 Byres Road, Glasgow, W.2.
Telephone: WEStern 8474-5.

Advert for sale of shops at top end of Byres Road, 1966.

Changing shop use - No. 102 being converted in 2008 from the newsagent and tobacconist shop run by J. Benson to a convenience store run by the Best One chain.

© *Robin Gillett, photo@brocweb.com*

New thoroughfare off Byres Road created as part of the new Glasgow University campus.   *Author*

development of the Western Infirmary and University within the next few years and I'd hoped that I could recover some of that money. I am going to close the shop at the end of this month. I just cannot go on. It is appalling to think that your livelihood can be taken away like this. I will have to seek public assistance or get a job as a housekeeper.

Her shop closed as did other long-standing businesses, including Price's Garage. Rates and higher rents have continued to be an issue for many traders, reflected by the number of empty shops at the Partick Cross end in 2023. Stuart Richardson who owns Graham's Auto Centre at No. 81

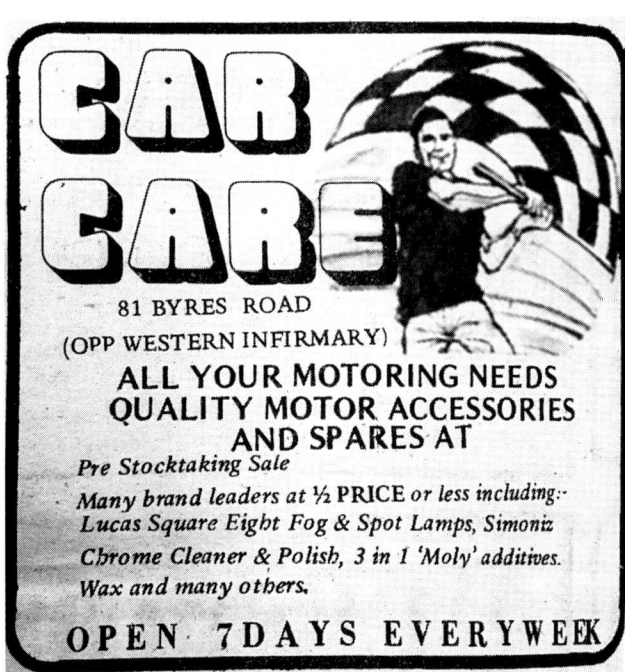

Advert for Car Care, No. 81, 1975.

explained: 'All too often people rent shops around here, but soon discover that business is not enough to cover the high cost of rent and rates. Fortunately, my father bought this shop almost sixty years ago so even if I have a slow day, I can survive.'

It may be that the redevelopment by Glasgow University of the site of the Western Infirmary that closed in 2015 may help revitalise and regenerate the bottom end of Byres Road; although rents may just increase further. The impressive Clarice Pears Building is the first completed building in this extension to Glasgow University's campus and already has dramatically changed the look of the bottom end of the road. Appropriately, given it is on part of the old Infirmary site, the new building houses the University's School of Health & Wellbeing. Still unclear is the fate of the disused swimming baths that were part of Church Street School. Built in 1904 the baths continued in use for 20 years after the school closed, but were shut in 1997 and only saved from demolition by a public campaign. Work is also under way on Byres Road's major roadway development that is designed to create: 'a people-focused place that improves the pedestrian experience, enhances the economic vibrancy of shops and services, and makes the area more cycle and environment-friendly.'

Chapter Two

Hidden Gems

Map showing Elliot Lane (later Cresswell Lane), 1890s.   *National Library of Scotland*

Parallel with the east side of Byres Road are five lanes that run south from behind Kelvinside Free Church to University Avenue: Vinicombe, Burgh, Cresswell (originally Elliott), Great George and Ashton. When built these contained a mix of stables and coachmen's houses, workshops and stores. Ashton Lane is the only one that has an entrance on to Byres Road.

Vinicombe Lane originally contained stables and the workshop of Alexander Kennedy's cabinetmaking and upholstery business, but none of those original buildings survive. The east side was redeveloped when the Botanic Gardens garage was built and those on the west side disappeared when the tenement on the corner with Byres Road had to be dismantled due to subsidence. Burgh Lane gave access to the yards and buildings erected behind Hillhead Burgh Hall that were demolished when the library replaced it. The brick building on the corner with Vinicombe Street was probably part of the Hillhead Cleansing Department.

The long single storey building on the west side of Cresswell Lane nearest Great George Street forms the back wall of what originally was the premises of James Henderson Ltd, cab and carriage hirers. The property was entered by an open archway at Nos. 302/304 Byres Road below the tenements. The premises probably consisted of an open courtyard with spaces for cabs and stables round the sides.

> In Glasgow there is always a considerable demand for cabs, carriages, &c., and the firm of Mr. James Henderson is widely known throughout the Glasgow district for the conveyances that are both reliable and comfortable, and horses thoroughly able to perform the necessary work.

Henderson's business was established in 1869 in Crookston Street and the firm opened branches throughout the city. By 1909, when horse-carriages began to be replaced by motor vehicles, the firm moved its Byres Road branch to No. 202 on the corner with Ashton Lane, with an office on Byres Road and a garage behind. Henderson's former property at Nos. 302/304 was roofed over and became the Hillhead Garage. In the late 1950s the Byres Road entryway was reconstructed and became a Woolworths store. Part of the rear area behind was used for auctions from the 1960s to the

1980s. The two-storey building next to it – now Bar Budda – was created around 1905 as the mail sorting office when the Post Office moved to No. 314. It closed along with the Post Office in 2008. In the basement of the corner tenement on Cresswell Street (No. 2 Cresswell Lane) was a billiard hall through to the 1940s. In the 1950s and 60s it was the workshop of Hillhead Vinyls, which produced plastic-covered folders, travel bags, etc. The single-storey building on the east side was erected around 1890 as a store for James Todd, a cabinetmaker who had a shop at No. 327. There also was a joiner's workshop there. The two-storey block on that side had been built by around 1900, probably as stables, although they soon became motor garages. One of the earliest to house a car there was Professor Archibald Barr, Professor of Civil Engineering & Mechanics at Glasgow University and the co-founder of Barr & Stroud, which had its first workshops in Byres Road and Ashton Lane. Another early user of a garage there was Peter Ridge-Beedle, a merchant who published one book, *Why not English?* This was described as 'a new alphabet for the English language enabling each word to be spelled as it is pronounced'. After the Second World War the run of properties housed Ross Motors.

In 1980 Jude McArdle obtained planning permission to convert the east side premises into De

Advert for De Coury's Arcade, 1980.

Courcy's Antique & Craft Arcade with small units on the ground and first floor. 'The planning people were very helpful', she said. 'My only complaint is that local tenants are not allowing us to display posters advertising the market.' Today, the arcade is regularly featured in magazines: 'This cute cobbled lane by day plays host to some of Glasgow's finest independent shops and by night has restaurants well worth a visit.' One past occupant was a fortune teller by the name of Lenor who was visited by the comedienne, Elaine C. Smith. Lenor described to Smith a man who would change her career in the next few years and the description uncannily fitted Dave Anderson of Wildcat Theatre, who later helped Smith go on to great things. These affordable small units continue to provide a chance for people to test out a business idea. Of course, some failed, but others, such as Janet & John Turner who have been selling the work of artists and craftspeople there since 2013, happily survive. Gordon Montgomerie, who established Fopp music stores, began by opening a small second-hand record shop in the arcade.

Ashton Lane was built around 1878 and a number of local shopkeepers housed horses and delivery carts there. The coachmen of a number of local wealthy local residents resided in the upstairs flat, with their employer's carriage and horse stabled below. The coach owners included John Jamieson, owner of

Ashton Lane, c.1900.   *Henry Morton collection*

The Fairfield Shipbuilding and Engineering Company, who lived in Crown Terrace, and William Kennedy, managing director of Broxburn Oil Company who resided in Huntly Gardens. As motor cars replaced horse-drawn carriages, the ground coach-houses began to be converted into garages. From the First World War through the 1920s, one was rented by Marion Gilchrist and her chauffeur, John Brown, lived there. In 1894 Gilchrist was one of two women who were the first to graduate as doctors from a Scottish university. She established a general practice at No. 5 Buckingham Terrace and being a specialist in ophthalmology, held the post of Assistant Surgeon for Diseases of the Eye at the Glasgow Victoria Infirmary. Gilchrist was one of the founding members of the Glasgow & West of Scotland Association for Women's Suffrage.

Employees of Barr & Stroud in front of Aston Lane workshop, c.1900.

Barr & Stroud

A number of the Ashton Lane properties later became workshops. In 1888, in response to a War Office advertisement in the magazine, *Engineering*, inviting proposals for an infantry range-finder, Archibald Barr, who was teaching engineering at Glasgow University, and his friend, the physicist William Stroud, worked together to create an optical range-finder. After a successful trial of it in 1892 they were awarded a contract, and established the company, Barr & Stroud. They rented space above Hillhead Subway at No. 250, and set up a laboratory and workshop. By 1899 increased demand for their product required larger premises and they rented a three-storey workshop at No. 44 Ashton Lane. There the firm employed around 65 people. Barr recalled: 'The premises were adjacent to stables that emitted an intolerable odour and were overrun by flies in the daytime and rats at night.' In 1904, presumably much to the relief of the workforce, the firm moved to a purpose-built factory in Anniesland. The First World War brought even more work and among the products Barr & Stroud developed were a torpedo depth recorder and a dome sight for aircraft. After the war the company gained the contract to supply the British Navy with all its binoculars.

Part of the workshop space that Barr & Stroud vacated when it moved to Anniesland was taken by James B. Stevenson. He had begun an apprenticeship as a baker but, seeing the rising

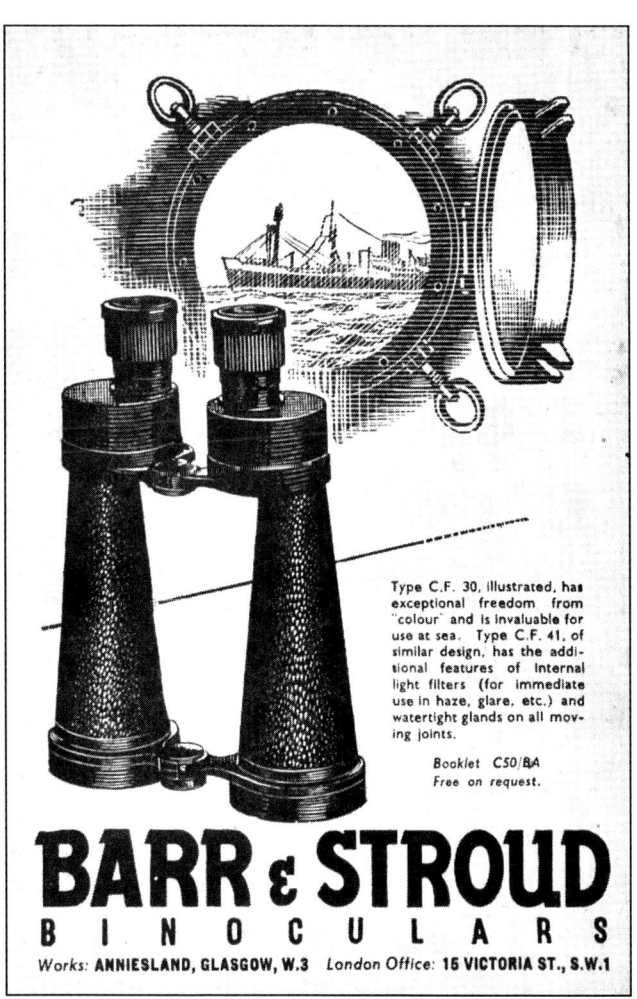

Type C.F. 30, illustrated, has exceptional freedom from "colour" and is invaluable for use at sea. Type C.F. 41, of similar design, has the additional features of internal light filters (for immediate use in haze, glare, etc.) and watertight glands on all moving joints.

Booklet C50/BA Free on request.

BARR ε STROUD
B I N O C U L A R S
Works: ANNIESLAND, GLASGOW, W.3 London Office: 15 VICTORIA ST., S.W.1

Advert for Barr & Stroud, 1933.

popularity of the motor car, left baking and established the Kelvinside Garage and Motor Company: 'All classes of repairs carried out by competent engineers.' Given many in Hillhead and Kelvinside were early purchasers of cars, his business quickly expanded and he opened premises in other parts of Glasgow. The business flourished into the early 1970s. In 1973 Stevenson's Ashton Lane workshop was advertised: 'Workshop with car hoist to each of the two upper floors. 1900 sq. ft each floor. Heating.' Another advert for premises in the lane offered: 'Mews cottage above two lock-up garages. Very suitable for someone wishing to combine workshop premises with living accommodation. 3 rooms, kitchen and bathroom plus separate W.C. Offers over £5,000.'

In 1910 the newly-formed Scottish Aeronautical Society rented space in the lane.

A large workshop for the use of members has been rented at No. 45 Ashton Lane and has been fitted up with all the necessary machinery for the building of aeroplanes including lathe, drilling machine. a smith's forge brazing furnace. The building of gliders and full-sized flying machines will be proceded with at once.

The property about to be converted into Grosvenor Café, *c.1978.*
Courtesy of Zanotti family

Sadly, the Society did not remain in the lane for long, perhaps because of an ill-fated event in January 1912. One evening around seven pm, George Riddoch, a keen club member, was walking through Ashton Lane when he was attacked. A young woman living in one of the mews houses, hearing his cries, opened her window. Seeing Riddoch being assaulted by another man, she shouted out and his assailant ran off leaving Riddoch seriously wounded from blows to the head, from which he died shortly after. In spite of an extensive police investigation, this murder that shocked the city remains one of Glasgow's unsolved cases.

The lane's evolution into today's fashionable destination started by chance. The redevelopment of Hillhead Underground Station in the late 1970s involved the demolition of a row of shops next to the old entrance, one of which was the popular Grosvenor Café. Unable to afford Byres Road rents, the owners took over a disused, dilapidated workshop in Ashton Lane and converted it into the New Grosvenor Cafe. Around the same time the Grosvenor Cinema was remodelled and the original Byres Road entrance closed, with a new entrance created in the lane. With two former popular Byres Road destinations now in the lane, other old properties in the lane began to be revamped into bars and restaurants. In 1980 the highly regarded restaurant, the Ubiquitous Chip moved there from Ruthven Lane.

The section of Ashton Lane that leads into Byres Road was the boundary between the Hillhead and Partick Burghs, and Dowanside Lane was the boundary between Partick Burgh and Kelvinside. The entrance to Dowanside Lane goes under what was part of the tearoom of Colquhouns and the firm had a bakery in the building on the left, probably where Revolution Spin is today. The brick building further

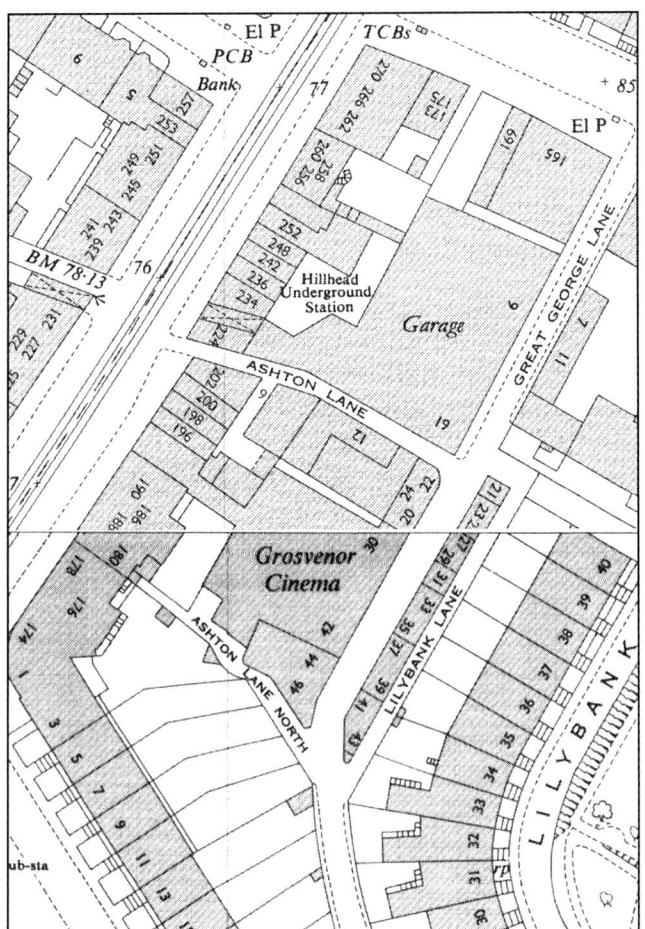

Map showing Aston Lane, *c.1940.*
National Library of Scotland

Joe Mulholland and the team that published the *West End News & Partick Advertiser*, 1975.

West End News & Partick Advertiser, 1974.
National Library of Scotland

down was erected in 1890 as a workshop. The unusual green wooden building (No. 19) was built as a joiner's workshop in the 1930s. In 1971 it was rented by Joe Mulholland as the base for printing his weekly Scottish newspaper, the *West End News and Partick Advertiser*. 'For the past six months Mulholland has been working on average fifteen hours a day cutting leads, fixing fuses, learning how to set type, chasing up advertising and, latterly, writing headlines and editorials. Tomorrow the paper launches.' Mulholland published his local newspaper through to 1981. Since 1989 the building has housed Starry, Starry Night, a vintage clothes shop.

In 1870 Alexander and Mary Steel, then in their late fifties, built the first property in Ruthven Lane, a dairy consisting of a house, byre, stables and other work buildings. Steel described himself as a cowfeeder (the contemporary term for a dairyman who kept cows) and had previously owned a dairy in Partick. The house was named Maryfield after his wife. Living with them in 1881 was a twenty-year-old dairymaid. The dairy later was owned by the McGrelis family and may have housed cows up to the Second World War. In 1979, the house became the Puppet Theatre restaurant: 'It consists of an engagingly lop-sided conservatory with a rabbit warren of tiny rooms and snuggeries which may seem charming or claustrophobic, depending on your frame of mind.' Today, the building is The Bothy restaurant. The building opposite, which famously became the first home of the Ubiquitous Chip in 1971, probably was built in the 1890s, and used as stables and store by some of the Byres Road shops, including Todd's fruit and flower shop. Before being converted to become the Chip, the building had been used as an electrician's workshop.

Around the same time as Steel built his dairy, Joseph Price built large Livery Stables at the Saltoun Street end of the lane. This consisted of carriage garages formed around an open yard with stables above, which horses reached by a ramp. The building incorporated a family house and two mews-style houses. Joseph began his career as one of eight grooms working for the Duke of Hamilton at Hamilton Palace in Lanarkshire. In 1857 he, his wife Jane and their eight children moved to Glasgow, where he opened a Livery Stable in Charing Cross

Starry, Starry Night at Nos. 19 to 21 Ashton Lane, 2023.
Author

Maryfield House, now Bothy
Restaurant, Ruthven Lane, 2020.
Author

Dance Glasgow & Ruthven Lane Mews, 2023.
Author

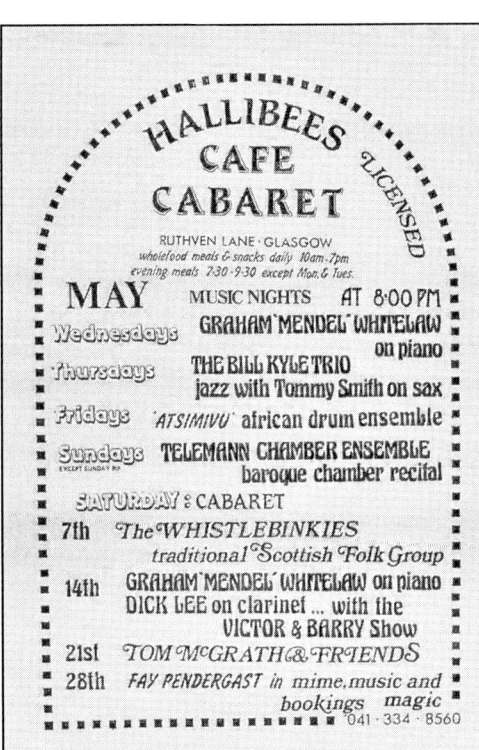

Poster for Hallibees Café Cabaret, 1984.

Ruthven Mews Arcade – Chaako restaurant in
former coach mews, 2020.
Photo by Robert Perry

Lane. The Ruthven Lane stables were initially called 'Victoria Stables', but soon renamed Price's Stables. With the shift from horse power to motor power, the business changed to Price's Garage. One of those whose car was kept in the garage was Hugh Fraser, who lived at Kingsborough Gardens. He was the son of the founder of House of Fraser department stores, and took over running the company; Price's Garage built additional premises in Victoria Crescent Lane to house a fleet of House of Fraser delivery vans. In the 1950s and '60s, the empty stable lofts of Price's Garage were used by various organisations, including the Glasgow Aquarium Society and the Glasgow & West of Scotland Model Railway Club. As first-time visitors to the model railway had to walk through two garage spaces and then climb an old ladder, they must have wondered if they were in the right place, only to beam in delight at encountering a forty-foot-long model railway that snaked through hand-made miniature fields, lochs and hills. When Prices's Garage closed in the 1960s it had over 20,000 square feet of car repair and storage space.

In 1978 Pat Halliburton obtained planning permission to convert parts of the former family house and garage, and opened a vegetarian restaurant, Hallibees coffee house and an arcade of antique shops, now called The Mews. For five years in the early 1980s Hallibees Cabaret Café presented a wide range of shows. The venue presented early performances by Victor & Barry, the comedy double act created by Alan Cumming and Forbes Masson, and music by such luminaries as The Whistlebinkies. In 1984 the Mews Arcade received a Civic Trust award for its conversion and continues to delight seekers of unusual objects:

Puma bas relief sculpture on back wall of Ruthven Street tenement, 2023.   *Author*

Laissez-vous transporter dans le passé dans ce vrai joyau du West End de Glasgow! Ruthven Mews Arcade est une galerie marchande dans une arcade sur deux étages où vous trouverez des magasins d'antiquités et des petites galeries indépendantes.

The rear section of Price's Garage became Mr Singh's Garage, and in the 1980s Singh converted part of his property into a small shopping arcade. There, in the 1990s, Louise Welsh sold second-hand books while writing her successful first novel, *The Cutting Room*. One of her regular customers was the writer Bernard MacLaverty who lived in a tenement at the top of Saltoun Street. The building (Nos. 33 & 35) was included in a series of paintings created by Avril Paton in 1993. Called *Windows in the West*, the Saltoun Street tenement is depicted after a snowstorm with glimpses of residents in their lit rooms. The painting was bought by Glasgow Museums & Art Galleries for its collection and is still much-loved, having been described by the *Evening Times* as 'probably the most famous tenement in the world'.

In the 1880s two coach-houses and stables with houses above were built halfway along Ruthven Lane. The motor car of Sir Andrew Pettigrew later was housed in one with his chauffeur living above. Pettigrew, who lived in Marlborough Terrace, was a partner in Pettigrew & Stephens, at that time the largest department store in Scotland. It was based in a stylish building in Sauchiehall Street that had a gilt dome designed by Charles Rennie Mackintosh. These Ruthven Lane buildings were redeveloped in 2010 as studios for Glasgow Dance Studio.

From Ruthven Lane it is possible to see high up on the rear of one of the Ruthven Street tenements an unusual animal bas-relief that may be a puma or panther. The origins of this sculpture remain shrouded in mystery, but it was possibly put there by George Barlas, whose firm built the double tenement Nos. 13 & 15; he himself lived in one of the flats from 1876 to 1890. If the sculpture had been of a black Newfoundland dog, then the mystery would have been solved for at the Ayrshire Agricultural Show in April 1885, Barlas's Newfoundland gained third place in its class. Sadly, the following month he advertised: 'Strayed, a black Newfoundland bitch – Finder will be rewarded by returning same to George Barlas, Hillhead. If found in any person's possession after this date they will be prosecuted.' Dog thefts were frequent, so Barlas may never have been reunited with his pet.

Price's Livery Stables as in the 1870s.

Author's collection

Windows in the West by Avril Paton, 1993.
© *Avril Paton (collection - Glasgow Museums & Art Galleries)*

Chapter Three

Going for the Messages

Until the 1970s when refrigerators became common, fresh food had to be bought regularly, and in the 19th century residents in Byres Road, as elsewhere, obtained their milk from cows that were kept in small local byres. The Hillhead Burgh minutes record, 'the nuisance of cows trespassing on and so obstructing the pavement'. In 1880 when James Legatt's dairy next to Dowanvale House at the bottom of Byres Road was sold, it included 35 milk cows. In the same year the sale of the sequestrated estate of Duncan Ferguson at No. 2 Great George Street included, '18 milk cows, 1 sheep, 18 hens and the whole extensive dairy.' In Ruthven Lane (where The Bothy restaurant is today) there was a dairy from the 1870s to the Second World War, which was owned from 1918 by William McGrelis who previously had a dairy in Hyndland Street. That it was still a dairy with cows even by 1921 appears to be confirmed by that year's census as McGrelis's son, who was then running the dairy, described himself as a dairyman, and a dairymaid was listed as resident.

It was common for fresh milk to be delivered to the houses of customers and in the early days

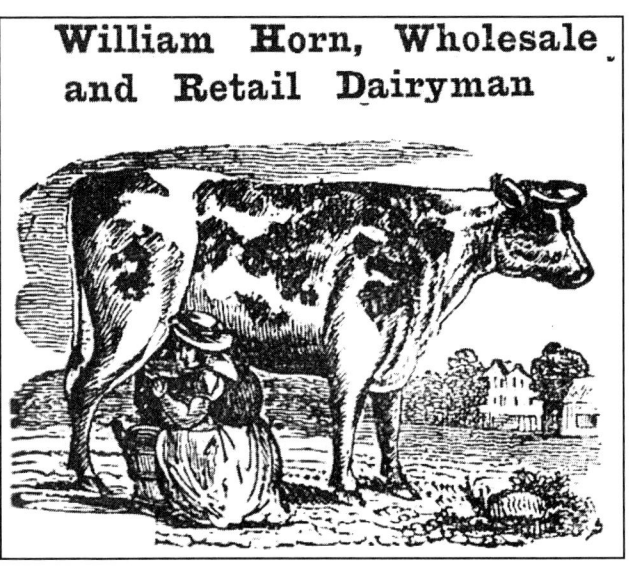

Advert for Horn's Dairy, date unknown.

deliveries might be made up to four times in a day. Until glass milk bottles were introduced from the early 1900s, the milk was carried in large churns and ladled directly into a customer's container. Local dairies, such as Horns at No. 200, delivered milk, but by 1900 most deliveries were made by larger milk firms. For decades the early morning clip, clop of hooves accompanied by the clink of milk bottles was a common sound around the city streets. Later electric 'milk floats' were introduced. The milk delivery depot of Ross's Dairies – that advertised with the catchphrase, 'It's Ross's, It's Right' – was on Crow Road, and the firm had two shops in Byres Road. But by the 1980s daily milk deliveries to customers' doorsteps began to die out.

The shops that sold dairy products were simply called dairies and mainly staffed by women: 'Mr Horn's three raven-haired, fresh-complexioned sisters in purple overalls diligently dispensed their dairy produce'. They also sold condensed milk, eggs, butter, cheese and margarine. Before individual packaging the butter was stored in large earthenware crocks and scooped out onto paper and then wrapped. Horns was a small family business, but most of the dairies in the road belonged to large firms. Around 1910 the Scottish firm, The Buttercup Dairy Company, opened at No. 306. It was founded by Andrew Ewing, a farmer's son who first worked as a grocer and by the 1920s had over 250 shops in Scotland. The architect James Davidson Cairns was commissioned to create a distinctive look to the company's dairies. The firm also had a poultry farm in Clermiston that contained around 200,000 hens: affectionately known as 'Hen City'. The economic

Sloan's Dairies No. 251, c.1940s.

Sloan's Dairies depot, Crow Road, *c.*1930.

Electric milk float and horse drawn milk cart, *c.*1950s.

Partick Camera Club

Milk crock, Maypole Dairy, date unknown

slump in the 1930s negatively affected the firm and some shops were closed, but the Byres Road shop continued into the early 1950s. In the 1910s the even larger British firm, The Maypole Dairy, opened a branch at No. 261. The Maypole Dairy Company was established in 1887 in Wolverhampton and was the first firm to promote the widespread use of margarine as an alternative to butter. The company expanded significantly in the early 1900s and its Byres Road shop was one of over 1,000 across Britain. Much of its produce came from Denmark. The logo of the company was a group of young people dancing around a maypole and the brand survived until 1964, when it was absorbed by Allied Suppliers, at which point the Byres Road shop closed.

Past residents of Byres Road who enjoyed a white coffee at one of the Italian cafes would be bemused by today's range of 'milks', such as coconut and soya. Even skimmed milk would have seemed strange, for in the past dairies often were fined for selling milk with insufficient fat content, and worse. In 1876 Mrs Glen wrote to the *Glasgow Herald* suggesting that Hillhead Burgh should appoint an analyst: 'My reason for this is that the milk sold by the dairies in the Kelvin neighbourhood is extremely adulterated with water, chalk and other substances.'

Before large bakeries became established, bread was baked locally. One of the first shops in the road was the bakers opened by Alexander and Archibald

A. & A. COLQUHOUN,
3 ASHTON PLACE, Dowanhill,
AND 123 GREAT WESTERN ROAD.
FAMILY BAKERS, COOKS, CONFECTIONERS, AND
LICENSED PURVEYORS OF
LUNCHEONS, DINNERS, AND SUPPERS.
MARRIAGE & EVENING PARTIES, in Town or Country,
Supplied with Requisites in every Variety of Style.
MARRIAGE and CHRISTENING CAKES,
In any Style or Size.
ICES, JELLIES, &c., &c.
SILVER PLATE, CRYSTAL, CHINAWARE, NAPERY,
TABLES, FORMS, &c., Lent on Hire.
GOODS ALWAYS ON HAND FOR LOAN.

A & A Colquhoun advert, 1876

Colquhoun in 1867. The brothers were born in Leith in the 1830s but soon after their baker father moved the family to Kilcreggan in Argyll and Bute. There the two brothers learnt their trade and in 1867 decided to set up in business in Byres Road. Before they left for Glasgow the residents of Kilcreggan treated Alexander to a dinner:

> To mark the occasion of his opening an establishment at Dowanhill, Glasgow. The chair presented to Mr Colquhoun a splendid service of silver plate, as recognition by the residents of the manner in which he conducted his business, and of his willingness to oblige all who resided in the district.

It is certain that soon after arriving in Glasgow the Colquhoun brothers would have become members of the Incorporation of Bakers of Glasgow, the trade body that traced its origins back to the 'Ancient Wheat Mill of Partick'. Partick Mill was given to the bakers of Glasgow by the Regent Moray in 1568, 'in reward for their zeal in the cause of the Protestant Reformation'. Until 1872, those wishing to join the Incorporation had to complete a form of 'Bake-Off' challenge called an 'Essay', which required applicants to produce satisfactory beef-steak pies, veal pies, pigeon pies, pork pies, mutton pies, rabbit pies, apple tarts, plum tarts, pear tarts, frouches, custards, and souffles. The brothers' first shop was the newly-built No. 3 Ashton Place (later No. 178), Having got the business underway, Alexander married Elizabeth Clark and they had two sons: James born in 1873 and Robert in 1877. Archibald, who never married, opened another bakery at No. 185 Great Western Road, and he managed that one, although both shops traded as A & A Colquhoun. Around 1875 the brothers paid for the block known as Albion Place (Nos, 215 to 235) to be built – the corner building is named Victoria Cross, as Byres Road was then named Victoria Street – and Alexander moved his business into the new

Front of what was Colquhoun Bakery, by the time of the photograph City Bakeries. Original baker's shop on corner with lane and the old Colquhoun restaurant sign still in place, *c.*1960.

building, Nos. 225/227. As well as a shop on the ground floor and a bakery next to it in Dowanside Lane, there was a stylish tearoom and restaurant on the first floor. For a time, Alexander and his family lived at No. 219. Their son, James, who was a keen boxer, became a volunteer in the Queens Own Company of Yeomanry and was in the first Yeomanry regiment sent to South African to fight in the Boer War. On his return he took over the family firm and lived with his wife and children in Dowanside Road. He died in 1938 but the firm continued through to the 1970s, at which point it was purchased by City Bakeries.

A & A Colquhoun bread cart in snow.

Glasgow Herald

Walter Hubbard's bakery, founded in Partick in 1847, expanded across Glasgow and had a branch at No. 149 from the 1920s to the 30s.

> Mr. Hubbard's name has been specially noted for many years in connection with the manufacture of rusks, a speciality which is known throughout Great Britain and in many of the colonies, &c. These, being intended as food for infants and invalids, are made in the most careful manner from selected materials, and their quality has always been their best advertisement.

Alexander McKay opened his baker's shop in 1879 at No. 53 and the premises housed bakers through to 1985. In 1965, when Hugh Tait was running it, the bakery was destroyed by fire in the middle of the night with the three families living in the flats above only being saved thanks to one of the residents waking up and smelling smoke. Tait got the bakery up and running again, and his son, Andrew took over; in the 1970s he renamed it The Pantry. In 1978 panic buyers scoured the Byres Road for a loaf of bread as 7,000 factory bakers in Glasgow and Strathclyde had gone on strike over pay, and long queues formed outside any shop that had a supply: 'Yesterday mid-morning at the Pantry Bakery where they bake their own loaves a spokesman said, "I've baked 600 since 11pm last night and they're all gone."' Andrew Tait's wife worked with a firm called Blue Sky Holidays owned by Brian Doran, and in 1980 Andrew and Doran decided to smuggle cocaine into Scotland from Holland. Doran acted as courier, and Tait hid the drugs in his baker's shop and acted as the dealer. One of Andrew Tait's bakes was named by him, 'The Pantry Partick Pie – 95% steak – Billy Connolly's favourite'. Whether or not Billy Connolly actually ever tasted it is not known, but others gave it glowing reviews: 'One of the best pies I ever tasted'. However, one can only wonder if its appeal might have been due to accidental contamination from the cocaine that the judge

Hubbard's Bakery in Smith Street later Otago Street, Hillhead, *c.*1905.

Lewis Hutton collection

The Pantry, bakers, *c*.1980s

Fairy Dell advert, 1970.

City Bakeries, Nos. 225-227 *c*.1960s.

at Tait's trial was informed induced, 'feelings of well-being, euphoria and sexual stimulus.' While Tait ended up in prison, Doran fled abroad, but was arrested six years later.

Alongside their loaves, bakers tempted their customers with an array of cakes, and few Byres Road customers – in the past or today – were immune to the temptation of the occasional sweet indulgence. Scottish classics sold at the branch of Peacock the Bakers at No. 248 included fern cakes, pineapple tarts, fly cemeteries, Eiffel towers, and that much-loved early summer treat, the characteristic Scottish strawberry tart with its single large strawberry standing proudly on its creamy base. Bakers, such as William Diggins at No.135, vied each year to have the first strawberry tarts on sale. In the 1970s, as Christmas approached, The Fairy Dell at No. 380 offered traditional mince pies and Christmas Cake, while Patisserie Francoise at No. 138 sold a 'Bouche de Noel'. Today, French pastries are available from Sugar Fall Patisserie at No. 153 and Valeria at No. 333, while Portuguese pastel de nata, made every day by Emma Airley and Sebastian Bacewiczm, can be enjoyed at Pastéis Lisboa, No. 280.

Of course, the health conscious will choose a piece of fruit rather than a cake, and the most famous fruit shop in Byres Road belonged to George Todd. He was born in 1879 and grew up at Rose Cottage in the village of Broomhouse, near Baillieston. There his father, who had a fruit shop in the Gallowgate, maintained a famed garden: 'The great rose garden, extending to three acres, at Broomhouse, and the property of Thomas Todd, fruiterer, is well known in city circles as "Tammie's Yard"'. When George married Helen Rankin in 1908, he was working as an

George Todd fruiterer & florist, Nos. 253/25, c.1950s.

advertising agent but decided instead to follow his father's trade. However, rather than take over his father's shop, he rented an empty shop at No. 262, and a flat above the shop at No. 266. The shop opened in 1912 and Henry Morton recalled assisting with its opening:

One day in the early 1910s, when a boy, I was passing what had been an empty shop and noted it had become a fruit and flower shop and at that moment a sturdy-looking man in a cap beckoned me to the entrance and gave me an apple and a penny to deliver a bouquet of flowers to a house in Hyndland Street. Without knowing it I had supplied the first delivery for George Todd.

George Todd's shop at 296 Byres Road, in the late 1960s.   *Guthrie Hutton*

From this small beginning, Todd's business flowered and around 1920 he opened a second shop at No. 253. This expanded into the next-door premises in 1930 when Solomon Stoll closed his tailor's business there. Todd retained No. 262 and in 1945 announced the opening of it as a 'super flower shop', and opened a further shop in Buchanan Street. Todd was a man of style and charm. In the summer he would dress in a cream linen jacket and wear a straw Panama hat, and always smoked small cheroots. One female customer recalled: 'Mr Todd often used to place a single fresh flower on the top of our vegetable baskets with such a pleasant smile to help raise our spirits.' Clearly his early involvement in advertising gave him a flair for promotion and he employed a man – it was said full-time – to create intricate designs of fruit and vegetables in his shop windows that were rated among the finest window displays in Glasgow, A tradition of George Todd was to buy and display the first Scottish tomatoes of the year:

'Tomatoes at £3 a lb! There were only 10 tomatoes in number and they were bought by George Todd. After being on display in Todd's shop in Byres Road they will be given to Eastpark Childrens' Home in Maryhill.' George and Helen later lived in Lauderdale Gardens, where George died in 1958. When his shops closed in 1965, one was taken by Carole Wilson, another florist.

George Todd clearly loved being a greengrocer but not everyone did. In the 1940s, Jackie Paterson, a Scottish boxer who in 1943 became world fly-weight champion, was living in Ashton Road and invested some of his winnings by buying the greengrocers shop at No. 113. However, he quickly found the life of a greengrocer rather dull after the excitement of the boxing ring, and left its running to his wife, who sold it after a few years. In spite of making lots of money, by 1952 Paterson was bankrupt having, 'frittered his money away in gambling and entertaining friends'.

Some of the vegetables and fruit that we take for granted today once were scarcely known. In 1963 an *Evening Times* article on exotic vegetables reported: 'George Todd's shops have courgettes which the manager tells me is a small type of marrow from France.' In the 1880s, Malcolm Campbell, a grocer and greengrocer, who established a chain of shops across Scotland, including one at No. 343 in the new Grosvenor Buildings block built in 1931, was the first to introduce Glaswegians to bananas. Campbell continued to introduce shoppers to new varieties by importing fruit and vegetables. In 1967 the company's buying director told the *Evening Times*: 'Anything very new we usually try out in our Byres Road shop. We find the shoppers in that district very interested in experimenting with new foodstuffs.' Thomas Neale, whose shop at No. 281 was called the Covent Garden Fruit Service, was another who in the 1980s introduced new varieties to the adventurous Byres Road shoppers:

Prickly Pears from Israel, leeches from Kenya, passion fruit from the East, and fat or thin chilies. These are just four of the world's unusual fruit and vegetables that Scottish house-wives are now buying. Mr Neale is the man who travels the world looking for the unusual,

and within days of returning to the city, he has them on sale in his shop. 'I'm just back from a trip to the Far East and brought back Coco Yams from Bangkok. They're a cross between ordinary potatoes and sweet potatoes,' says Mr Neale. 'I also introduced Chinese cabbage into Scotland. Housewives are quite prepared to try new fruit and vegetables, especially in summer when everyone is in a better frame of mind.' With customers, including the Duke of Argyll. coming from as far away as the Highlands and Islands, Mr. Neale is now importing fruit and vegetables from every country in the world except Red China and Japan. 'In the middle of winter I have fresh strawberries flown in from America and Israel, apples are sent from Russia, and from the East come all the exotic items.'

Most Italians who came to Scotland opened confectioners or cafes, but Dominic Demarco, who came from Italy to Glasgow around 1960, had a greengrocer's at No. 37 and traded there for over 40 years. One regular recalled its unusual shopping baskets: 'The most exciting thing about Demarco's is the leopard-print lining on the baskets that they use to keep fruit in. It gets me every time.' The arrival of supermarkets impacted on all the small shops selling fresh produce as Demarco observed in 2001:

I have half the number of customers I had twenty years ago. It is not the prices that the supermarkets beat us on, but the convenience that they offer. In winter time

Dominic Demarco, greengrocer, No. 38, c.1960s.

James W. Galloway, butcher's van, *c.*1920s.
J. W. Galloway collection

Robert Sloan & Son, No. 311 advert, 1967.

REAL SCOTCH HAGGIS

For 25th January

Secretaries of Burns Clubs and Caterers who are asked to provide Haggis should write at once to ANNACKER LTD., GLASGOW, who specialise in this article, and can give full information as to cooking and quantities required. As there is an enormous demand, orders should be placed well in advance in order to ensure delivery in time.

ANNACKER LTD.

19 William Street, Glasgow, :: Scotland

Telephone : Central 3814   Telegrams : " Annacker, Glasgow "

ESTABLISHED 1857

Advert for Annacker's Real Scotch Haggis.

PHEASANTS, PHEASANTS, PHEASANTS
CHEAP THIS WEEK,
AT WALKER'S,
OLD-ESTABLISHED FISH EMPORIUM,
245 BYARS ROAD, KELVINSIDE,
ESTABLISHED 1874.

Advert for Walkers Fish Emporium, No. 245, 1896.

Rodgers Butchers, No. 315.   *Author*

M'COMISKEY,

45 BYRES ROAD (near Partick Cross), and 18 STEVENSON ST.
ESTABLISHED 40 YEARS.
Nat. Tel., 232X6 Bridgeton and 213X4 Hillhead.

IRISH LUMP BUTTER A SPECIALITY.
Fresh Supplies Received Three Times a Week.

Advert for McComiskey, Egg Dealer, No.45, 1906.

people are simply not interested in trailing from shop to shop: supermarkets provide all shoppers' needs under one roof.

In spite of competition from supermarkets, Byres Road still has a quality butcher and an award-winning fishmonger in 2024, although many other shops selling meat, game and fish have come and gone. One of the first butchers in the road was John Watt who opened at No. 309 in 1880:

> The shop has a large plate-glass window, and bright steel fittings, tiled walls, substantial cutting blocks, corner office desks machine room at the rear, and modern sanitary appointments throughout. In addition, Mr. Watt has, at considerable expense, erected one of Roberts's patent refrigerators on the premises, thereby enabling him to supply thoroughly seasoned joints, well hung, and in as good condition in the middle of summer as in winter weather, home-fed ox beef, and wether mutton; house lamb, veal, and pork in their respective seasons; mixed collops and sausages freshly made day to day, together with prime pickled tongues and choicely corned beef. There can be no doubt that the large and liberal patronage enjoyed by Mr. Watt is the outcome of conscientiously catering to and studying the exact needs and requirements of his individual customers.'

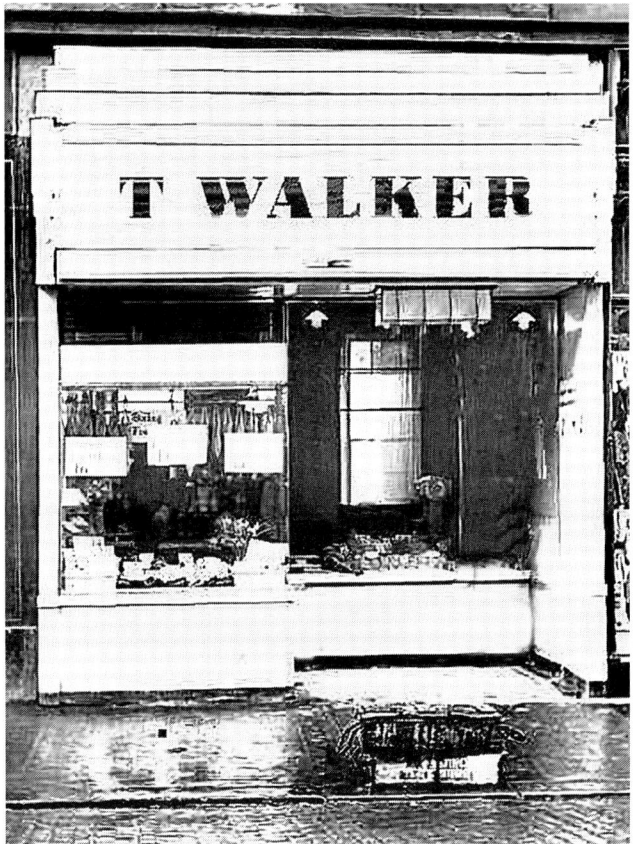

T. Walker, fishmonger, No.193, c.1950s.

Watt lived in Vinicombe Street until his death in 1909, at which point the shop closed. A number of Glasgow's butcher firms had branches in the road. J. W. Galloway, that had a shop at No. 231 from 1935 into the 1980s, was begun in 1888 by Robert Galloway in Cowcaddens. His son, James, who had opened his own shop in Partick, expanded the firm to more than 54 shops throughout the Central Belt. Galloways prided themselves on their friendly over-the-counter service and the shops were a regular meeting place for Glasgow housewives, leading to the slogan 'Meat at Galloways'. Another common Glaswegian phrase linked to a chain of butchers was, 'It's like Annacker's Midden in there' ('midden' being Scots for a refuse heap) to describe an untidy room. The firm was established by Peter (Pierre) Annacker, German sausage maker and ham curer, around 1850 and again it was his son William who built the business. At its height Annacker had a sausage factory near St. George's Cross and fifteen shops around Glasgow, including one in Byres Road at No. 15 Grosvenor Place (No. 267) from 1885 to around 1930. One theory for the slogan is that it was because Annacker's sold off bruised pies and sausages cheaply at the end of the day and hence were messy, but no one really knows the phrase's origin. The most recent butcher to open in Byres Road is Rodgers Butchers, first at No. 180 but now at No. 315. The firm was established in Clydebank in

1880 by James Rodgers and is now run by the family's fifth generation. 'Rodgers has become a favourite with the West Enders, who are known to like a good dinner party or two.'

Since 2013, dinner party hosts seeking quality fish have shopped at The Fish Plaice at No. 188 that was opened by David and Roma Scott. In 2022 their shop was voted one of the top ten British fishmongers. Not all past fishmongers have been as well regarded. John Duff, who opened his shop at No. 294 in 1875, appeared at the Hillhead Burgh Police Court charged with creating a nuisance within his shop. 'Dr Dobie, the medical officer of the Burgh stated that the obnoxious smells which proceeded from defender's shop were injurious to the health; and the Court ordered Mr Duff to abate the nuisance.' Duff's shop closed soon after. Gilmore & Son, whose main branch was at St George's Place, opened at No. 263 next door to Annacker in 1887, and advertised as, 'fish and ice merchants, poulterers, game dealers, sole agents for Chamberlin's pheasant food and dog biscuits.' The firm closed in 1905 but John Boyd took over. After his death in 1915, his wife, Jane, ran the shop until 1930, when it was purchased by Unkles Ltd, wholesale fish merchants. The firm had a number of fishmonger shops, but continued to trade in Byres

Road as Boyd's through to the late 1970s. In 1964 a royal sturgeon landed at Ayr and weighing between 25lb and 30lb was displayed in Boyd's window. 'By tradition, the fish, from which caviar comes, is offered to the queen, but as she is out of the country the fish will be on show for a few days and then sold.'

That Byres Road's shopkeepers always have prided themselves on their range of products is evidenced by a description from 1896 of George McVey's grocers at No. 333 that traded until the First World War:

> The supply of select general groceries and prime provisions to meet the daily demands of a large and essentially superior class of trade in the fashionable west end district of Hillhead, finds an able representative in the person of Mr. George McVey. All manner of everyday groceries, together with the numerous household sundries usually associated therewith; special lines in pure and choicely blended teas and coffees, conspicuous amongst which is the celebrated Cingalese Mazawattee tea; British and foreign tinned and bottled combustibles and table delicacies of the highest order; and prime provisions of every kind in the way – hams and bacon, butter and cheese, meal and flour, lard, and the freshest of country eggs, are all fully represented. Order, system, and courtesy are salient features of this carefully conducted business; and the large and liberal patronage enjoyed by Mr. McVey is ample evidence of the fact that his efforts have not failed to meet with deserved appreciation and support.

James & George Hunter, grocers and wine merchants, opened four shops through the 1870s: two on the south side, one in Hyndland Road and one at No. 215, and traded through to the 1960s. In 1910. William Kerr, another grocer and wine merchant, opened at No. 299 and also operated into the 1960s. When Giuliana Zanotti of the Grosvenor Café arrived in Glasgow from Italy in the 1950s, she went to Kerr's shop to buy olive oil. As her English was still limited, she pointed at a yellow bottle she presumed to be what she needed, only later to discover she had purchased Lucozade! At this time olive oil was only available from chemists in tiny bottles, as its use was generally limited to removing earwax.

Larger grocery chains had shops in Byres Road, including R. & J. Templeton, which opened its branch at No. 276 in 1912. The firm was begun by Robert Templeton in the 1880s and his brother John joined the business when it began to expand. By 1900 R. & J. Templeton, 'tea merchants and cash grocers', had 40 branches, mostly in Glasgow. In 1919 the firm was sold to Home & Colonial Stores, which had been founded by a grocer in London in 1883. The term, 'colonial stores' was widely used to describe retailers specialising in imported, non-perishable dry goods from abroad, such as coffee, tea, rice and sugar. Home & Colonial Stores began opening stores across England and by 1903 had 500. Templetons was one of a number of chains the company bought, including Maypole Dairies, and when it merged with Liptons' stores, the company began to evolve into one of the first food multiples businesses.

Like other shops, grocers were adversely affected by the arrival of Cooper's Fine Fare in 1962; the first Byres Road supermarket. It was on the corner of Ashton Lane, where Iceland Foods is today. The *Glasgow Herald's* food writer, Robin Orr popped in to the new store:

> The new supermarket in Byres Road makes an immediate and striking impression, being clean and bright. comfortably warm yet fresh and airy. It has hardware, books and stationery, as well as all manner of foodstuffs under the same roof including a good selection of cheese, a fine display of 'oven-ready' poultry, and beef, lamb, and pork, as well as groceries, fruit and vegetables.

James & George Hunter, Grocer & Wine Merchant, No. 215, *c.*1910.

Henry Morton collection

Coopers Fine Fare supermarket, corner of Ashton Lane, 1977.

Chris Doak

In 1969 the Scottish Final of the Miss Grocer UK competition was held in the Byres Road Fine Fare: 'Fifteen girls will be judged for their competence as grocery assistants, ability to handle awkward customers and personal charm. The three winners will go forward to the final in London.' Mercifully, there is no Miss Grocer competition these days, although handling awkward customers continues to be an essential skill for all those working at the various Byres Road stores. In 1988 the Byres Road branch of the Bejam Frozen Food company at Nos. 224/226 was the only Glasgow shop listed in *The Good Manners Guide* published by the Polite Society, an organisation founded by the Rev Ian Gregory in 1986 to promote a 'politer society'. The Bejam staff were praised for being 'notably friendly and knowledgeable. A triumph of personnel policy and training.' The store manager Stephen Howarth said, 'This has come as a complete surprise.' Perhaps Jack Lothian would have failed to win customer plaudits for, by his own admittance, while working for three years at the Byres Road Safeway store in the mid-1990s his mind was not always on the job:

I worked the trolleys for two years and was always finding scams to skive off. Sometimes I would have a mate phone the store and say that a trolley had been dumped in the Botanic Gardens, and could they send someone to retrieve it? I could usually make that trip last about an hour.

He had an ambition of becoming a film and TV writer, so, 'at other times I would disappear to the toilet for an hour at a time to work on my script.' The boring years finally paid off when his film, *Late Night Shopping* was commissioned by Channel 4, and he has gone on to have a hugely successful career; including many episodes of *Doc Martin* and more recently, *Who Is Erin Carter?* for Netflix.

By the 1980s, when Bejams opened, frozen food had become widely used and around two thirds of British homes owned a freezer. The frozen-food revolution could be said to have started in Britain in 1955 when Birds Eye launched its frozen fish fingers with the sales pitch 'No smell, no fuss'. Although initially mocked, frozen fish fingers swiftly became a family favourite. The first Byres Road shop specialising in selling frozen foods and freezers, was

Master Freeze Foods that opened at No. 101 in 1972. At that time less than 5% of homes owned a freezer. Around 1990, Bejams was taken over by Iceland, which still trades at Nos. 224/226.

In response to the challenge from supermarkets, when Tony Johnston opened Peckham's in 1982 he focused on stocking specialist food and drink products, and styled his shop as, 'vintners, victuallers and delicatessen'. Johnston began his career running a hamburger stall in Saracen's Head before opening the first Peckham's in Clarence Drive. Its success enabled Johnson to open more branches, including one at No. 100 that later moved to Nos. 124/126. Part of Johnston's ethos was for his shops to remain open until late and the Byres Road shop did not close until midnight. In 1992 the *Evening Times* described Peckham's success as, 'satisfying the discerning and sophisticated tastes of a small army of Glasgow's *bon viveurs*.' Perhaps the opening in Byres Road of Waitrose and M&S Food Hall, each with their expanding range of specialist foods, was part of the reason that by 2010 Johnson's business was struggling, and in 2017 the Byres Road shop closed.

Interior of Peckhams, vintners & delicatessen, No.124/126, *c*.2000.

View up Byres Road from Ashton Lane, 1910.   *Lewis Hutton collection.*

Chapter Four

Looking One's Best

Dressing well has always been important to West End residents and Glasgow's stylish central city stores of the past, which included Wylie & Lochhead, Copland & Lye and Pettigrew & Stephens, offered the most up-to-date fashions. However, in earlier times people usually shopped for everyday wear at the local drapers' shop, such as David Lawrie's at No. 116 that opened in in 1893:

> The spacious double-fronted shop is handsomely appointed throughout in the best modern style with a stock that is remarkable for its richness in fashionable novelties and articles of standard worth and excellence. All manner of everyday drapery goods, in the way of household linens, calicoes, sheetings, shirtings, flannels, blankets and heavy Manchester wares generally; hosiery, gloves, and corsets; fancy drapery goods of every conceivable kind; baby linen, and children's and gentlemen's underwear and outfitting items of every kind; and the numerous sundries coming under the designation of small wares and haberdashery, are all fully represented.

In past times hats were essential wear for both women and men, and Byres Road had a number of milliners over the early decades. Miss Marion Rowand opened her hat shop at No. 303 in 1888 and by the early 1920s the shop was trading under the name of Madam Rosalie. There was a vogue for fashion shops to have French sounding names but the owner at that time was in fact Ada Eastaugh. The shop's Frenchified name was not enough to stave off bankruptcy and in 1925 the shop was under new ownership. Irene and Edna McLaughlan were more successful and traded through to the 1960s. The shop then became Jacqueline Children's Boutique, which sold 'clothes for babies, tots and grown-up eight-to-ten-year olds' and in its adverts claimed, 'where it's easy to shop by car.'

It is not known if Mademoiselle Agier who opened her dress shop at No. 1 University Avenue in 1900 was really called that or if again it was a PR pseudonym. She advertised: 'Just returned from

Advert for Jacqueline, No. 303, 1964.

Paris with all the latest novelties for spring and summer wear in day, evening and reception, and tailor-made gowns, millinery, mantles and underclothing.' The shop was short-lived but Mademoiselle Agier continued as a corsetiere and her corsets were advertised for sale at Jenners in Edinburgh. To the relief of many women, the wearing of corsets went out of fashion, but became trendy among some in the 2000s due to the burgeoning interest in Burlesque. For a number of years from 2008 Hayley MacLennan's shop, Betsy Labelle at No. 57, was a favourite with many seeking vintage-style lingerie: 'Walking into this gorgeous lingerie shop is like stepping into a fantasy bedroom. The shop feels romantic and nostalgic, with floral flocked wallpaper, vintage furniture and Marlene Dietrich LPs on the record player.' The hosiery and undergarments on sale at the Scotch Wool & Hosiery Stores at No. 195 from the 1930s through to the '60s were rather more utilitarian (and often scratchy). This was one of over 300 shops opened by the Greenock firm, Fleming, Reid & Company. As well as the firm's own knitwear, the

Advert for Mademoiselle Agier, No, 1 University Avenue, 1900.

Betsy la Belle, No. 57. 2010

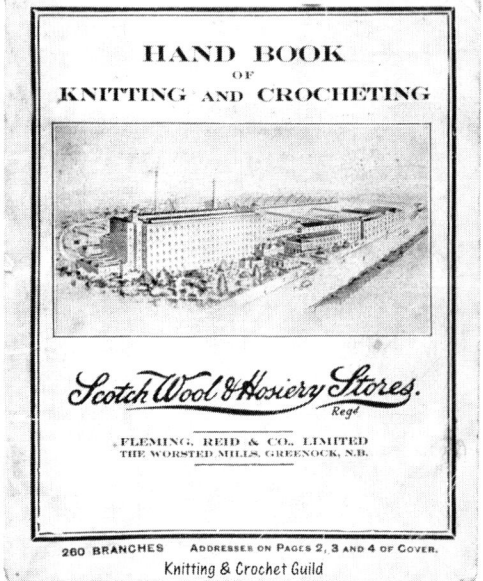

Scotch Wool & Hosiery Stores' Knitting & Crochet book, c.1930s.

Scotch Wool & Hosiery Stores, c.1930s.

Advert for Aquarius, No. 134, 1983.

Interior of a Bayne & Duckett shoe shop, c.1960s.

shops stocked hand-knitting wools and pattern books for home knitting and crochet.

That fur coats are now thought inappropriate is understandable given the wide range of animals hunted to provide the pelts. An advert in 1915 by Mrs Crichton, who lived in a flat at No. 142, offered coats, capes. muffs and other garments made from ermine, skunk, opossum, otter, fox, wolf and musquash. For those who could not afford the expensive furs, cheaper pelts were used, such as those Mrs Crichton advertised to buy: 'Last season's moleskins wanted.' Through the 1960s and '70s Henri Bordaud furriers at No. 242 offered fur coats that were, 'young modern styling at reasonable prices.' In 1966 raiders smashed the fur shop's window and escaped with a number of coats. In 1957 Susie Stewart opened her dress shop at Nos. 157/159:

> Monopolies, mergers, multiples, take-overs are no doubt very important to tycoons but are not worth a row of pins to the woman of fashion! What matters to you is personal individual service and by maintaining this policy Susie Stewart is receiving an even greater share of West End trade.

By the mid-1960s young people were seeking new styles, influenced by the 'Swinging London' fashion explosion. To cater for them Aquarius opened at No. 311 selling 'ethnic curiosities' and clothing. It was one of the earliest shops to sell clothes designed by the young Marion Donaldson who, with her husband David, returned from London to Glasgow

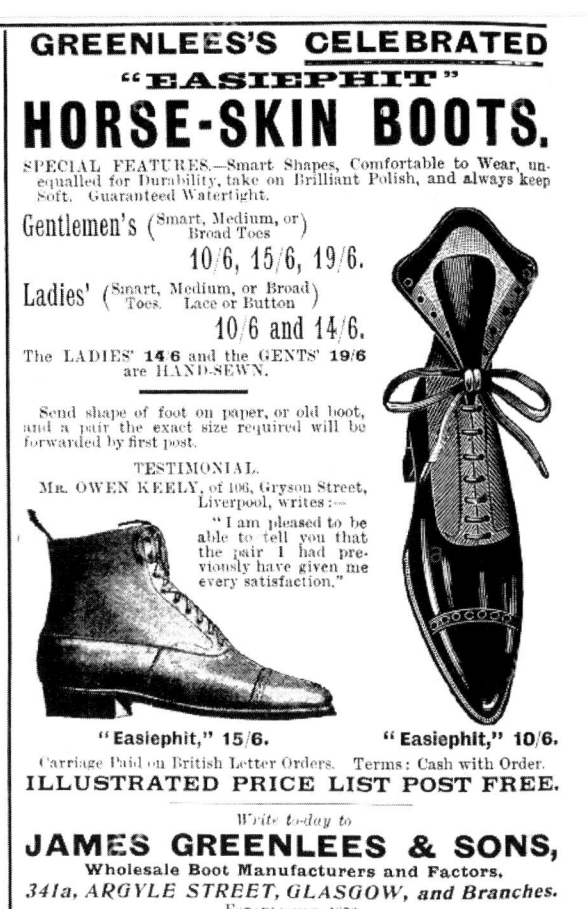

Advert for Greenlees Boots, 1899.

Advert for Bordaud, No. 242, 1972.

and began making her clothes from a small flat in Hill Street. Such was the influence of her fashion designs that the Marion Donaldson brand has been credited with bringing 'Swinging London' to Scotland, and by 1979, from an initial £50 capital, the brand was turning over £1 million. As then, today's Byres Road clothes shops reflect current trends. At No. 305 is Finnieston Clothing, established by Ross Geddes and Luke Miller, that 'offers functional lifestyle garments, each telling a story of the industrial workforce of Glasgow's past'.

Bayne & Duckett, that had a shop at Nos. 319/321 and another on the corner of Byres Road and Dumbarton Road, was one of three Glasgow-based shoe companies with branches in Byres Road. Another was A & W Paterson, which opened a branch at No. 284 in 1880 and traded there until the late 1930s. Greenlees shoes was established in Argyle Street in 1858 by James Greenlees, a chemist turned boot-maker, and expanded hugely after the First World War; its Byres Road shop at No. 283 was one of over 200. It became known for its 'Easiephit' brand. The Leeds firm, Stead & Simpson, which by

1875 was the largest shoe manufacturer in the world, opened its Byres Road shop at No. 217 in the 1920s and traded through to the 1980s. From the 1920s to the 1950s many shoe shops had an 'X-Ray Pedoscope':

The machine seemed to me to be a wonderful device to show how well the shoes were fitting. We put our feet into it and looked down onto a screen which showed the outlines of the shoes and our bones inside them. I thought it quite fun to look down this device, waggle my toes and watch them move.

However, concerns about radiation led to the machines' removal. A few independent shoe shops traded in the road, such as James White, who opened No. 384 in 1880 and traded till 1900:

The spacious double-fronted shop, with its neatly contrived separate departments for ladies and gentlemen, and well-equipped workshop adjoining, is admirably appointed throughout in the best modern style, and displays a large and first-class stock of ready-made boots, shoes in a great diversity of styles, shapes, and sizes at moderate cost. Mr. White and his picked staff also make all kinds of high-class boots, shoes, and slippers, of perfect fit and faultless in construction.

After the Second World War, Charles Archibald moved his shoemaking and repair business from Govan to No. 138 and by the 1970s it was run by his son, Leonard. While still offering shoe repairs, Leonard had stopped making shoes and instead made sporrans. His shop was described in the *Evening News*:

Archibald's shop smells of leather, thread, wax, and adhesive. An enormous wooden shoe at the door symbolises his trade and in the window is a display of old hand-craft tools. Inside is a marvellous clutter of shoes and boots and contains a most magnificent piece of Victorian engineering – a Blake insole stitcher dated 1889. The business, founded by Leonard's grandfather at White Street towards the end of the last century, moved to Byres Road in the early 1950s. He told me, 'Our proper title in my day was Bespoke Shoemakers and all were members of the Shoemakers' Society. Before the Second World War there were around 30,000 members in the Shoemakers' Society but in 1955. a meeting was called and only twelve attended.'

In 1978 Archibald's business failed; a warrant sale of all his equipment took place to pay off his debts, and the business closed.

The first jewellery shop in the road was opened in 1891 by John Kerr at No. 287, and in 1901 the business was taken over by Matthew Pollock, 'optician, watchmaker and jeweller'. Matthew, his wife, Margaret, and their three young children lived

Shoe shop advert explaining the marvel of the X-ray shoe fitting machine,. *c.*1920s.

above at No. 279, where Matthew died in 1949. He had retired in 1939 but the shop continued to trade under his name into the 1960s. In the 1940s, Thomas Harkins, who had become fascinated by gemstones, decided to open a jewellery shop and bought No. 11, which had been a newsagent. His son, Michael who took over the shop when his father died, recalled:

Michael Harkins outside his jewellers shop, No. 11, 2023.   *Glasgow Live*

Jewellery shops have always been a prime target for thieves. In 1975 a young woman was employed as a shop assistant at Hannah Jewellers at No. 257 and assisted in a theft of jewellery worth £14,000. In court she claimed an older man, described as 'a former pub and restaurant manager', had coerced her into the crime by threatening to harm her if she refused to assist. This claim did not save her from going to prison. Stevenson Jewellers took over the business and in 2007 it was scammed out of thousands of pounds of jewellery by three men and two women, 'wearing colourful African-style robes'. The group asked to see a number of items, including gold chains and rings. Having said they wanted to buy them, the items were placed in a bag, but when they offered to pay with euros,

Part of the deal, which I could never understand, was that my father had to run it as a newsagents for a couple of years to get rid of the guy's stock. Gradually he introduced watches, clocks, necklaces and built it up from there.

Michael remembered the time in 1973 when his father was having to cope with the economic crisis of the miner's strike that was known as 'the winter of discontent', during which power to shops and homes was restricted on certain days:

My father would check the newspaper to see when our lights would be switched off at 3pm. He was very ingenious and bought caravan gas lights and had a big gas canister. He rigged up a copper pipe which fed into the lights and it was like we were in the Victorian times. Once the lights were off, he switched on the gas and it would light the mantles so we could still trade. Just before Christmas time my father came into the shop where my brother and I were working away. He had a camping gas canister which had to be renewed. He walked through the back door where we had a gas fire. I was attending to a customer and there was an almighty explosion. I turned round and flames came out through the back door. I thought, my God, what has happened to my father. I opened the door and he looked like a cartoon. He had his cigarette hanging out of his mouth, his bushy eyebrows were ash, he was in shock.

Fortunately, Thomas survived to enjoy his retirement, as did Michael, who closed the business when he retired in 2023.

Advert for Hannah & Sons, jewellers, No. 257, 1977.

the shop assistant explained that the shop could not accept foreign currency. So, they said they would go and exchange their currency for sterling and return. To show faith they left a small deposit. However, unseen by the unfortunate assistant, they had slickly swopped the bag containing the jewellery with a dummy one, and absconded with the valuable goods. 'Detective Inspector Alister McCreadie, of Partick police station, said: "This is a well-organised team who have practised this scam."

While many small businesses in the road have closed in the face of competition from supermarkets, new technology and on-line shopping, hairdressers continue to thrive. Edward Graham – Traditional Scottish Barber – first opened at No. 99 in 1915, and for a time had four barber shops. Walter McCallum worked for the Graham family for over forty years: 'People didn't just come into a barber shop for a haircut, but for a laugh and a blether. … In those early days it was all short back and sides.' Graham's

barbers shop is now at No. 29, and in charge of the scissors today is Edward's granddaughter, Elizabeth. It is now the longest continuous family business in Byres Road.

In 1898 John Stafford Gregson, 'hairdresser, perfumer, hair-worker and wigmaker', opened No. at 290 and lived with his wife, Kate above at No. 286. Gregson was born in Berwick-on-Tweed and trained with his father before moving to Glasgow. He became one of Scotland's leading hairdressers, and an expert in creating the 'postiche': hairpieces that clip into biological hair to cover thinning or balding spots on the head, and add volume to the hair. He founded the Glasgow College of Hairdressers, which eventually became the Stow College of Hairdressing and was president of the National Federation of Hairdressers for many years. He had a love of the arts and in 1910 helped establish the Glasgow Music Festival that continues to this day. Also in the 1920s, he supported the setting-up of the Scottish National Players, a non-professional touring theatre company that aimed to pioneer the establishment of a Scottish National Theatre along the lines of Dublin's Abbey Theatre. The company performed early plays by James Bridie and a number of its productions were directed by the young Tyrone Guthrie. Gregson, who died in 1944, passed his business on in 1930 to Robert Thomson, a colleague who assisted Gregson with establishing the Glasgow College of Hairdressers. Thomson later was chairman of the Advisory Committee for Courses for Hairdressers at Stow College. He too gained an international reputation, serving on juries for international hairdressing competitions and as an examiner for the City and Guilds of London Institute. He died in 1958 but his salon at No. 290 continued through to the early 1970s.

While Gregson and Thomson gained fame in the world of hairdressing, Gordon Smith, who had his men's hairdressing business at No. 65 in the 1990s, became renowned for quite a different sphere of operation. By 2013 his fame as a Spiritualist led to appearances on TV, a series of successful books and invitations to attend Spiritualist meetings around the world. His appearances at venues, including the Pavilion Theatre in Glasgow, were sell-outs.

Edwards Graham & David Bingham outside Graham's hairdressers, No. 99, c.1920s

Thomsons hairdressing, No. 290, in the late 1960s.

Guthrie Hutton

Advert for Gordon Smith, Psychic barber.

Mary Hair Nail & Beauty, No. 37.

Botanic Gardens, *c.*1910.
Lewis Hutton collection

Postcard showing Kibble Palace and hothouses, *c.*1930.

Sunday afternoon at the Botanic Gardens, *c.*1920s.

Chapter Five

Sporting Pastimes

Those living and working in Byres Road have been able to enjoy the delights of strolling through the Botanic Gardens since the road's earliest days. Glasgow's first Botanic Gardens were established in 1817 by Thomas Hopkirk, a distinguished Glasgow botanist, with the support of a number of local dignitaries and the University of Glasgow. They were originally sited at the western end of Sauchiehall Street, at that time on the edge of the city. The Royal Botanical Institution of Glasgow owned and ran the Gardens, and provided the university with a supply of plants for medical and botanical classes. In 1821, William Jackson Hooker, one of the most eminent botanists in the world at the time, was appointed Professor of Botany at the University and Curator of the Gardens, and in 1839 the Gardens moved to the present site. Members of the Royal Botanic Institution of Glasgow had the right to free entrance, while the public were admitted only at weekends and had to pay a penny.

Botanics in the snow, 1936.   *Daily Record*

The Kibble Palace originally was a private conservatory built for John Kibble at his house in Coulport on Loch Long. Kibble had a plan to make money by moving the structure to Glasgow and holding paid events within it. He tried to persuade Glasgow to give him a free site in Queen's Park but the city declined. So he then offered it to the Royal Botanical Institution on the basis that after allowing him to manage it for 20 years, the glasshouse would pass to the Institution. The deal was agreed and all went fine for a time. In May 1874, an event featuring Moody and Sankey, two famous North American evangelists, took place in Kibble Palace and an estimated 6,000 people were inside the glasshouse and around 20,000 outside. The building also was used for the installation as rectors of Glasgow University of both Benjamin Disraeli in 1873 and William Ewart Gladstone in 1879. In 1883 the Institution ran into financial difficulties and had to borrow money from Glasgow Corporation. Two years later, mainly because of the loan repayments, the Institution ran into further debt and had to curtail use of the Gardens. As this was a breach of the contract with John Kibble, they had to pay him £11,000 for the glasshouse. This was the final straw and the Institution folded in 1887, the Gardens closed permanently and the site passed to Glasgow Corporation.

Although the city continued basic maintenance work, the Gardens remained closed and their future became intertwined with Glasgow's push to annex Hillhead Burgh. The city proposed that the Gardens become a public park for Hillhead but the Burgh instead offered to pay a share of the loan and maintenance expenses to ensure it remained a botanic garden. 'The question is shall Glasgow, the second city of the Empire, possess botanic gardens which rank next to Kew?' The stand-off was resolved when annexation was agreed in 1891, for as part of that agreement an act was passed vesting the gardens in Glasgow Corporation, on the condition that the Gardens, 'be kept open, preserved and maintained as a public area and botanic gardens to Glasgow.' Today the Gardens are visited by over 400,000 visitors each year.

Partick Curling Club was established in 1842 and in 1848 was given permission by James Gibson of Hillhead House to make a curling pond on his land at a rent of £2 per annum. Gibson also agreed to become the club's patron. The club's rink lay between today's Ruthven Street and Roxburgh Street, and in 1855 the club played a charity match there:

This spirited club, successful in all its matches this season with one exception, got up last month a very laudable match among themselves, members residing in the east against those in the west, for the excellent purpose of giving the poor of Partick a supply of coals – the losing side to subscribe double the amount of the winning side. We shall only say regarding the game that it was a delightful one, and neither side won. Upwards of sixty carts of coals were distributed among the poor. Part of the funds was most cheerfully and kindly contributed by inhabitants of Partick and neighbourhood not connected with the club.

The curling pond was still in use through to the early 1870s as on 29 December 1869:

The competition for the Royal Caledonian Club's silver medal, between the Partick and Maryhill Clubs, took place on Monday on the pond at Byar's Road, when three rinks too part, and after some very exciting play the Maryhill representatives were defeated by nineteen shots.

Curlers, *c.*1900.

'Long John Anderson who was President in 1843 when the Partick Curling Club opened the rink off Byres Road.
History of Partick Bowling Club

The pond was shared with the Glasgow Skating Club. In January 1868, the club advertised: 'If the frost holds, there will be skating on the Club's pond, Byars Road', and later: 'Wanted an intelligent able-bodied man to act as Club officer and take charge of the pond at Byars Road.' Skating was a popular pastime throughout Scotland in the nineteenth century and the Glasgow Skating Club was founded in 1830. The Club's President George Anderson published *The Art of Skating; with Plain Directions for The Acquirement of the Most Difficult and Elegant Movements* in 1852 and in it wrote:

In Glasgow, there is probably less skating than in any town in the kingdom of near its size; the inhabitants are so much engaged with business all day, and there is so total an absence of idle people, that the ice has only a few devotees.

Club members could pay by annual subscription of 10s. 6d. or take out a life membership for £7.7s. Skates at that time had a wooden sole affixed to the boot and members wore a badge with a flying eagle holding a skate in its claws. There also were informal skating ponds created when water froze in the pits that had been left from extracting clay: 'There we skated after school hours on weekdays and Sundays.' However, such informal skating had its dangers. In December 1867 a young boy who had been skating on a frozen clay pit fell through the ice. Having been alerted to the plight of the boy, who was struggling to keep himself afloat, John Orr, a decorator who worked in Byres Road. rushed to the pond with a ladder and rope, and saved the lad.

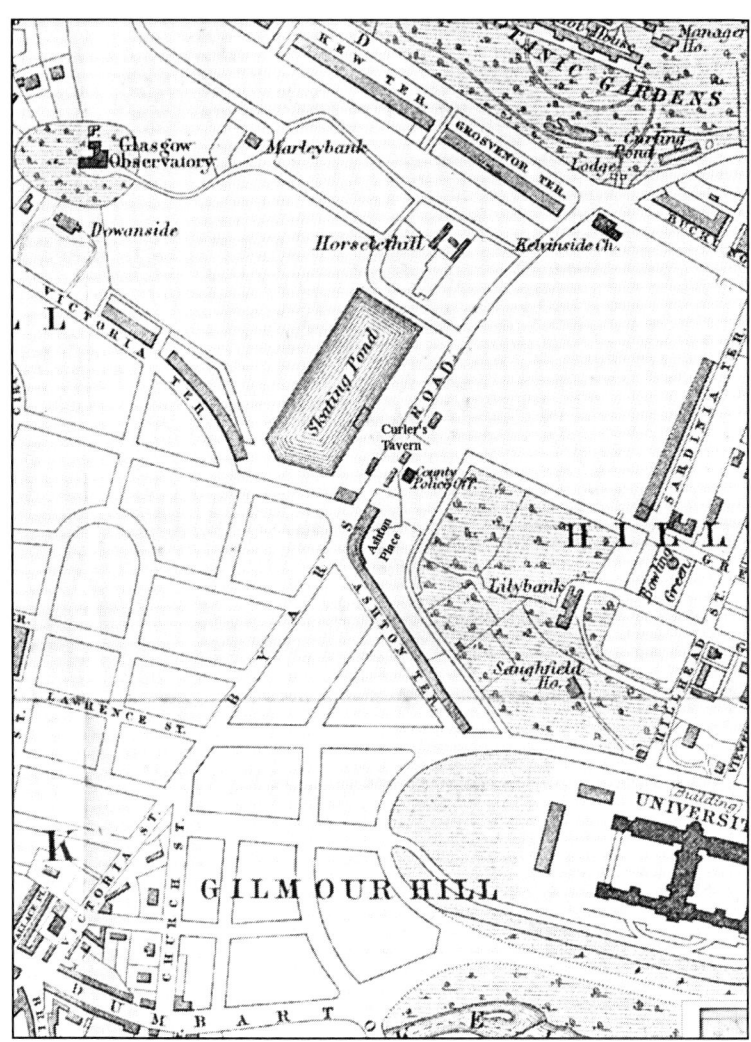

Extract of 1852 map showing skating pond
National Library of Scotland

The Art Of Skating; with Plain Directions For The Acquirement Of The Most Difficult And Elegant Movements by George Anderson, published 1852

A new form of skating began to become popular among youngsters in the 1970s but the *Glasgow Herald* warned: 'If all your kids want for Christmas is a skateboard, don't give in. Let your child keep their front teeth. That's the message from safety organisations.' The article included interviews with owners of sports shops including David Bell of Sportstoys at No. 381, who said, 'I doubt if we would market them even if there was a craze.'

In 1869 there was a 'velocipede mania', although that craze for what were the first pedal-driven two-wheel bicycles was among adults. Gustavus Alsing was the first in Glasgow to import one of the Parisian inventions:

Yesterday, Mr Alsing, with one or two friends, proceeded to Partick and tried the machine. Though quite unpractised in such a mode of locomotion, they succeeded in preserving their balance on the somewhat ticklish saddle, and getting along satisfactorily and at a considerable speed.

While the velocipede may not have been invented in Scotland, it is probable that the first piece of British music honouring the first bicycle model was composed in Partick by Gustavus Alsing. He was a musician – he played the mouth harmonium – and in early 1869 he composed *Alsing's Velocipede Galop* and sold the sheet music from his shop in Sauchiehall Street. The tune was described as: 'pleasing and lively, the time is good and well-marked, and, we doubt not, it will become a favourite addition to the dance music of the season.' Within months the Glasgow Velocipede Club, was formed with headquarters at 94 Buchanan Street. The club kept a number of velocipedes that could be borrowed by members at stables in Byres Road, and its regulations stated that the machines, 'must not be used by those who are not yet proficient.' There were issues over the borrowing:

The two members who took number 3 and 4 velocipedes without having previously entered their names in the Club's Engagement Book on Monday afternoon and had not returned them by this (Wednesday) morning, will please communicate with the Secretary, as several disappointments ensued in consequence.

Advert for Sportstoys, No. 381, 1974.

Velocipediana.

GLASGOW VELOCIPEDE CLUB.

Several of the Club's new Velocipedes have been Stationed at the Club's Stables, Byres Road. They will be available for Members on and after TO-DAY, the 7TH INSTANT. Members, before taking out the Machines, must enter their Names in the Club's Engagement Book (which lies at 94 Buchanan Street), stating what Machine they want, and when they mean to take it out and return it. These Machines must not be used by those who are not yet proficient, as Machines for Learning are kept in the Club's Practising Hall, 138 Stirling Road. A. G. C., Hon. Secy.

THE VELOCIPEDE COMPANY'S
BURNBANK RIDING SCHOOL,
GREAT WESTERN ROAD,
(Burnbank Drill Hall,)
AND
THEIR BRANCH RIDING SCHOOL,
AT
44 MITCHELL STREET,
ARE OPEN DAILY FOR VELOCIPEDING.

Velocipedes (with Lessons), 2s. per Hour.—Visitors, 6d.

N. B.—Velocipedes for Hire or Sale on Moderate Terms—large Stock to select from.

Advert for Glasgow Velocipede club, 1869.

Cycle Cycles,
Cresswell Lane, 2023.
Author

Man riding a Velocipede, 1869.

UCI cycling World Championship race in Byres Road, 2023.

Within a few years the velocipede gave way to the next bicycle model, the 'Penny-farthing', and the club closed, and its eight velocipedes sold. The 'Penny-farthing' was tricky to ride due to its very large front wheel, and many who were more safety-minded took to riding tricycles. In 1884, twenty tricycles ridden by members of the Glasgow Tricycling Club travelled up Byres Road on their way to the Botanic Gardens. By the mid-1880s the 'safety bicycle' displaced the 'penny-farthing'. This was the form that exists today and being easy to ride it quickly became widely used, and Joseph Darroch opened his cycle shop in 1897:

> Our representative called at the establishment of the New Windsor Cycle Company, 98 Byres Road, Hillhead, and found them busy and reporting good business during the recent fine weather. This company holds the agency for the well-known Trent machines, which are going well. This company makes speciality of the hire of machines. Anyone requiring a machine by the hour, day, week, or month should pay them a visit and inspect their large stock of both ladies' and gents' machines.

With the roadway of Byres Road being revamped to include bicycle lanes, no doubt local

Opening of the baths by A. S. Boyd, 1876.

THE WESTERN BATHS COMPANY
(LIMITED).
To be Registered under The Companies Acts, 1862 and 1867.
CAPITAL, £10,000, DIVIDED INTO 2000 SHARES OF £5 EACH.
5s per Share to be Paid on Application; 5s on Allotment; and the Remainder in Instalments as required.

Chairman.
H. E. CRUM EWING, Jun., Esq., 20 Belhaven Terrace.

Directors.
JAMES BUCHANAN MIRRLEES, Esq., Redlands.
HENRY COWAN, Esq., 13 St. James' Terrace.
ROBERT GOURLAY, Esq., 11 Crown Gardens.
GEORGE M. PLAYFAIR, Esq., 14 Rosslyn Terrace.
GEORGE R. ALEXANDER, Esq., 42 Sardinia Terrace.
FREDERIC J. HALLOWS, Esq., 37 Hamilton Drive.
ALEXANDER A. FERGUSSON, Esq., 11 Grosvenor Terrace.
HUGH STEVEN, Esq., 4 Buckingham Terrace.
JAMES ALEXANDER, Jun., Esq., 7 Great Kelvin Terrace.
WILLIAM WALLS, Esq., 2 Belhaven Terrace.
Professor COWAN, M.D., 159 Bath Street.
THOMAS WHARRIE, Esq., 5 Kew Terrace.

This Company has for its object the Erection of Swimming, Turkish, and other Baths, for the accommodation of the Suburbs West of the Kelvin.

An eligible Site has been secured in Cranworth Street (a New Street being formed parallel to Kersland Street, and between that Street and Byars Road).

As the Shareholders of the Company will probably form too limited a body to retain exclusively the use of the Baths, a Swimming Club will also be formed, with the object of taking the Baths in Lease from the Company on such terms as will insure a fair Dividend to the Shareholders; the Members of the Club having the sole right of using them during the Lease, on such terms as may be arranged.

A considerable portion of the Capital is already Subscribed for, and Applications should be lodged on or before 31st December, 1875.

Prospectuses and Forms of Application for Shares may be obtained from the Interim Secretary, D. Hill-Jack, Accountant, 138 Hope Street; or from the Solicitors, Dill, Smillie & Wilson, 51 West Nile Street.

Advert for shares in the Western Bath Company, 1875.

bicycle shops, such Cycle Cycles at Unit 14 in Cresswell Lane, will flourish. Byres Road itself has been used as part of the course for a number of bicycle races over the years, including the UCI Cycling World Championships in 2023.

Those in Hillhead and the surrounding area who sought regular exercise, but were less taken with chilly outdoor pursuits, would have been thrilled to read the 1875 advert for a new company:

> It has for its object the erection of swimming, Turkish and other baths on a site in Cranworth Street. As the Shareholders of the Company will probably form too limited a body to retain exclusive use of the Baths, a Swimming Club will also be formed.

The shares were swiftly taken up by the well-off residents of the West End and the architects Clarke and Bell created an ornamental building in the style of a Venetian palazzo. The baths opened in 1876 and at the time included the largest swimming pool in Scotland. Some of the wealthier members would be collected by carriage and driven to the baths for an early morning swim – it is said some in their dressing gowns. There they could obtain a shave from the baths' barber after

Western Baths, c.1900

their swim before departing for work. In 1881 the third annual swimming competition was held:

> There was a large and fashionable assemblage of ladies and gentlemen. Music was discoursed by an orchestra stationed at the South end of the bath, and as the place was profusely decked with flags, everything had a happy appearance.

However, by 1884 the baths were in financial trouble, partly due to a recurrent leak in the pool, and closed: 'Extensive public sale of the whole superior and elegant billiard room, reading room and bathroom furniture and fittings. Originally cost upwards of £500.' In 1886, the building which had cost £30,000, was sold to a private company for £6,000 and the baths reopened in October with many improvements:

> A complete set of gymnasium apparatus has been fitted up over the bath, including flying trapeze and travelling rings. In the Turkish bath a great improvement has been affected. Another hot-room has been added, in which the temperature can be raised to 150 degrees. A plunge bath has also been constructed in connection with this department, while the shampooing room, which has been remodelled, will be exclusively set apart for members who are using the Turkish, Vapour, and Russian baths, the latter of which is a new feature. A dressing room has been fitted up for the use of ladies, for whom the whole of the establishment will be reserved during the middle part

of each weekday. There is a billiard-room (which contains two tables), spacious reading-room, smoking-room, and two rooms set apart for card-playing.

However, not everyone was happy: 'I would beg draw attention, in your valuable paper, to a crying nuisance in Hillhead. Since the Western Baths were opened about a month ago, the tall chimney stack attached to the premises, belches out dense columns of smoke, morn, noon, and night.' In 1887 the first Ladies Swimming and Diving Contests were held:

BATHS	Tickets	3 months. Not transferable
Aix Massage Douche, - - -	4/	3 for 10/6
Bier's Hot Air Treatment, - -	2/6	5 ,, 10/6
Brine Bath, - - - -	4/	3 ,, 10/6
Dowsing Radiant Heat and Light Bath :		
Full Treatment, - - -	6/	4 ,, 21/
Local Applications, - -	3/	4 ,, 10/6
Liver Pack, with Needle Bath, -	2/6	5 ,, 10/6
Local Douche, - - - -	2/	6 ,, 10/6
Medicated Vapour, with Needle Bath,	2/6	5 ,, 10/6
Mustard Compress, - - -	2/6	5 ,, 10/6
Nauheim Bath, - - - -	4/	3 ,, 10/6
Needle Bath, - - - -	1/	—
Oxygen Bath, - - - -	4/	3 ,, 10/6
Plombières, - - - -	5/	5 ,, 21/
Rectal Douche, - - - -	2/	6 ,, 10/6
Russian Bath, - - - -	—	6 ,, 21/
Schwalbach Bath, - - -	4/	3 ,, 10/6
Sulphur Bath, - - - -	3/6	4 ,, 12/
Turkish Bath, - - - -	—	6 ,, 21/
Vibratory Massage (ten minutes), -	2/6	5 ,, 10/6
Vichy Massage Douche, - -	4/	3 ,, 10/6

List of charges for visitors at Western Baths.

Western Baths Archive

'Nearly 400 ladies attended. The only members of the sterner sex present were two club masters who acted as judges.' Although women were able to use the baths at certain times it was not until 1965 that mixed bathing was allowed. Today the club has 2,500 members and a waiting list. In 1995, in response to the growing interest in keep-fit, a gymnasium and sports hall were added by the creation of an extension on the corner of Cranworth Street. This is now just one of a number of local gymnasiums, including Revolution Spin in Dowanhill Lane that advertises: 'Banging playlists and amazing lighting…. Ride to the beat and get that full body workout.'

Advert for Cecil Billiard Rooms, 1903.

Western Baths, c.1900

George Snooker Hall, Great George Street, c.1950s.

Those who were not members of the Western Baths could play billiards or snooker in various dimly-lit dark, nicotine-stained halls in the area. One opened in the 1920s in the basement of No. 2 Cresswell Lane and, from the 1950s the George Snooker Hall, owned by William Devlin, was sited at the bottom of Great George Street (where M&S is now). The oldest was the Cecil Billiards Hall that opened at No. 17 in 1903. Raymond Miquel, who headed Bells Whisky through the 1970s and 80s, and in 1982 orchestrated a £300,000 sponsorship package to save the golfing Ryder Cup, often recounted that his skill in managing people had come from working evenings in the Cecil Billiards Hall for a shilling a night. In the early 2000s the billiard hall became PJ Champs and one disgruntled former denizen expressed disappointment: 'the demise of the snooker tables was the saddest part, as the focus of the venue shifted more towards student-friendly pool tables, and bright lighting drove away the old team.'

Partick Police Station and its associated courtrooms were built in 1853

Below left: William Cameron, Partick Chief Superintendent, *c.*1900.

Below right: Constable Alexander Cameron.

Cover of *Ecce Homo*, poems by James Chapman, published 1883

Courtyard behind Hillhead Burgh Hall.
Henry Morton

Chapter Six

Burgh Services

On becoming a Burgh in 1852, Partick created its own police force and within a year built a police station plus associated courtrooms on the corner of Anderson Street and Gullane Street. An early test for the capability of the still small force came in 1855 when they were called to a fracas at the Curlers Tavern.

A group of colliers and bricklayers were in the tavern and after partaking of some liquor they exhibited a disposition to wanton mischief. Remonstrance only rendered them more furious. Meanwhile, a boy was dispatched by the occupants to give the alarm at the Partick Police Office, and Captain M'Coll proceeded to the spot with seven of the night force. On the appearance of the constables the ruffians decamped. As is usual among small neighbouring towns, a spirit of jealousy prevails between the inhabitants of Partick and those of Maryhill and its suburb Kelvindock. Accordingly, the lower class of the populace in the latter villages took part with the rioters against the foreign invasion. In a very short time a riotous mob assembled, to the number of almost 2,000. The men hastily armed themselves with any weapons that chanced to be nearest the hand – pickaxes, shovels, brickbats, paling posts, etc. – and even females rushed into the melee with the ferocity of harpies. The police maintained their ground at first with the utmost firmness and no little success. Dashing into the mob they captured three of the ringleaders. Upon this, the mob became actively excited, and made desperate use of their rugged weapons. After fighting for about half an hour, the police saw that it was hopeless for them to continue the struggle against such odds, and betook themselves to places of concealment as fast as they could. About 200 inhabitants belonging to Partick, including not a few of the more respectable inhabitants, marched to the rescue of their police from the ruthless hands of the rival townsmen. Before, however, they could reach the scene of the action the actors on both sides had dispersed.

In 1865 the Burgh advertised for new constables:

Wanted one or two active, sober and intelligent men to act as constables. Wages to begin with, 18s per week besides uniform. None need apply above forty years of age, nor under 5 feet 9 inches in height. Apply in own handwriting, enclosing copies of testimonials.

Partick was known for employing Highlanders as constables and many were well in excess of the minimum height requirement. One local Partick resident who, on the occasion of another large-scale disturbance, was temporarily engaged as a special constable to augment the force, would have matched most of the Highland constables in height,

Rachel Hamilton, c.1880.

although this temporary constable was a woman. Rachel Hamilton, known as 'Big Rachel', was 6ft 4in tall and weighed seventeen stone, and was the first female ever to be employed for such police duties. Her historical employment took place on 8 August 1875. The day before there had been a riot that became known as 'the Battle of Partick Cross'. As was often the case in Glasgow, religious bigotry was the cause. Roman Catholic Irish immigrants were celebrating the centenary of the birth of Daniel O'Connell, an Irish politician who had been instrumental in securing Catholic Emancipation in 1829. On 7 August, 900 Catholics were returning from the event at Glasgow Green and entered Partick around 8pm. Among the watching crowd was a large number of Orangemen. 'A processionist struck one of the bystanders, who returned the blow by giving his assailant a smack on the face. This was the signal for a free fight between the processionists and the crowd.' A riot ensued and the Partick police struggled to control events. Eventually after a few hours the fighting groups faded away, leaving a trail of damage. However, the police were informed that further trouble was planned for the following evening. So, with support of the Hillhead police and 30 local special constables, including Mrs Hamilton, the combined force confronted the mob and dispersed it without violence.

By 1881 the Partick police force consisted of a Chief Superintendent, his deputy, three sergeants, three detectives and 27 constables. William Cameron became chief superintendent in 1892, having previously been superintendent of the Burgh of Broughty Ferry Police Force. At the time he took charge, police operated a two-shift system of night and day, and he altered that to a system of two day shifts and one night shift, thereby shortening the constables' duty to nine hours each day. He also formed a police athletic club and instituted an annual police sports day. The Partick Police Sports Club quickly gained a reputation for producing top quality athletes, none more successful than Constable Alexander Cameron in the early 1900s. Being a Highlander, it was in the traditional Highland Games events that Cameron excelled. He smashed the world records in the putt shot, throwing the hammer and throwing a 29lb weight, and was reputed to be the best heavyweight athlete of his generation. He toured to Highland Games in Australia and Canada. While little remembered today, another Partick policeman also made his mark: 'The name of James Chapman is already well and favourably known to a large section of the Scottish public.' Chapman served with the Partick police force for 25 years from 1859 and his repute was earned for an activity less common among the police – poetry. 'Half amused, half amazed at the daring of mine', is the first line of his poetic introduction to his book, *Ecce Homo*, published in 1883.

The Hillhead Burgh police force was established in 1869 and when the Burgh Hall was built a few years later, it included a police station, cells and accommodation for the police superintendent and two constables. The last superintendent in 1895, before the force was amalgamated into Glasgow's, was James Cairns. Born in Ireland, Cairns came to Glasgow around 1878 when 27 years old and joined Glasgow Police as a constable. When he moved to take up his position at Hillhead, he, his wife and six children moved into the police flat behind the Burgh Hall. In 1912, policing of Byres Road became the responsibility of 'L' or Partick Division of the Glasgow Police.

The first street police telephones in Britain appeared in Glasgow in 1891. These were tall, hexagonal, cast-iron boxes painted red with large gas lanterns fixed to the roof, which could be switched on from the central police station to signal to police officers in the vicinity to call the station for instructions. In 1933 Glasgow replaced these with concrete police boxes and Byres Road had three: at Partick Cross, on the corner of Ruthven Street and Byres Road, and at the Botanic Gardens the latter being one of only five surviving in the city. The police Boxes had a telephone connected to the central police station and a first aid kit. The small room inside provided the police on the beat with a place to hold arrested individuals while waiting for a police vehicle and, more importantly, somewhere for a

Looking north along Byres Road from Partick Cross, c.1900, with boys clustered around the police signal box.

Lewis Hutton collection

Police box at Botanic Gardens.

and as none could pay their fine of 5s. were removed to Duke Street Prison.

Possibly the most tragic and shocking murder to occur in Byres Road took place in 1937. Two years earlier, Alma Millar, the daughter of a dentist who lived at No. 1 Lawrence Street, married Uprenda Biswas, an Indian who was working as a gymnastics instructor. After Alma had a baby, the marriage broke down and in May 1937 Alma and her child went to stay with her parents and four siblings in Lawrence Street. She then obtained a court separation order from her husband on grounds of cruelty. The day after, Biswas arrived at Lawrence Street by taxi, having had the driver take him to various addresses in a hunt for his wife. He rang the doorbell, and Alma came down and opened the door. A few words were exchanged before Biswas suddenly produced a revolver and shot his wife, seriously wounding her. As the taxi driver rushed to help her, Biswas shot him and he staggered into Byres Road where he fell dead. Biswas then ran upstairs into the Millars' flat. Mrs Millar and three of her children were out but Alma's father, one of her sisters and the Biswas's baby were there, and Biswas shot all three dead before killing himself. Alma survived.

Following the Second World War many left-over armaments were stored unguarded. In 1948 three nineteen-year-olds were arrested for possessing large amounts of explosives that they had stolen from one such unguarded ammunition dump. One of the lads stored his stash in the coal cellar of the tenement at No. 160; this was found to consist of 127 hand grenades, 132 detonators, 68 gelignite cartridges, seven packets of gelignite, and 125 feet of safety fuse. Among the armaments stored by his confederates were phosphorus bombs and anti-tank mines. The court heard that the young men professed to be members of 'Young Scotland' a youth group that some years earlier had been linked to the SNP but then formally disbanded. 'They apparently take an even more nationalistic view of the claims of Scotland than others in the movement, and formed themselves into a militant group,' their defence lawyer said. He then claimed that their theft of the arms was 'merely stupid adolescent curiosity and thirst for adventure, and that the three wished to make it clear that it was not their intention to injure anyone.' They were imprisoned.

The territorial antagonism that had sparked the 1855 riot evolved into local gangs that were particularly prevalent in the 1920s and 1930s. While these had mainly died out by the Second World War, in the 1960s new youth gangs emerged, linked to two conflicting British youth subcultures, Mods and

sheltered smoke or cup of tea. Unlike elsewhere in Britain, the Glasgow ones were painted red, but in the 1960s, in response to the popularity of the BBC TV series, *Dr Who*, they were repainted blue.

The crimes that the Partick and Hillhead police had to deal with remained similar over the decades: break-ins, petty pilfering, domestic quarrels, acts of violence – more often than not drink-related, and even the occasional murder. One unusual police alert took place in 1884:

The aristocratic burgh of Hillhead was invaded by a crowd of sturdy beggars. They ranged from all ages and there were sweeps, dock labourers, shoeblacks, broken-down tailors, &c. The men had taken up residence in an old building and the Hillhead and Partick police were called to arrest them. They resented the interference of the police, and immediately armed themselves with bricks, and held the officers at bay. After some difficulty, twenty-five were arrested. The inspector was unable to procure a prison van, and he could not ask the Tramway Company to convey them to the city as they were too ragged and dirty to mix with ordinary people. The difficulty was overcome by hiring a drag and a closed family carriage. The men were packed into these machines and taken to the city court, where they were convicted of malicious mischief,

Rockers. In the mid-1960s, the Curlers Tavern again was the starting point for a major brawl. One evening, two of the Mod gangs, the Maryhill Fleet and the Partick Cross Boys, arrived at the pub to discover the local Rockers' gang, the Blue Angels, drinking there. One member of the Blue Angels recounted the mayhem that ensued:

> The mods ran in, slashing with their razors and the Blue Angels retaliated with flick knives, switchblades and tyre levers; there was bawling and shouting, guys were slashed and stabbed and several guys collapsed with weapon wounds. Soon the police arrived in droves and waded into all and sundry and making no distinctions, some were captured and some got away.

Glasgow Police van, c.1900.

The Curlers also suffered a number of burglaries. In 1961 thieves made off with the pub's hefty safe containing £300 and the police's investigation led to the less-than-startling conclusion: 'We believe the thieves used a van'.

While all crime has regrettable impacts, there are occasions where the criminal act has an audacity that one can but admire. Such was the case with a crime in 1926. The shop awnings, often called sunshades, (although this being Glasgow 'rainshades' might be a more accurate term), were winched out over the pavement by a long-handled winder. One day Christopher Wiseman went into a Byres Road shop and told the shop assistant he had been sent by the factor (those who looked after property on behalf of owners) to examine the sunshade's springs as they had been reported as out of order. After being given the winding pole, he borrowed a step-ladder from a nearby resident and unfurled the shade. Wiseman then coolly got the assistance of a passer-by to hold the ladder steady, removed the canvas from the frame, rolled it up and as he walked off with it asked his obliging 'assistant' to keep an eye on the step-ladder until he returned. Which he never did. Instead, he walked down to Partick and sold the shade to a shop there for £3. He was arrested, and this being his fifth conviction for the same offence, sentenced to eight months' hard labour. Clearly the police had a sneaking admiration for Wiseman's bravura as they gave him the nickname 'The Sunshade King'.

There also are crimes which even in court are described as comic. When 22 year-old Brian Seagar

Constable William Joyner, c.1950.

Henry Morton

appeared in court in 1981 on a charge of theft, his defence lawyer described it as, 'one of the daftest crimes and straight out of the Keystone Cops'. The court heard that Seagar, who lived in Kersland Street, was returning home from a party with a friend at 2am. No doubt having partaken of a drink or five, he smashed a Byres Road TV hire shop window and stole a colour television. Soutar's friend was in a wheelchair and Soutar dumped the television set in his lap, and began wheeling both up the road. However, the crash of the glass had alerted two police constables and they pursued Soutar and his 'getaway vehicle', and arrested Soutar and his reluctant partner in crime.

Another crime that involved smashing a Byres Road shop window was carried out by an unlikely perpetrator: the Chair of Psychology at Glasgow University. The court heard that the professor had been angered when he heard his son had been sacked from the Aquarius Boutique at No. 170. A few days after the sacking, having drunk almost three quarters of a bottle of whisky on top of a number of Valium tablets he had been prescribed for stress, the professor hurled a rock at the Aquarius's shop window and then threw a lighted petrol bomb inside. Fortunately, it failed to set the shop ablaze.

Given the number of writers in the Byres Road locality it is unsurprising that the road often features in crime fiction, such as Angus MacVicar's 1949 novel *Fugitive's Road*:

> Should you have lunched at the Unicorn in Byres Road and are sitting idly in your car wondering how to pass the next few hours, do not, as Peter Campbell did, offer to give a lift to the bank, to a dark-haired girl wearing a print frock and a big cool-looking hat, even if she asks the favour in a slow, husky voice. There's just the chance that, like Peter Campbell, you'll land yourself into the most dreadful trouble, including bank robbery and murder.

Partick Burgh's Fire Brigade was created in 1855 and Hillhead's in 1871. Partick's first fire station was in Wilson Street (now Gullane Street) and Hillhead's was housed in the yard behind the Burgh Hall. Each had a horse-drawn cart containing a hose and a ladder. The only full-time member of staff was the firemaster who lived next to the station. The other firemen – three to four in the early days – were part-time and lived elsewhere. In the event of a fire, the firemen were summoned from home or work by a bell on the roof of the police station. The rules for the Hillhead firemen included:

> On receipt of information of a fire occurring in the Burgh he shall proceed to the place with all possible speed. He shall make himself acquainted with the positions of all the fire-plugs in the Burgh, and shall at

Glasgow Fire Brigade's Chief Officer William Patterson, in 1884. He was based in the Central Station of the brigade in Ingram street and was responsible for many improvements to Glasgow's Fire Brigade in the late 19th century.

all times carry with him a printed list of the various plugs and their situations.

The part-timers had to attend the fire station for drill once a month, and also were responsible for cleaning and over-hauling the appliances on a monthly basis. They were provided with 'one helmet, one tunic and trousers, one hatchet, one coil rope, one belt. one pair hose and boots.' In 1905, by which time Partick's fire service was full-time and consisted of a firemaster, a deputy firemaster, and ten firemen, it moved to a new station on the corner of Clyde Street and Hozier Street:

> The New Station is designed to meet all requirements for some time to come. In addition to accommodation for the permanent staff of firemen and their families, the buildings include an engine Room, stables for eight horses, watchroom, workshops, hose tower, and recreation rooms. In the watchroom is a switchboard and apparatus for complete communication with every part of the Burgh, and also with each fireman's house. The switchboard is one of the most complete and latest devices in the kingdom, and has both alarm and telephonic connection from each fire box on the streets.

Hillhead Fire Station – new motorised fire engine and the about to be retired, Kelvin and Tweed.

Glasgow Fire Service

The 'fire box' was a street fire alarm and Glasgow was the first city in UK to install these from 1878. They were discontinued in 1960 with the increasing availability of the telephone emergency service. Hillhead Fire Station was the last in Glasgow to have a horse-drawn appliance and in 1913 its two horses, Kelvin and Tweed, were retired when a shiny new 4-cylinder, 24hp motor fire-engine with a maximum speed of 22mph arrived. The Hillhead station was closed soon after and amalgamated with the Partick station.

In 1884 the Hillhead firemen were only called out five times, one a false alarm, but by 1892 the brigade was called out almost every day. In 1900 around a quarter of the call-outs were linked to fires in commercial premises – many in pubs – and the rest were split between fires in dwelling houses and fires in ash-pits. In the days when the majority of houses were heated by coal fires the ash (dust) was deposited by householders in holes in the back courts, called ash-pits or dust-pits. Coal ash was in demand as a fertiliser so after collection by the 'dust-men' the material was taken to dust-yards where the coal ash and other materials were separated in a form of early recycling. It was not

unusual for the ash thrown out still to contain smouldering embers and cause fires. Moreover, most occupants tossed food scraps and flammable rubbish onto the kitchen fire, and often these set off chimney fires. When such fires occurred, onlookers often would gather to view the thick yellow smoke belching out of the tenement chimney. These were dangerous as they could set alight to the beams inside the house. The fire brigade was also called to assist in accidents, including helping to help raise up horses that had fallen. In the days before radio or TV, such events were the excitements of a day, as one message boy remarked to his chum: 'This has been a gran' day. A horse coupit, a lum ablaze, and a man fell off a lorry.'

Larger fires often required all the fire stations in the city to attend. When Kelvin Hall went on fire in 1925, embers from the blaze in the roof were lifted high by the heat of the fire and carried around the locality, starting roof-fires in nine tenements and a church. The Clydebank Blitz of the Second World War was an especially testing time for Partick's firefighters and a number died, including a part-time volunteer with the Fire Service, Neil Leitch, who lived in Hyndland. He was sixteen and worked

Glasgow street fire alarm.

Silver Slipper Café/Sgt Pepper's Club fire, 1970.

Fire above Tennents pub, 2012.

Clydebank Blitz damage, 1941.   *Daily Record*

as a bicycle messenger. Hearing the siren, Neil cycled to the local fire watch station to assist and the fire warden sent him to Partick Fire Station for help. As he cycled, Neil was thrown repeatedly from his bicycle by bomb blasts. After one explosion he had to be treated by local first-aid workers and although advised to take shelter, set off again. He sustained further injures from another bomb blast, but managed to reach Partick Fire Station and deliver his message, before dying from his injuries.

A different form of the Blitz happened in January 1968 when 'Hurricane Low Q', a ferocious storm, ripped through Glasgow and devastated buildings. Over 1,000 chimney stacks crashed through roofs; thousands of slates were ripped from rooftops, streets were strewn with rubble; and parked cars reduced to heaps of tangled scrap metal. Twenty people died and over 100,000 buildings were damaged, and all of Glasgow's firemen and police were required to rescue people and make buildings safe. 'On his visit to Glasgow, Prime Minister Edward Heath will examine storm damage in Hillhead and Pollock before he flies back to London.'

In 1974 the most devastating fire in Byres Road's history occurred during a period when Glasgow's firemen were on strike. Fire broke out in a kitchen of the Grosvenor Hotel on Grosvenor Terrace and swiftly took hold. Navy and Royal Marine firefighters who had been placed on emergency fire cover, rushed to the blaze. However, they lacked the essential equipment for such a fire and the 300-room hotel, and buildings next to it on Byres Road, were reduced to charred rubble. While the hotel was rebuilt, another of Byres Road landmarks that burnt down was not. In 1970 a blaze occurred in the former Botanic Gardens railway station, which by then was Sergeant Pepper's music club. 'The fire broke out in the building a few hours after a pop concert had been held on behalf of the Police Dependants' Fund.'

The Burghs were responsible for street lighting and essential workers were the 'leeries' – the Scots term for the lamplighters – who lit the gas lamps at dusk with a wick on the end of a long pole and returned at dawn to extinguish the lamp using a small hook. Although electric light began to be introduced from the 1890s – in 1911 Partick Burgh's

Wreckage after Hurricane Low Q, in Gourley Street Springburn, 1968.

Grosvenor Hotel fire, 1974.   *Glasgow Herald*

Hillhead Burgh poster 1890.

BURGH OF HILLHEAD.

STAIR LIGHTING.

NOTICE IS HEREBY GIVEN, That the Commissioners of Police have, in terms of the General Police and Improvement (Scotland) Act, 1862, and particularly clause 131 thereof, resolved that the Lamps in all common stairs, passages, and private courts within the Burgh, shall in future be lighted all the year round from sunset to sunrise.

Under the clause above referred to, every occupier failing to have such Lamps lighted during the hours above fixed, will be liable to a penalty not exceeding 10s. for each offence.

By order of the Commissioners,

JAMES MUIRHEAD,
CLERK.

BURGH CHAMBERS, HILLHEAD,
9th June, 1890.

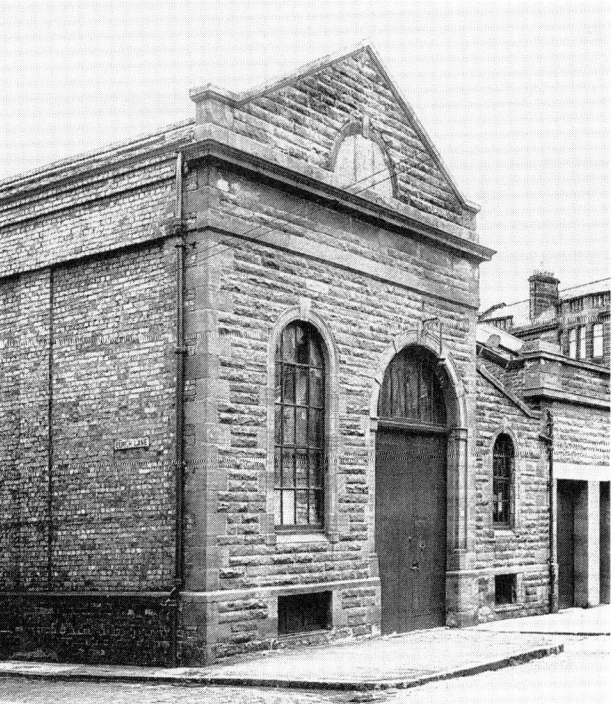

Former Hillhead Burgh cleansing department.

A dustcart, *c.*1890.

Commissioners proudly announced that all its main streets were by then lit by electricity – in smaller streets and in tenement closes gas lamps remained for decades: 'As a student I lived off the Byres Rd in 1975 and was amazed that the leerie still came round to light the lamps in the close.' At one point, the Corporation employed 1,050 workers in the Lighting Department, to maintain almost 25,000 gas lights.

Gas began to be supplied to Scottish cities in the early 19th century. The first large-scale gasworks was built at Townhead in Glasgow in 1818 by The Glasgow Gas Light Company and in 1841 the company erected the Partick Gas Works, opposite the bottom of Byres Road. The works closed in 1879. Premises lit and heated by gas were prone to fires and even explosions. In 1893 it was reported:

> Shortly after one o'clock this morning a serious explosion of gas occurred on the second floor flat of 160 Byars Road. The window was blown into the street, the door blown out and the rooms wrecked. The plate glass window of the shop directly below was smashed and two shops on the other side of the street badly damaged.

In the flat were Charles McLaren, his wife, two young sons and a servant, but, luckily, apart from Charles being 'severely cut about the face and hands', all escaped serious injury, though badly shocked.

The carts and horses of Hillhead Burgh's Cleansing Department were housed in buildings behind the Burgh Hall, and in its early years the Burgh proudly boasted that its carters, as the term for dustmen then was, collected rubbish on a daily basis, whereas in Glasgow collections were just weekly. However, it failed to boast that the collected refuse, including meat and fish remnants, was tipped into the old quarry and clay-pits around the neighbourhood. Eventually, complaints from nearby residents at the summer stench forced the Burgh to deposit its refuse elsewhere. In 1927 a Hillhead resident complained about what he saw as over-staffing in Glasgow's Cleaning Department. 'Is it really necessary for a uniformed foreman to supervise the actions of two dustmen, a carter and his horse and cart, collecting house refuse?' Behind the tenements in the back lanes were the dust-pits in which the tenement residents disposed of their household waste, these later replaced by concrete 'middens'. In spite of their smell and dirtiness, the concrete structures often doubled as play areas for children.

In 1960 the *Evening Times* reported on a young man who had given up teaching after just two days and instead got a job as a dustman at the Byres Road cleansing depot. Like all new employees his job at first was sweeping the streets and one day, while he

Alasdair Grant Taylor, Self-Portrait.
Jean Camplisson and Anna McCabe collection

was sweeping in Observatory Road, a reporter from the *Evening Times* interviewed him:

> Contemplating a pile of leaves, the serious young man said, 'I am an artist and I want to experiment. If I had remained as a teacher I would have got into a rut, and the longer you stay, the deeper the rut becomes. After fifteen years teachers often become cynics. They say "If only I had had the chance to paint." I am giving myself that chance'.

Alasdair Grant Taylor was true to his word. Through to his death in 2007, he created an impressive body of paintings, collages and sculptures. Yet during his lifetime his work was little recognised. He became friends with Alasdair Gray, who wrote about him in his book, *Portrait of a Painter*; the story of an artist who persists in his painting though he remains unrecognised and unrewarded. In 2023 the Maclaurin Gallery in Ayr mounted a retrospective of Taylor's work and it was opened by another who long promoted the artist's work: Booker-winning author James Kelman. The young Byres Road sweeper is now considered one of the foremost Scottish abstract expressionist painters of the late 20th century.

Chapter Seven

Getting Around

While the old Byres Road would have been traversed by a few horse riders and horse-drawn carts, the opening of the new, improved turnpike road would have seen traffic increase. Thus, the sight, sound and smell of horses would have been an integral part of Byres Road until horse-drawn transportation was replaced by motor vehicles. Building the new houses in the area required large amounts of stone, wood, slate and other building materials to be hauled in by horses, and later, horse-drawn vehicles were used by local shops to deliver commodities to customers. There were many reports of individuals, particularly children, being injured or killed by horse-drawn carts. In 1887 the *Glasgow Herald* reported:

> Donald McGregor, four-years of age, son of James McGregor, clerk, 172 Great George Street, died in an accident in Byres Road. While playing with other boys, he went to cross the street, and was knocked down by a heavy spring van. The driver, John Wherry, absconded, leaving his van in charge of a gardener who was with him at the time, but was later apprehended in Huntly Gardens by Constable Halliday.

Four years earlier, Wherry had been fined for knocking down a child having driven his cart 'recklessly and carelessly'.

A number of the wealthier residents in the area owned a saddle-horse or horse-drawn carriage, and apart from the few who had a stable as part of their property, these were kept in the mews in the Byres Road lanes or in local livery stables. One of the first stables was opened in 1870 in Ruthven Lane, facing on to Saltoun Street, by Joseph Price. He had been a coachman to the Duke of Hamilton at Hamilton Palace in Lanarkshire, but in the 1860s left the Duke's employ and initially opened a livery stable in Charing Cross Lane. The Ruthven Street stables was a large two-storey property that included a family house on the first floor above the entrance to the stables, and two mews-style houses. The entrance to the stables led into an open courtyard, round which were individual carriage garages and work spaces, such as a harness room, while on the first floor above was stabling for the horses that was reached by sloping ramps. Although originally named Victoria's Stables, as Byres Road then was called Victoria

Street, it soon became known as Price's Stables. The stables also sold horses on behalf of clients: 'Hunter for sale, 16 hands, 6 years old. Has been hunted two seasons in Ayrshire Renfrewshire, splendid fencer and fast: has been driven in single harness.'

For those who did not have their own carriage, cabs could be hired and one of the largest firms in the city was owned by James Henderson. Among his many premises were two in Byres Road; Nos. 300/304 and No. 377. Alison Blood recalled ordering a cab around 1900 from Henderson's cab office at No. 377.

> A delightful errand that, because of the fine, pungent smell of horses that came through the side door of the office from the stables and because of the friendly 'cabbies' that were always ready to exchange a word at the stable archway, their jolly faces topped by (possibly) one's own father's old silk hats. Taxi-drivers are not the same. Jocularity and a red face seem to have gone out with horse cabs.

The jolly faces of the cabmen who drove the open horse-cabs may have been partly to do with weathering as they had to brave all conditions. In 1903 it was reported that:

> through the enterprise of ladies in the west end of Glasgow a barrow has been designed and built for the purpose of supplying coffee, tea, etc, to cabmen who are waiting in the late hours of night and the early hours of morning. The barrow is fitted after the fashion

James Price in Athole Gardens, c.1900.   *Author's collection*

JAMES HENDERSON,
JOB MASTER, CAB AND CARRIAGE HIRER,
6 GOVAN ROAD, GLASGOW
4 SHIELDS ROAD, POLLOKSHIELDS,
Telephone No. 1539.
QUEEN STREET STATION,
Telephone No. 1370.
97 BYARS ROAD, HILLHEAD,
elephone No. 2091.
116 ST GEORGE'S ROAD GLASGOW,
Telephone No. 288.
TELEPHONES FOR NIGHT WORK, Nos. 288 & 1539.

Open and Close Carriages.
BRAKES FOR EXCURSIONS.
Broughams for Marriages, Shopping &c.

Advert for James Henderson Cab & Carriage Hirer, 1896.

Hansom Cab, *c.*1900.

Tram in Byres Road, *c.*1905.
Lewis Hutton collection

Glasgow bike shop on corner of Haldane Street and Dumbarton Road, *c.*1930s

of a yacht pantry, with a small stove and coal box, water tank and basin. The driver and steward all in one can handle his pony from inside the barrow and serve the coffee from the open half of the door on the side.

The earliest versions of bicycles – the velocipede and then the penny-farthing – were difficult to ride and so mainly ridden by young people for pleasure or sport. Early tricycles were more generally popular, although not with horses, who often were startled by the new machines. Matthew Williamson, a butcher in Byres Road, owned a two-person tricycle and in 1879, when he and his wife were pedalling through the town, they were involved in a serious accident. An omnibus and its three horses were waiting at the terminus and the horses, temporarily unharnessed from the bus, took fright and bolted. The driver, who was standing on the footpath, unsuccessfully tried to catch the reins, and the horses rushed off, knocking over one of the street lamps. As they careered down the street they collided with the Williamsons' tricycle:

> Mr Williamson and his wife, who were in the machine, were both pitched out, Mrs Williamson falling among the horses' feet where she lay for about a minute. She had a marvellous escape, her right arm only being somewhat injured. Mr Williamson, however, had his right arm broken and head severely hurt.

When the version of the bicycle that we know today – first called 'the safety bicycle' – came into common use, as well as getting people about, bicycles became much used by shop and telegraph delivery boys. police constables, postmen and the lamplighters who would cycle with their long pole held like a knight's lance.

Robert Wylie and William Lochhead, who opened their first Glasgow department store in the 1830s, introduced the first bus service between Partick and

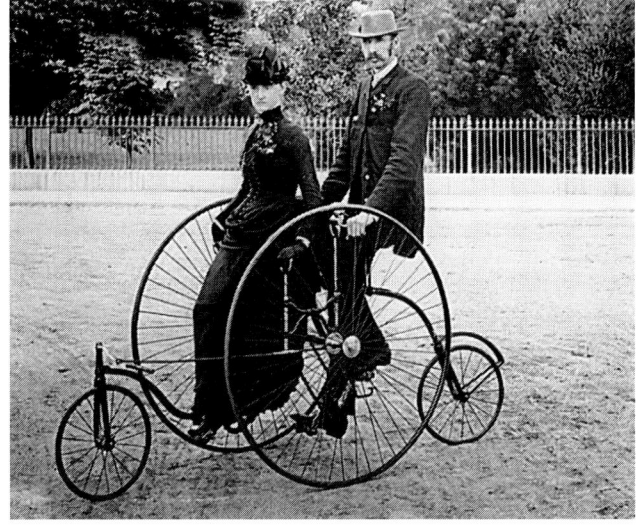
Two person tricycle, *c*.1880.

Glasgow using a stagecoach. By 1844 it had been replaced by a horse-drawn omnibus, and the service ran every two or three hours with a single fare of four pence. The Wylie & Lochhead blue buses, including the de-luxe model 'The Favourite', were popular and their success led James Walker, better known as 'Hookie', to set up the Glasgow & Partick Omnibus Company in opposition. Around 1870 Wylie & Lochhead withdrew from operating buses to concentrate on carriage hiring and funerals. The Glasgow & Partick Omnibus Company introduced the first ever Sunday service in the city; in response to an outcry from the church authorities, Hookie claimed that his service was aimed at those who lived in Partick but went to church in Glasgow.

Glasgow was one of the first cities to develop a tram network and in 1872 the first horse-drawn tram ran from St. George's Cross to Eglinton Toll. By 1880 one of the city's tram routes travelled from Great Western Road down Byres Road and via Church Street to Dumbarton Road. Although a horse-drawn tram ran along University Avenue into Byres Road, when it was decided to replace the horse-trams with electric ones, the University expressed concern that the electricity would cause magnetic disturbances and disturb their scientific instruments. Because of this the electric tram line did not go ahead and a bus service was introduced instead. The tram route down Byres Road via Church Street was

First Partick horse-drawn omnibus, *c*.1860.

Traffic on Great Western Road passing Botanic Gardens Railway Station, *c.*1960s.

joined by a line from Hyndland that came along Highburgh Road. Problems with the rails or points caused a number of tram accidents. In 1940, two trams collided at the junction of Great Western Road and Byres Road when one failed to negotiate the points and crashed into the other. Again in 1955, at the same junction, the automatic points failed and a tram turned the wrong way, crashing into a bus and a motor-cycle and side car, killing both its driver and passenger. Motorbuses were introduced in the 1920s and given the cost of maintaining the tram rails and cables, tram routes began to be replaced by buses; trams were finally phased out by 1962.

The Glasgow Central Railway opened a line between Queen Street and Maryhill in 1896 that included a station next to the Botanic Gardens entrance. The line at that point ran through a very long tunnel that was smoky from the steam trains, and thus unpopular. With the introduction of electric trams and the building of the subway, use of the railway line declined and the station closed in 1939. The attractive railway station building later became the Silver Slipper restaurant and then a music club before being destroyed by fire.

The original plan for the Glasgow subway included a station next to the Botanic Gardens entrance but this was omitted in the final route due to the existence of the railway tunnel, which forced the subway company to excavate its deepest tunnel – 100 feet below street level – between Kelvinbridge and Hillhead. The circular subway system opened in 1896 and was the third underground railway in the world. It first operated by cable but later was electrified. The original carriages, mostly dating back to 1896, were still in use through to the late

A Glasgow Underground carriage, 1976.

Partick Camera Club

Entrance to Hillhead Underground Station, 1970s .
Partick Camera Club

Platform at Hillhead Underground Station, 1962.
Mrs A. Robertson/Strathclyde Transport collection

Ticket machines in the Underground station.
Partick Camera Club

Revamped Hillhead Subway Station, 2012.

The first motor car in Scotland was licensed in 1902 and many of the wealthy residents of Hillhead and the neighbouring areas soon swapped their horse and carriage for one of the new marvels. In the early years it was forbidden to keep motor cars parked on the street so garaging was required. Even when that restriction was lifted, for decades many owners of expensive cars garaged them to avoid the risk of rust to the bodywork from Glasgow's climate, and from theft. Price's Stables enlarged its premises to enable it to garage motor cars – charging a fee as they had done for housing carriages and horses – and evolved into Price's Garage, adding petrol pumps and a vehicle workshop. Hendersons cab premises at No. 306 was converted into the Hillhead garage in 1910 and was still entered from Byres Road through an opening below the tenements above. When the garage closed, the entrance was converted to shop premises. An ambitious garage for cars was built by the entrepreneurial Alexander Kennedy who owned Castlebank Laundries. In 1906 he commissioned the architect David V. Wyllie to build the Botanic Garage in Vinicombe Street and the first section opened around 1907. In 1911 Kennedy purchased the premises next door that at the time housed the Hillhead Academy for Young Ladies and the garage was expanded. Wyllie's inclusion of a faïence façade was innovative for the time, as was the internal construction. He borrowed the idea of the ramps used to take horses up to first floor stables to enable the cars to drive up to the upper floors and down into the basement. An earlier

1960s, though adapted for electric traction in 1935. The system was completely revamped in the 1970s when Hillhead Station was enlarged and an additional platform added. Originally known as the Glasgow District Subway, in 1936 it was renamed the Glasgow Underground, although when the old carriages were replaced by modern bright orange ones it became locally known as the 'Clockwork Orange'. In 2012 the entrance was refurbished and renowned Scottish writer and artist, Alasdair Gray was commissioned to create an artwork as part of the work. He said of his larger mural depicting the area, 'I have lived and worked in the district since 1969, and I knew I would enjoy depicting it, and those who use the subway, in a symbolic and humorous way.'

Price's Garage, Ruthven Lane, c.1960.   *Author's collection*

Wylie Lochhead garage.　　　　*John Orr, FRAS, University of Glasgow Archive*

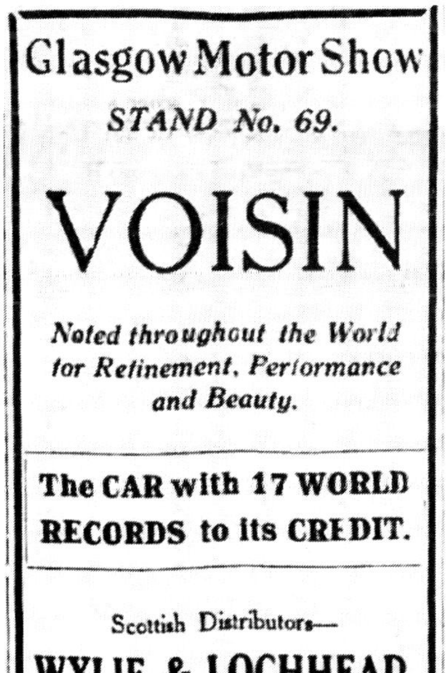

1927 advert for Voisin cars on sale at Wylie & Lochhead, No. 377.

Botanic Garage, Vinicombe Street.

HILLHEADERS HATE NEW TRAFFIC SCHEME

SHOPKEEPERS and business people on and around Great Western Road are so incensed by the new Hillhead traffic management and parking scheme that they have formed an association to deal with it.

The Hillhead Business and Professional Persons Association formed last Friday in the cloth shop owned by Tom and Sheila Miller on Great Western Road after caterer Ken Sumner, Belgrave Terrace, stormed in threatening to bulldoze the red

the once private drive had been taken over ...   striped poles that have been ...   uncertain terms ...

Headline in the *West News and Partick Advertiser*, 1975, berating the Hillhead traffic management and parking scheme.

Trams at the Botanic Gardens junction, *c.*1900.
Lewis Hutton collection

Byres Road, 1956.   *Old Glasgow*

Coal delivery cart, *c.*1920 in Derby Street.

one built by Augustus Perret in Paris in 1905 used hydraulic lifts to access the upper floors. With a basement and two upper floors, the Botanic Garage was one of the first multi-storey car parks in Europe.

For a few years in the 1920s, No. 100 housed the premises of Barron & Younger, motor engineers, and in 1922 the firm advertised: 'To be let for the Motor Show. Large shop, two windows can accommodate six cars.' Cars were still extremely expensive but there was no lack of well-off residents in the West End and in 1920 Wylie & Lochhead, whose stores catered for the fashionable, decided to convert its premises at No. 377, originally built as a base for its

funeral carriages, into a showroom. There the firm sold both new and second-hand cars: 'For sale a second-hand 6-cylinder 15 Horsepower Delage. Fitted with 4–5 seater touring body. Hood and lighting set. Thoroughly overhauled. Fast and powerful. £650. Also a new 10/20 H.P. Cluley, the sturdiest and best of light cars. 4 seater with all-weather side curtains. £270.' In the 1930s the car showroom was revamped but it closed in the 1960s, when the building was demolished to build flats.

After the Second World War, the majority of horse-drawn carts and vans were replaced by motor vehicles, although some milk floats, coal and beer lorries, and rag and bone men's carts were still pulled by horses into the 1960s. Renato Zanotti remembers the Dunns lemonade still being delivered by horse and cart to the Grosvenor Café in the early 1950s until the police objected that it was blocking the traffic.

The rising number of motor cars brought frequent accidents and in earlier times a number were the result of hand-brakes not being properly applied on the hilly slopes to the east of Byres Road. In 1910 a delivery van belonging to the grocer William Kerr rolled down the hill

A rag and bone man.

while unmanned, collided with a motor car and then both vehicles ran down into Loudon Terrace: 'The van ran into the railings, but the car, after knocking over a lamp-post, knocked down and ran over Louise Sherry, daughter of a local wine merchant, who was walking on the pavement, and severely injured her.' In 1932, dozens of people 'ran for their lives in Cresswell Street' when a parked motor car began to run down towards Byres Road. Kenneth Hurll, a sixteen-year-old boy, of Huntly Gardens. acted promptly: 'With great courage, he rushed towards the runaway, leapt on the running board, and applying the handbrake with all his strength, brought the runaway to a stop.'

Although motor car drivers were required to have a driving licence from 1903, it was not until 1934 that drivers had to pass a driving test, and many accidents occurred due to drivers' poor driving skills. One day's newspaper in 1909 carried various reports of accidents. A woman was killed by a car at the bottom of Church Street, and elsewhere in Scotland a cyclist and a young boy both had been killed when struck by cars, and a driver seriously injured when he lost control on a steep hill. Many Byres Road residents have lost their licence on being convicted for drink driving, but in 1981 George Moore who lived in Kersland Street made

history by being the first person in Britain to be disqualified for 'driving under the influence of cigarette lighter fuel', seventeen empty butane gas cylinders having been found in his car. Of course, it is not always drivers who are responsible for accidents, as one letter writer to the *Evening Times* in 1979 pointed out: 'I nominate that thoroughfare, Byres Road, as being easily the worst in the country for pedestrians, who are seemingly hell bent on *hari-kari.*'

Many would contend that for decades Byres Road has suffered from pollution, noise and risk due to the dominance of motor vehicle traffic, and a major report into the future of Byres Road agreed:

> The impression is of pedestrians and shoppers being constrained at the edges of the street and the rest of the space being taken up by cars, lorries and buses. The on-street parking adds to this feeling. Traffic movement through Byres Road can be slow and this leads to high concentrations of fumes and pollutants at busy times with high air pollution levels.

In response to this report, in 2023 work began on 'public realm work' that aims to 'rejuvenate the quality of Byres Road streetscape' and make it a safer place for pedestrians and cyclists, and generally enhance the quality of the road.

New road layout with bicycle lane at bottom of Byres Road, 2022. *Author*

Chapter Eight

Entertainments

MARCH 27, 1916.

"SHE,"

By Sir H. RIDER HAGGARD.

SHOWING ALL THIS WEEK at 3, 5, 6.45, and 8.45.

Can only be seen at

HILLHEAD PICTURE SALON.

Advert for Hillhead Picture Salon. 1916.

The success of the first dedicated cinema in Glasgow that opened in 1907 encouraged the building of other cinemas, and in December 1912 *The Entertainer and Scottish Kinema Record* reported:

In the aristocratic neighbourhood of Hillhead, we are to have a luxurious picture house. It will be opened this month, and will be known as the Hillhead Picture Salon. Seating accommodation will be provided for 630 persons in the stalls and 133 in the balcony. The new building is of beautiful design with luxurious accommodation. The best pictures the world can supply will be projected in the most up-to-date fashion. Mr Herr Iff's celebrated orchestra will provide the music, an attraction in itself.

The Salon was one of the first suburban cinemas in Glasgow and was designed by the architectural firm, Brand & Lithgow. In the early days, tea and biscuits were served between the short films while Herr Iff's orchestra played. This orchestra was very fashionable at the time and performed across Britain through to the 1930s. The Salon had local events filmed and in late December 1913, 'the hall was crowded nightly with a very fashionable audience, the attraction being a picture of the Christmas Day Inter-City Rugby Match between Glasgow and Edinburgh'. In October 1915, the cinema showed a seven-minute film of what locally was known as 'The Church Parade on Great Western Road'; a regular Sunday morning promenade by the great and the good dressed in their Sunday best along the then traffic-free road between Byres Road and Bingham's Pond. It was filmed by one of the Salon's projectionists,

James Hart, from the back of an open car as it travelled along the middle of the road. The film can be viewed online as part of the National Library of Scotland Moving Image Archive. During the First World War there was a Cinema Day in November each year to raise money for the Red Cross and in 1915 the Hillhead Picture Salon organised a special showing for wounded soldiers:

The soldiers, who were from one of the hospitals in the neighbourhood, were conveyed to the hall in motor cars kindly lent for the occasion, and were suffering from almost every description of wound, but were all as cheerful as sandboys, and once safely ensconced in the comfortable tip-ups, proceeded to enjoy the splendid programme. During intervals a sumptuous tea was served, and every Tommy was presented with packets of cigarettes by the directors. The picture programme was 'special' for the afternoon, and, of course, comedy predominated, and it did one good to hear the hearty laughter of the wounded when a particularly comic incident tickled their fancy. The projection was in the hands of Mr. Dunlop, himself an old soldier of thirteen years' service, and he gave of his best.

In 1919 the Salon's musical accompaniment was modernised:

Already two kinemas in Glasgow have installed and are widely advertising a Jazz Band. These are the Hillhead Salon and the Theatre De Luxe in Sauchiehall Street. Judging from the amount of interest manifested in this comparatively new form of entertainment, and

Hillhead Salon cinema.

The Grosvenor Picture House, 1929 showing the Frank Capra movie *Flight*.

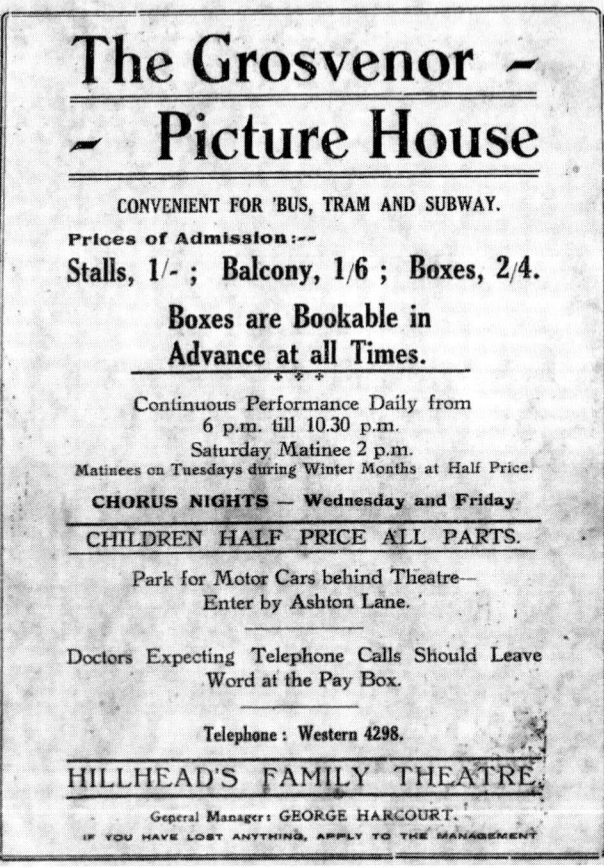

Poster for The Grosvenor Picture House, 1920s.

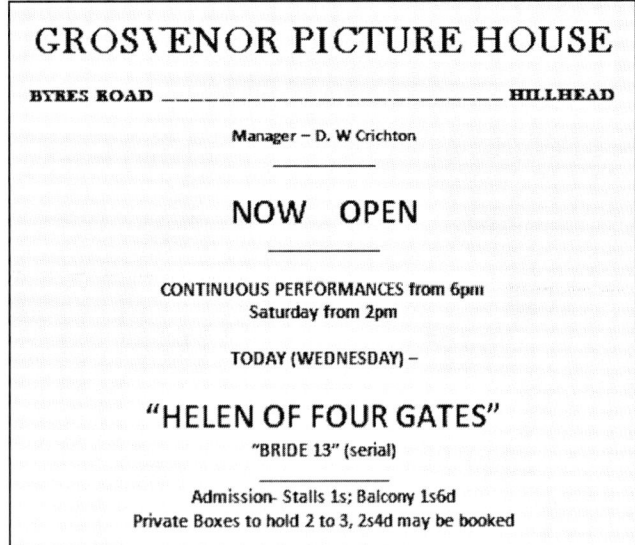

Advert for the Grosvenor Picture House, 1921.

Poster for ABC Minors Fancy Dress Competition, *c.*1970.

from the business being done by both of these theatres, the step has been justified.

By the 1960s the Salon had become rather run down and in the back row was a broken seat. At the time people often came in halfway through the film and had to find a seat in the dark, and knowing locals would burst into laughter as an unsuspecting patron crashed to the floor. Around 1970 the cinema was renovated and re-opened with *The Sound of Music* but finally closed in October 1992. It now is a restaurant, the Hillhead Bookclub.

In 1920 an advert appeared offering shares in the Grosvenor Picture House, a new cinema to be built on Byres Road and these were swiftly snapped up. When opened, the Grosvenor Picture House seated 1,300 in the stalls and circle levels, had private boxes at the rear of the stalls, and a cafe and soda fountain in its foyer. At the opening in May 1921 at which two films, *Helen of Four Gates* and *Eastward Ho!* were shown, 'the manager, Mr Lomax, was in full evening dress and Richard Daeblitz conducted the orchestra.' Daeblitz introduced Chorus Nights – audience sing-alongs – that took place every Wednesday and Friday. One attendee recalled, 'the singing nights at the Grosvenor when we all "tip-toed through the tulips" in loyal support of one or two invited people who led the singing in paper hats.' In November 1930 the cinema's manager sent sandwich-men round the Scottish Motor Show that was taking place in the Kelvin Hall with placards saying, 'After visiting the show why not take a walk up to the Grosvenor Cinema and see George Clark in the film, *Buying His Car.*'

The ABC chain bought the cinema in 1929, and carried out internal alterations and installed sound equipment: 'The Grosvenor in Byres Road is going for the latest "craze" and the manager expects to show talkies sometime in October'. In the 1940s the company introduced a Saturday cinema club for children, 'The ABC Minors', and excited local children would crowd into the Grosvenor every week to see cartoons, regular films and serials; such as *Flash Gordon*, in which each episode would end with the intrepid space hero appearing to be doomed, only to be seen to have escaped the peril the following week.

Each Saturday, before the films began, we all sang the ABC Minors Song to the tune of *Blaze Away* by Abe Holzmann, whilst the lyrics were projected on the screen with a bouncing red ball above the words

to help us all keep in time. There also was an annual Fancy Dress Competition and my mother made me a jockey's costume that gained me third place.

In 1980, allegedly after subsidence caused by extensions to the nearby subway station, the original foyer was closed (and later demolished) and a new entrance created on Ashton Lane. In 2002 the interior was restructured to create two small luxury cinemas, the Ashton (276 seats) and the Kelvin (253 seats), with a restaurant upstairs.

In 1923 there was a proposal to build a large cinema on the corner of Observatory Road and Byres Road to replace the existing row of one-storey shops. The new venture, the Botanic Gardens Picture House, that was to include a dance hall and tea-rooms, received initial planning permission, but there were local protests. Objectors claimed it, 'would be injurious to the amenity of the district', and that the land feu forbade any building on the site other than a tenement. For seven years the scheme was fought over until eventually being abandoned.

When the delightful comedy film, *Whisky Galore*, in which a ship carrying 50,000 cases of whisky is shipwrecked off the coast of a small Scottish island and the islanders hatch a plan to steal the whisky, was first shown at the Grosvenor Cinema in August 1949, a number of teachers and ex-pupils of Hillhead High School would have had a particular interest in going along for Gordon Jackson, who acted in it, attended the school in the 1930s, and the film's director Alexander Mackendrick, ten years earlier. Jackson left school to work as a draughtsman for Rolls Royce before becoming a film and TV actor best known for his role as the butler, Mr Hudson in the series, *Upstairs, Downstairs*. Mackendrick was born in Boston in 1912 but after his father died in the 1918 flu

Planned Botanic Gardens Picture House

Bill Forsyth making his mark at the Grosvenor Cinema, 1985.
Daily Mirror

Bill Forsyth, the director of other classic Scottish films, including *Gregory's Girl* and *Local Hero*, is no stranger to Byres Road and Ashton Lane a regular rendezvous. In 1982 he was interviewed for the *Glasgow Herald*:

> Forsyth suggested we meet for a cup of coffee in the Grosvenor Café. The place is full of family groups, young couples, a senior citizen or two. There is a mixture of Glasgow patter of the kind he has observed so lovingly in his films.'

Three years later his place in Scottish film-making was honoured in Ashton Lane, when he was invited to make an impression of his hands in a paving stone outside the Grosvenor Cinema.

Local patter has fed into much of Glaswegian comedy, and four of the greatest and most loved comedians have at some point in their lives lived within strolling distance of Byres Road: Stanley Baxter in Fergus Drive, Billy Connolly in Hyndland Road, Rikki Fulton in Byres Road and Chic Murray in Cecil Street. Murray regularly used the underground and on one occasion, while waiting on the platform at Hillhead, asked a member of the underground staff, 'Is there a dining car in the next train?' The puzzled member of staff said there wasn't. 'In that case I'll wait for the next one,' Chic replied, straight-faced. The actor, Robbie Coltrane recalled a day when he was walking down Byres Road and bumped into Murray. 'He grabbed my arm and said I was a funny boy. My dad would have loved that. We should have a Chic Murray Day...tartan bunnets compulsory.'

epidemic and his father's brother was murdered a few weeks later, his distressed grandparents decided to return home to Glasgow, and Mackendrick went with them, leaving his mother, whom he never saw again. He lived with his grandparents just off Hamilton Drive while attending Hillhead School. His move into film-making began by making animated cartoons, and later he joined Ealing Studios. In 1967, by a wonderfully perfect coincidence, on Great Western Road, just a few streets away from where Mackendrick grew up, two hogsheads of whisky each containing 50 gallons of whisky fell from a lorry when the driver had to break suddenly. The barrels broke and the 'water of life' began leaking from the cracked barrels:

> It was Whisky Galore in Glasgow today as dozens of people, with cups, kettles and anything that would hold liquid pushed and jostled each other to get their fill. Men and women rushed into shops to buy bottles of lemonade which they quickly poured down the street drains and queued to fill them with best whisky – and all of it free.

Chic Murray, a regular around Byres Road.

When, on 16 May 1938, the BBC broadcast the Dundee comedian Will Fyffe singing his famous song, *I Belong to Glasgow* it is likely that some of those listening on their wireless sets in Byres Road would have considered the moment as being of special interest as the programme was being broadcast from just across Great Western Road at the new BBC Scotland studios in Queen Margaret House. The BBC opened its first Scottish base in 1923 and although it was a small studio in an attic in Bath Street, orchestras, pipe bands and choirs often squeezed in to play live. In 1929, BBC Scotland's headquarters moved to Edinburgh, but it was decided there also should be a Glasgow base and after looking at various sites, the BBC bought Queen Margaret House in 1935. Previously the property had housed The Glasgow Association for the Higher Education of Women, a college established in 1868 by Jessie Campbell, the wife of the owner of a prosperous department store in Glasgow, to provide university-level education for women who were not permitted to study at Scottish universities. The building was enlarged by the BBC and with its eight studios was, at the time, one of the most modern broadcasting centres in Europe. Further buildings were erected in 1964 to provide television studios.

From 1938 until 2005, when the BBC moved to Pacific Quay, the location of the Corporation's Scottish studios in Queen Margaret Drive brought broadcasters and celebrities to Byres Road. Krishnan Guru-Murthy, later the presenter of *Channel 4 News*, recalled coming to Glasgow from his home in

Orchestral studio and listening room at BBC House, Queen Margaret Drive, 1938.

BBC

Burnley when eighteen years old, having been offered a spell of work experience with BBC Scotland during the Glasgow Garden Festival.

> Glasgow was a really fun place in 1988, It was preparing for its year as City of Culture, and there was a lot going on. I stayed in a rented flat on Belhaven Terrace in the West End and hung about on Byres Road – it was great. I was just amazed by Glasgow restaurants, like the Ubiquitous Chip.

Tam Cowan recalled how every Monday for six years in the early 2000s, after recording his football show *Offside*, the production team would wander down to Bonham's Bar at No. 192, while Sally Magnusson told the *Scottish Field*,

> I found a great little hairdresser called Graeme Reid on Byres Road just across the road from the BBC. Now the BBC has moved to the Pacific Quay on the Clyde but I still go there. I go there to get a haircut and then I love to just wander along Byres Road.

With radio growing in popularity, McLaren & Wallace opened a wireless shop at No. 302 in the 1930s. No doubt one of their best sellers was the advertised Philco 444, dubbed 'the People's Set' although as it cost £6.6s (around £300 today) it would have been beyond the means of many Byres Road residents. Jack Hastie's recollections of his family's radio listening in the 1940s and 50s mirrored that of many:

> There stood in the corner of our family living room a big brown wooden box two feet square. It was, I was told, a Marconi. It was a 'wireless'. The Marconi was

Krishnan Guru-Murthy presenting Open to Question, 1988,
BBC

the wonder of the age. It had dials which could change channels and I seem to remember trying to tune in to Leipzig or Dresden or Munich to listen to crackly German voices. This was quite an adventure as we were at war with Germany at the time. We didn't cluster round this marvel of technology in the way we line up today to goggle at the TV. The focus of our room was the fireplace, replete with coal scuttle, tongs and poker and there the family gathered with our backs to the Marconi.

The BBC programmes that Byres Road residents could listen to in the 1930s were mainly music. The Scottish regional station on Tuesday 12 February 1935 was typical. Programmes commenced at 2pm with 'gramophone records' – on that day opera highlights. Then there were schools programmes (including French) followed at 5.15 by Scottish Children's Hour. The evening included a short news bulletin, a twenty-minute Gaelic language lesson, a piano recital, the Wireless Military Band, a classical concert from the Scottish Studio Orchestra, and to round things off, the Rhythmic Serenaders and the Novelty Accordion Band. Popular among Scottish listeners was the highly-regarded Glasgow Orpheus Choir so listeners were mystified when the choir

Recording *The MacFlannels*: Left to Right – Jean Stoddart as Maisie; John Morton as Willie; Arthur Shaw as Peter; and Meg Buchanan as Sarah. *BBC*

vanished off the air in late 1939. It transpired that the Ministry of Information had instructed the BBC to no longer allow the choir to perform on the radio due to the pacifist views of its founder, Sir Hugh Robertson. It was not until 1941 that the choir was welcomed back when Winston Churchill hearing of the ban said mockingly, 'I see no reason that the holding of pacifist views would make him play flat'. One Scottish programme transmitted live from the Queen Margaret Studios across Britain during the war that was welcomed by the Ministry was *Up in the Morning Early*, a keep fit programme presented by J. Coleman Smith, a PT instructor from Glasgow Academy, and May Brown accompanying the exercises on the piano. From 1948, Brown presented *The Way to Dance*, a series of broadcast lessons in the steps and movements of the Scottish Country Dances, accompanied by Tim Wright and his Band, and many listeners rolled back the carpet and tried out the dances.

In the 1940s and 50s, the programmes became more diverse. One of the most popular series was *The MacFlannels* – a radio equivalent of the comic strip, *The Broons* – that at its peak in 1948 attracted nearly half of the listening audience in Scotland. Other popular programmes included *Housewives' Choice*, *Mrs Dale's Diary*, *It's That Man Again* (ITMA) and *The Goons*, while youngsters tuned in for the next exciting adventure of *Dick Barton Special Agent* or *Journey into Space*. However, the arrival of television in the 1950s began to lead to a reduction in radio audiences. The first television programme broadcast in Scotland was the funeral of King George VI on 15 February 1952. A month later the first programme broadcast nationally from Scotland was aired. Given that it featured a prayer of dedication, a vote of

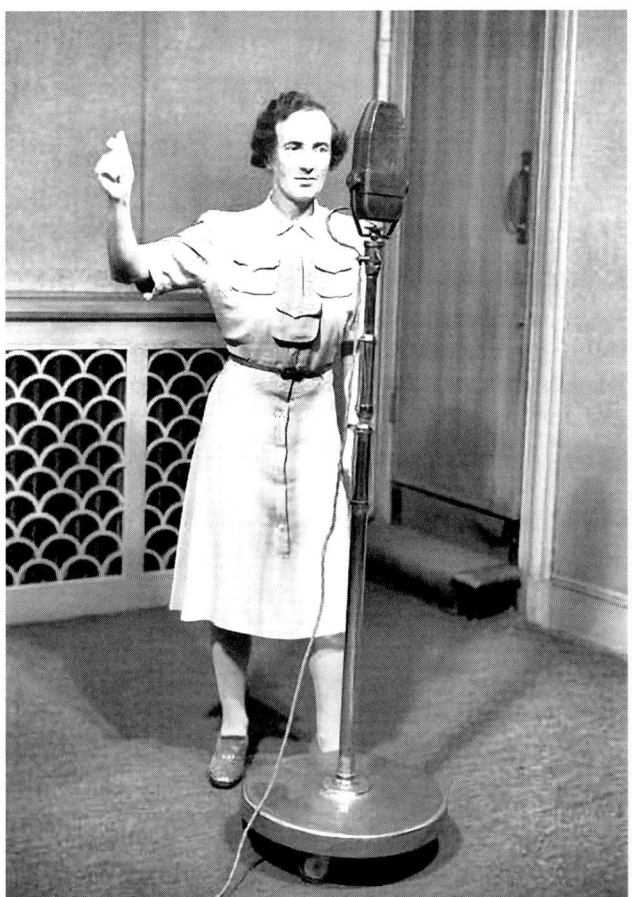

May Brown recording *Up in the Morning*, August 1941. *BBC*

thanks from the Lord Provost of Edinburgh, and ten minutes of Scottish country dancing, it is no surprise that one critic wrote: 'Need the BBC's Scottish opening have been so impeccably dull?' Fortunately, few in Scotland at the time owned a TV set. It was the Coronation of Queen Elizabeth II, broadcast live on 2 June 1953, that spurred interest in TV ownership, and more than twenty million people watched the service on television, outnumbering the radio audience for the first time. As television sets were still scarce, a large percentage of those who watched were crowded into rooms of friends or neighbours who owned a TV. When Scottish Television (STV) launched in 1957, its opening programme was more successful than the BBC's as although it also featured Scottish dancing, the inclusion of stars such as Alastair Sim and Stanley Baxter ensured it was watched by 750,000.

For a long time television sets were expensive and often unreliable, so companies began offering sets for hire. Such was the demand that at one point Byres Road had six competing television rental firms. In 1962, of the twelve million television sets

Radio Rentals on corner of Byres Road and Great Western Road, 1984.
Courtesy of Stuart McKenna

operating in Britain, half were rented. 'Subscribers', as those who rented sets were called, paid a monthly fee and if the original set was retained, the rental charge reduced every six months over the first years. Hiring also had the advantage of offering the opportunity to upgrade as better models came onto the market, as one rental firm advertised: 'You'll be glued to our sets, not stuck with them.' In 1977 The *Glasgow Herald* reported under the headline, 'Only in Glasgow':

Three young men, apparently unable to watch in more homely circumstances the Brazil-Scotland football match being transmitted at 2am were seen comfortably sitting on boxes on the pavement, drinking cans of beer, while watching the game through a TV rental shop window in an otherwise deserted Byres Road. A radio provided commentary.

In 1980, with video recorders becoming more widely owned, Video World opened at No. 398, renting and selling films on video. As the recorders also could record TV programmes, for those who owned one the dread of missing an episode of a favourite programme became a thing of the past, as did household arguments over which competing programme on BBC and STV should be watched.

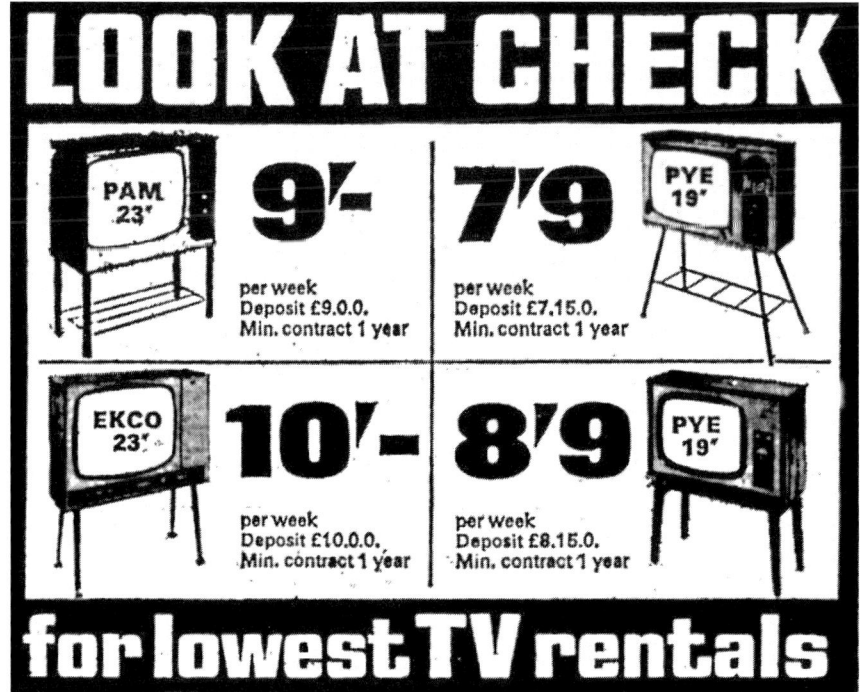

Advert for TV rentals at Robert Harris, No. 5.

Byres Road also had a direct link with the rise of pirate radio in the mid-1960s. At that time only the BBC was allowed to transmit radio programmes in Britain and this featured little pop music. The only option for teenagers was Radio Luxembourg, where disc-jockeys such as the American Alan Freed played the records they wanted to hear. However, reception was patchy and more often than not Glaswegian listeners would hear more hiss than music. A number of entrepreneurs got round the BBC's monopoly by opening radio stations on ships or disused sea forts in international waters to transmit pop and rock music to Britain. In Scotland Tommy Shields launched Radio Scotland from the *Comet*, a former lightship and a land office was opened in Cranworth House, renamed Radio Scotland House. Jack McLaughlin who worked as a DJ recalled the experience:

> The *Comet*, which had been lovingly described to me as somewhere between a luxury yacht and the *QE2*, was nearer in looks to the Govan Ferry. It was a rusting hulk with only the barest of accommodation – no carpets, no hot water, and worst of all on this freezing night, no heating.

The first shop in the road to sell gramophone records was No. 162, opened by Robert and Sophia Rae in 1892. A few years earlier Rae had moved into the flat above, from where he gave piano music lessons and worked as a piano tuner. When he married Sophia Saich, at that time working as a bookkeeper, in 1893 they opened the music shop and there sold pianos, other musical instruments, gramophone cabinets with fluted horns and gramophone records. While Robert continued to teach piano Sophia staffed the shop: 'Mrs Rae, crowned by a large feathered hat like ferns in a miniature conservatory and surrounded by a jumbled variety of musical instruments, was fussy and excitable, but had an eagerness to please.' Walter Hyslop ran a similar business at No. 132 and advertised 'Columbia Granfonlas and New Process records', but both shops closed in the 1920s.

It was not until the rise of pop and rock music that Byres Road again had a shop selling records. Robert Harris who had two shops, Nos. 5 and 9, where he sold radios, television sets and electrical appliances, turned No. 5 into a record shop in the late 1950s. It was run by his son who was in his early 30s and seemingly not particularly interested in the new pop music he sold.

> I and my mates used to hang around in his shop many days after school until it closed, listening to whatever he decided to play. On 5 July 1960, after a lengthy period of no new records from Elvis Presley as he had been in the army, his new record was due for release. It had not yet

Advert announcing launch of Radio Scotland pirate station, 1966.

been broadcast so we stood in Mr Harris's shop for hours waiting for it to arrive. At last, a box of the new single was delivered and we excitedly listened to *It's Now or Never*, though it was clear that Mr Harris was less impressed with Elvis's reworking of *O Sole Mio*.

The 1970s, '80s and '90s saw a number of specialist record shops open where buyers could seek out obscure music. Unlike Mr Harris's shop, these were staffed by people who knew about, and actually cared for, the music the shop stocked, and places where enthusiasts could meet, talk and argue about records. One was Listen, later renamed Echo, at No. 305, and in 1975 Richard Stenlake applied for a summer job there:

> To get a job at Listen you had to score high on various questions about the stuff they were selling, such as what label a band was on and what instruments musicians played. There also was an arithmetic test as although the shop had tills you had to add it in your head first before you rang it up.

The upstairs of the John Smith Bookshop at No. 252 was a mecca for indie music lovers. The record shop there was managed by Stephen McRobbie, singer with the band, The Pastels, and founder of the legendary 53rd and 3rd record label that helped to launch the careers of Scottish bands, such as the Jesus & Mary Chain and Teenage Fanclub. Journalist Nadine McBay recalled visiting it in 1996:

The west end of Glasgow bristled with heady romance and possibility. Bounding up the stairs to the record store in John Smith's Bookshop, I felt giddy. McRobbie, known to me and my friend as frontman of The Pastels, was behind the counter. It seemed implausibly glamorous to two kids used to getting records we wanted on order, or scavenged from record fairs. As we scanned the racks, we laughed with disbelief at what was available. I promptly blew my entire weekend budget on two records.

Echo Records, No. 305, 1980s.

Woolworths also began to stock records, although it focused solely on the popular hits of the day. The song, *Young at Heart* by The Bluebells, a Glasgow group that after some success disbanded in the mid-1980s, was used in 1993 in an advert for Volkswagen and the record re-released. Soon after, Robert Hidgens, aka Bobby Bluebell, who had founded the group, was shopping in Byres Road:

I remember standing in Woolworths, and I looked down the queue and every single person in it was holding the single. Even now I get a tingle thinking about that moment. The record went to Number One in the charts. Being at Number One a long time after we had first written the song was incredible.

Listen record shop carrier bag.

Some fellow shoppers may have recognised Bobby Bluebell, but four years earlier no one would have taken note of the elderly woman admiring the plastic utensils in the household section of Woolworths as she turned to her younger companion and said,

It is so long since I have been in a shop that I look at everything with greedy eyes. Do I want this? Do I want that? This is sweet but what would I use it for? An exhausted old woman doesn't need a scarlet cooking bowl.

The eighty-eight-year-old woman was Lina Prokofiev, the first wife of Russian composer Sergei Prokofiev. She was in Glasgow to perform as the narrator in a recording being made of Prokofiev' composition, *Peter and the Wolf* by the Scottish National Orchestra. She was suffering from a swollen foot, so had been taken to Byres Road to buy new shoes by Anne Simpson, a *Glasgow Herald* journalist, and was taking the chance to explore the road's other shops.

One who wanted to be recognised but wasn't, was Ciara MacLaverty. In 1996, *If You're Feeling Sinister*, the second album by Belle & Sebastian was released and its cover sleeve featured a photograph of MacLaverty taken by the band's lead singer, Stuart Murdoch. Soon after the record came out, Ciara saw it for the first time in the window of the Fopp store in Byres Road. Next to the shop was a flower stall and in her excitement, Ciara excitedly pointed to the record in the window and said to the guy on the stall, 'Look! That's me!' 'Yes, it looks a lot like you!' he replied, clearly humouring what he thought was a crazy young woman.

Byres Road's record shops have introduced many local musicians to influential music, and stocked great records they made. Ricky Ross, lead singer with Deacon Blue, recalled:

> I went in to the old Listen in Byres Road and bought every album I could find by Nanci Griffith. From memory I came home with five or six and just played them all. I loved them all. I loved the songs, her voice and I loved the fact that it opened me up to a whole new world of other writers and performers. if this was country music, then bring it on.

The actor and comedian, Craig Ferguson who achieved Stateside fame as the host of *The Late Late Show* said in an article celebrating thirty years of Deacon Blue:

> I owe my career to Byres Road. In the mid-1980s there was a newer sense of pride burgeoning, and not just in Scottish music. There really was a force in Glasgow at the time. Something very powerful was happening, and I think it still exists. There was a change in the artistic zeitgeist. Every dollar I made in America was from stealing stuff from pantomimes in Scotland and really clever fuckers I knew in the west end around that time. I owe my entire career to that little kernel of creativity that was really forging some spectacular artists. Deacon Blue not being the least of them — they were giants, and they still are. I tell my wife that even now it's still 1987 on Byres Road. They're still dressing like it's 1987 and they're still listening to Deacon Blue.

Ricky Ross may not still be dressing as he did in 1987 but Byres Road still feeds into his creativity as the *Glasgow Herald* reported in 2017:

> This is the difference between experienced songwriters and the likes of you and me. Ricky Ross was waiting at traffic lights on Byres Road when a dog – boundlessly happy, its tail wagging – crossed the road on its own. Its owners, Ross noticed, were a couple of homeless men. It was the sort of thing that would detain anyone else for a few seconds, but Ross's mind clicked into gear, and a lyric began to form. Which is why there is a poignant song called *Only God and Dogs* on his rather fine new solo album, *Short Stories Volume One*.

For most musicians, success, if it comes at all, is hard won. Paul Buchanan, singer with The Blue Nile, recalled that in 1981, some years before the band broke through and they were just a three piece – Robert Bell, Paul Moore and Buchanan – they played a gig at Di Maggio's, then an Italian restaurant in the former Price's Garage in Ruthven Lane. 'We played to two people. I remember thinking, this is astonishing, the band outnumber the audience.'

Sadly, the records being made by Ricky Ross, Paul Buchanan and others can no longer be bought in Byres Road as the last record shop, a branch of Fopp at No. 358, closed in 2000. The Byres Road shop had a special significance, for the chain's origins were in Cresswell Lane. In 1981 Gordon Montgomerie, who had been

Fopp, No. 358, 1990s.

working for Virgin record store in Glasgow, decided to start up on his own selling discounted records, and began secretly buying records from wholesalers and storing them at home. When Virgin found out they gave him an ultimatum: give up your idea and keep your job, or leave with 12 weeks' pay. He took the pay-off and rented a market stall in De Courcey's Arcade. After three years he decided to open a shop and with borrowed money, opened the first Fopp store in Renfield Street; named after a track by the Ohio Players – 'Fopped last night and the night before'. Fopp's prices were kept simple – most rounded to whole-pound figures – and Montgomerie introduced a policy called 'suck it and see', whereby any purchase could be returned to the shop within twenty-eight days for a full refund. Montgomerie began opening other shops – the Byres Road branch at No. 358 was one of the earliest – and by 2007 he had over 100 Fopp stores across Britain with combined sales of about £30 million. Unfortunately, the expansion coincided with competition from internet downloads and an economic downturn, and the company ran into financial problems. The chain was sold to HMV, who later closed the Byres Road shop. Among the many who bemoaned its loss was the broadcaster, Janice Forsyth: 'More than a shop, a much-loved Glasgow institution – a busy hub with brilliant staff, fab books and music – frequented by music fans of all ages, bands, musicians including big names.'

Still flying the flag for music is the Oxfam Music Shop at No. 171 where avid music collectors seek out second-hand gems. In 2018 Andrew McWhinnie, the shop manager, recounted that the shop had had visits from such luminaries as Franz Ferdinand and Jarvis Cocker. In that year the shop took in around £100,000, with half of that coming from sales of vinyl records. The staff's expertise in recognising rare items paid dividends when among a box of cassettes, they spotted a gem: a rare Celine Dion cassette. 'It sold for £700 to a gynaecologist in Hollywood', McWhinnie recounted, 'Who would have thought that?'

Chapter Nine

Processions and Parades

Queen Victoria first visited Glasgow in 1849. To commemorate the visit the city commissioned Baron Marochetti to create a statue of her sitting side-saddle on a horse, although initially there had been concern that the queen's small stature and feminine figure might be dwarfed by the horse. It was the first equestrian statue of a woman in Britain. Glasgow later commissioned Marochetti to create a further equestrian statue in memory of Victoria's deceased husband, Prince Albert, and in 1866 Prince Alfred, the Prince of Wales, came to Glasgow to unveil it. On the day of the unveiling the prince travelled down Byres Road on his way to the house of John Blackie, Glasgow's Provost, in Lilybank Terrace, prior to being honoured with the Freedom of the City.

The queen's second, and last, visit to Glasgow took place on 24 August 1888 when she came to inaugurate the new City Chambers and visit the International Exhibition of Science, Art and Industry, held in Kelvingrove Park below the University. This was the first of four major international exhibitions that took place in Glasgow during the late 19th and early 20th centuries mounted to draw international attention to Glasgow's achievements in applied sciences, industry and the arts. The 1888 Exhibition was housed in temporary buildings designed by the Glaswegian architect James Sellars in an oriental style, and featured a 170 ft high dome erected on an iron framework covered in galvanised sheet iron.

After visiting the exhibition, the queen travelled up Byres Road as her itinerary included a visit to Queen Margaret College in Queen Margaret Drive, home to the Glasgow Association for the Higher Education of Women. The pavements of Byres Road were thronged with cheering onlookers as the Queen's procession passed and the crowd standing in front of Queen Margaret's College took up the cheers as the Queen approached.

> Then, to the undisguised horror – no other word can express the feelings expressed on the faces of the company inside the College grounds – the whole cavalcade swept past the gateway without stopping. The ladies looked into each other's faces with a distressed look. 'Is she really past?' Mrs Elder who was patiently standing at the foot of the college steps with an enormous bouquet ready to present to her Majesty, concerningly enquired from those around her what was wrong, and there were a few murmurs of dissatisfaction at what was considered a decided slight on the part of the Queen.

The 1888 exhibition looking from Park Circus. The main exibition hall is on the left. On the right, below the university are the the Bishop's Castle Cafe and facsimile of the Bishop's Castle, with the Royal Bungalow Dining Room in front of them towards the photographer.

Lewis Hutton collection

It transpired that her carriage driver had got confused and missed the turn-in. The crowds were so thick that the Queen's carriage, and the cavalcade following, had to circuitously wend their way round the streets to arrive back at the gates. Given that Queen Victoria only visited Glasgow twice during her 64 years on the throne, Byres Road was extremely fortunate to have been graced by her even once, and the crowds in Queen Margaret Drive especially blessed that she passed by twice. Sadly, Byres Road did not make sufficient impression on Victoria for her to mention it in her daily journal:

I left by the Grand Entrance, & we drove up to the University, a very fine building, just above & overlooking the Exhibition grounds. We stopped there, but did not get out, & Lord Stair, the Chancellor handed me an address, without reading it. He presented some of the principal people, including Dr (Principal) Caird & Sir William Thompson, who was the only remaining member, who had been there on our visit to Glasgow in 1849. Stopped also at Queen Margaret College, where Mrs Campbell (Vice President) presented an address & a large nosegay was given by another lady. Several were presented to me. From here, we drove straight to the station, greeted everywhere by the same enormous, enthusiastic crowds.

On 18 October 2000 Byres Road's pavements were again lined with onlookers, but on this occasion there was just respectful silence as the funeral cortege of Donald Dewar passed on its journey from Glasgow Cathedral to Clydebank Crematorium. Called by many, 'The Father of the Nation' in respect for his significant role in masterminding Scottish devolution, his unexpected death only eighteen months after being appointed First Minister in the new Scottish Parliament shocked the nation. Many across Scotland, and further afield, mourned the passing of a man regarded as a political legend, but few more than those standing in Byres Road for Donald Dewar was a local, having been born, grown up,

Queen Victoria visiting the Glasgow Association for the Higher Education of Women in Queen Margaret Drive, 1888. *Illustrated London News*

King Edward VII and Queen Alexandra visiting Glasgow University, 1903.
Annan Photographers

studied and lived in the West End, serving as MP and then MSP for Glasgow Anniesland.

For twenty-five years from 1996 the West End Festival, established and organised by Michael Dale, brought thousands of people to Byres Road every June to revel in the free events and watch the Byres Road Mardi Gras. Dale recounted its beginnings:

I'd been in London and people there were discussing launching local festivals and I thought that Byres Road

Donald Dewar election poster, 1983.

Michael Dale.

courtesy Michael Dale

Glasgow West End Festival, 2019, and the first one in 1996 (*right*).

courtesy Michael Dale

Poster for Belle & Sebastian and West End Festival free concert in the Botanic Gardens, 12 June 2004

would be a great place for such an event. Then by chance I met Lindsay John and Karen Wood who had been thinking about a form of Mardi Gras style costume parade and we agreed to join forces.

Having run the Festival Fringe in Edinburgh and the Garden Festival in Glasgow, Dale was the perfect person to make the idea a reality. Yet his enthusiastic vision was not shared by everyone.

I rang Glasgow Council and said, 'I'm planning a festival on a Sunday this June and I'd like to have the road closed.' After a lengthy silence the man on the other end of the phone simply responded, 'You have to be joking, Mr Dale. Suppose there was a sewer collapse?'

In spite of the city being keen to promote Glasgow as a tourist destination under the slogan 'Glasgow's miles better', council assistance was hard to obtain. However, local artists and community groups agreed to participate and Dale's friends came on board to help. It's hard to imagine anyone could have envisaged the success of that first one-day event that saw thousands of spectators packing Byres Road to watch the vibrant parade of colourful costumes, music, theatre and dance, while buses and other traffic squeezed past.

Òran Mór.

The event became annual and in the fourth year the council eventually agreed to road closures. The programme expanded to run for a fortnight with over 400 free events in some 80 venues across the West End of Glasgow, involving a diversity of local community groups, and the Sunday Mardi Grass parade from the Botanic Gardens down Byres Road into Kelvingrove Park. The West End Festival was rated one of the top thirty festivals in Europe by *The Independent* newspaper and in 2007 voted the number one reason to visit Glasgow by Trip Advisor. Such success was remarkable given the relatively small budget available, and one that constantly required seeking fresh support. The management of an event of such scale is enormous and Dale's professionalism and expertise ensured the required coordination with the police, fire and ambulance services, bus services, and many more, was relatively problem free. He recognised that feeding all the services' personnel was important so managed to get the Hilton Hotel on Grosvenor Terrace to provide free space on the Sunday as a feeding point. Then, the day before, clutching a large wad of notes, he ordered hundreds of sausage rolls and pies from Greggs. 'Each year the buzz was terrific, Dale said, but one day after the 24th festival was over, one of the team said to me, "You know, Michael, it's just not the fun it used to be." I realised he was right so I decided to make the 25th festival my last.'

Dale also organised a range of other successful events around the West End including a free one-day music festival on 12 June 2004 in the Botanic Gardens at which he persuaded Glasgow indie rockers Belle and Sebastian to headline for free, and 15,000 people turned up. Dale recalls: 'That same day Òran Mór opened and I remember feeling that Byres Road was the centre of the universe.'

Òran Mór was opened in the then disused Kelvinside Church at the top of Byres Road by entrepreneur Colin Beattie who over two years lovingly refurbished the building, including commissioning local artist, Alasdair Gray to paint impressive murals inside. The building, an arts and leisure centre with stylish bars, launched a variety of events including comedy nights, cabaret and live music. In its first year Beattie was approached by the theatrical innovator David MacLennan, who proposed a series of one-act plays at lunchtime to be called, A Play, a Pie & a Pint. Many doubted if the idea could succeed but succeed it did, and it has gone on to become a Scottish institution. Yet this enterprise too was only realised through 'small resources and huge imagination' and unpaid effort. Mounting around thirty-five new shows annually, as well as summer and winter pantomimes, it has become the most prolific producer of new drama in the UK, championing emerging writers and enticing famous acting names to appear. As one regular said: 'It's great value for money. You get your lunch, you get to see new plays, some you like, some you don't, but that doesn't matter because the whole event is great enjoyment.'

From the 1870s through to the 1930s the Jones family shared this impulse to overcome any obstacle to entertain people as they toured their Punch & Judy show round Glasgow's streets. They often performed in Byres Road, as they were fond of a drink in the Curlers and while there refreshing themselves stashed their portable theatre and props in a store in the yard at the back of Hillhead Burgh Hall. Professor Henry, the honorary title bestowed on Punch & Judy men, and then his sons, Henry, junior and John, assisted by their small dog(s) Toby would set up their portable booth in the street and then beat a drum to gather a crowd. Once a sufficient audience had assembled the show would begin with the anarchic star, Mr Punch and his relentless baton, his annoying baby and wife, and much knockabout comedy. At the end Toby would carry the hat round, but given many of the streets they played in were populated by Glasgow's poor, takings must have been slim on numerous occasions.

Not everyone who sets out to entertain in the streets is welcome. In 1909 an elderly Italian

Performance at A Play, A Pie & A Pint, Òran Mór.

A Play, A Pie & A Pint

accordionist, Guiseppe Olive, who frequented Byres Road was jailed for a week on the charge of begging although perhaps his arrest was the result of complaints from shop-owners over his musical prowess as the court was told, 'He cannot play many tunes on his instrument.' Quite unlike the street accordionist, Arthur Manton, whose musical skills entertained the passing shoppers outside the Curlers Tavern through the 1950s, with his dog, Dukesey patiently holding a hat for appreciative coins.

Left: John Jones, 1957.
Henry Morton collection

Right: Arthur Manton and Dukesey outside the Curlers, 1950s

Beatrice Clugson.

Broomhill Home for Incurables.

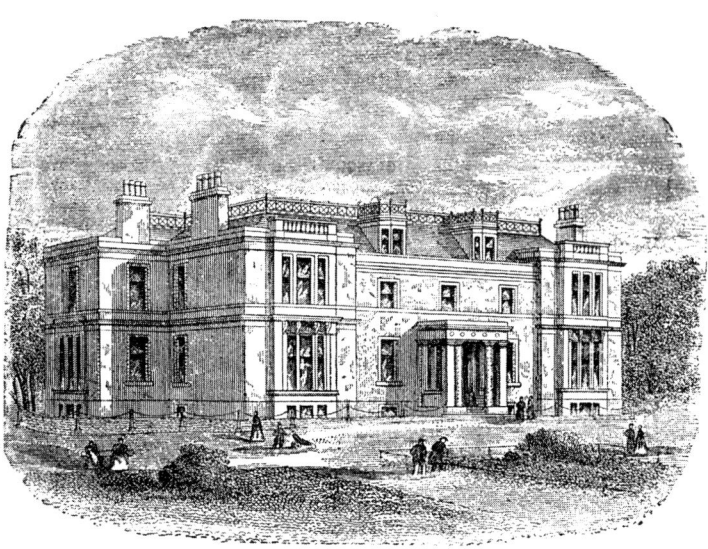

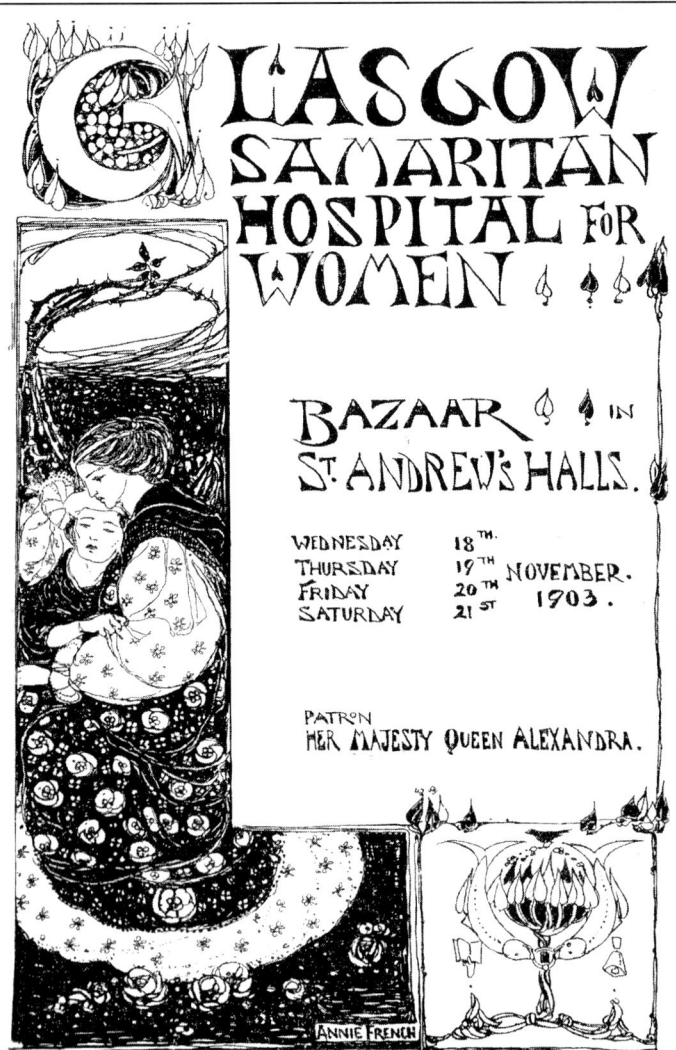

Advert for Belmont Street Church Bazaar, 1891.

BELMONT CHURCH, HILLHEAD.

THE GRAND

CLASSIC BAZAAR,

IN THE FORM OF AN

OLD ROMAN MARKET PLACE,

Will be held in

ST ANDREW'S HALLS, GLASGOW,

ON

THURSDAY, FRIDAY, and SATURDAY,

12TH, 13TH, and 14TH CURT.

OPENING ARRANGEMENTS

The Bazaar will be Opened at Noon Each Day by the
following Gentlemen:—

THURSDAY, 12TH MARCH.

THE EARL OF GLASGOW.

SIR J. N. CUTHBERTSON.

S. W. SHAND HARVEY, Esq., of Castle-Semple.

REV. DAVID STRONG, D.D., Hillhead Parish Church.

FRIDAY, 13TH MARCH.

R. W. COCHRAN PATRICK, Esq., LL.D.,

Under-Secretary for Scotland.

BAILIE M'LENNAN.

JAMES TULLIS, Esq., Ex-Deacon-Convener.

REV. GEORGE STEWART BURNS, D.D.,

Glasgow Cathedral.

SATURDAY, 14TH MARCH.

J. G. A. BAIRD, Esq., M.P.

CESSAR GILBERT, Esq., of Yorkhill.

COUNCILLOR GUTHRIE.

REV. DONALD MACLEOD, D.D., Park Church.

LARGE AND VARIED DISPLAY OF
USEFUL AND ARTISTIC WORK.

NOVEL AND ATTRACTIVE ENTERTAINMENTS,

COMPRISING

WAXWORKS,

VARIETY ENTERTAINMENT,

CHRISTY MINSTRELS,

MILITARY BANDS,

ORGAN RECITALS, &c., &c.

ADMISSION.

THURSDAY—From Noon till 3 o'clock .... 2s 6d.

From 3 till 10 o'clock 1s

FRIDAY—From Noon till 3 o'clock 1s

Advert for Glasgow Samaritan Hospital for Women Bazaar, (design by Annie French), 1903.

Glasgow Caledonian University Archives

Chapter Ten

For Charity's Sake

In 1882 Miss Clugston held a public meeting in the Burgh Hall Hillhead attended by 'the ladies of Dowanhill, Hillhead and Kelvinside' to raise support for a grand bazaar to be held in St Andrew's Halls in aid of the Broomhill Home for Incurables. In his opening remarks the Provost warmly commended Miss Clugston's work and, 'expressed the hope that the sympathy of the people of Hillhead would embody itself in abundant, not to say overflowing, aid to the contemplated bazaar.' Beatrice Clugston, who lived in Lansdowne Crescent, was known as a 'prodigious fundraiser' and in 1874 it was she who founded the Association for the Relief of Incurables for Glasgow, of which Broomhill Home was part. Among her many fund-raising bazaars was an earlier one held in 1875 in the Kibble Palace that over one week attracted 30,000 visitors and raised more than £23,000 (over £2 million today). Bazaars became a fashionable way to raise money for charitable causes after receiving royal endorsement in 1833 when Queen Adelaide, William IV's wife, attended one in London. They were often grand affairs, with entertainment and up-market catering, targeted at the great and the good. One in 1891 in aid of Belmont Church in Hillhead, also held in the St Andrew's Halls, was billed as 'The Grand Classic Bazaar in the form of an Old Roman Market Place' and featured waxworks, Christy Minstrels and military bands.

More common as charity fund-raisers in the 20th century were 'sales of work' and in 1942 one held in Hillhead Burgh Hall raised £191,2s,4d for the People's Dispensary for Sick Animals Refuge for Destitute Animals in Glasgow. Sales of work almost always included a white elephant stall, the

forerunner of today's charity shops. Surprisingly, it was as early as 1893 that the first charity shop, the Ladies' Repository, opened in Byres Road, and it traded until 1899:

> The shop is not yet largely enough patronised to allow of its being placed in one of the more populous and therefore more highly-rented parts of the town, but a journey to the end of Ashton Terrace, where it is situated, will well repay the caller's trouble, besides helping poor ladies, many of whose incomes are falling year by year. Some of the ladies are old as well as poor, and are solely dependent on their needlework.

However, it was not until the late 1960s that the next Byres Road charity shop opened. In that year Save the Children used No. 215 for ten days to sell items to raise money: 'Please bring your unwanted Treasures (Old and New). No jumble please.' While similar short-term use of shops for charitable purposes took place later, it was not until the 1980s that permanent charity shops began to open. At that time the changing nature of retail, increased rates and rents, and competition from large chains and supermarkets, were resulting in shop premises lying empty. Concerned at this increasing blight on shopping streets the government gave charities significant incentives to take up retailing spaces, providing exemptions from Corporation Tax on profits, zero rating donated goods and allowing 80% rate relief. So, in 1983, Save the Children opened a permanent shop at No. 327, now at No.165. The charity's President, Princess Anne, visited the Byres Road shop on at least two occasions when visiting Glasgow, the first in 1986. In 2009 TV retail advisor and Save the Children Ambassador Mary Portas brought her flair to enhancing the charity's shops: 'We want to create a real buzz around second-hand shopping and make the old-fashioned charity shop a thing of the past'. The success of this and the other charity shops is tribute to the long history of West End residents' generosity. In 1983 during the Ethiopian famine, an envelope with £1,000 was put through the Save the Children shop's letterbox.

Oxfam opened its first Byres Road shop at No. 195 in the 1980s and was one of the first to set up a dedicated second-hand bookshop, with later a music shop. In 2023, to mark Record Store Day, the Los Angeles-based Scottish producer Hudson Mohawke donated over 500 records to Oxfam's Byres Road music shop and, in 2022, the shop received a donation that must rank as one of Oxfam's most unusual: a Hungarian Cimbalom, a hammer dulcimer, made in 1904 by master craftsman Mogyoróssy Gyula that was then auctioned.

NORTH - WESTERN REFUGE
FOR
DESTITUTE ANIMALS,
5 WINDSOR TERRACE, GLASGOW, N.W.

A SALE OF WORK
will be held in the
HILLHEAD HALLS, BYRES ROAD, W.2,
TO-MORROW (THURSDAY),
from Noon to 5 p.m.
USEFUL GOODS AT KEENEST PRICES.
Donations in Cash or Kind will be gratefully received by Mr MEWAN, Hon. Treasurer,
31 WILLOWBANK CRESCENT, C.4
C. M. ROBINSON, Hon. Secretary.

Advert for Sale of Work in Hillhead Burgh Hall, 1940.

Annually, from 1904 until 1913, several hundred Boy Scouts acted as collectors at a fancy dress parade organised in Glasgow to raise money for the city's three hospitals. The parade's procession around the main streets always included Byres Road. The event grew in scale and after a few years those in fancy dress were joined by members of over fifty cycling clubs, with the cyclists also in fancy dress and riding decorated bicycles; members of roller-skating clubs in a variety of costumes and on skates; local brass bands; and floats on lorries and horse-drawn carts. A report of the 1912 parade offers a flavour of the event:

Three young women collectors for a flag day in aid of prisoners of war, 1915.

> The Indian Summer which we are told generally sets in during September is being eagerly looked for, but so far has not put in an appearance. Saturday was wet, but the wretched weather did not prevent the Fancy Dress Association from holding their annual parade in the cause of charity, and the collection is expected to amount to over £1,100. During the afternoon the procession paraded the principal streets of the city, and the Indians, milkmaids, animals, rialtos, nurses, Dutch girls, suffragettes, and all the other characters created a great deal of amusement. The decorated cycles and lorries were a feature of the parade, and the prize for the most original design was won by Mr T. Macintyre for representation of the Comet of 1812 and the Titanic of 1912, bearing the motto, 'Joy and Sorrow'.

Although the collectors with their rattling tins wore fancy dress at the city parade that processed up Byres Road in January 1915, it was a less festive occasion than the previous events. That year the event was in aid of the Royal Society for Animals Wounded in War and comprised, 'lady and gentlemen horse riders in various uniforms, two stage coaches, over 200 horses, 100 vehicles

'Flag days', accompanied by the rattling of collection tins, to raise money for charities were once common in the road. One in 1915,

> was held in the Partick district of Glasgow on Saturday in aid of Belgian refugees who are in residence in Crosspark House and Broomhill House. A staff of about 80 collectors, most of whom were ladies, were engaged throughout the day and evening in selling miniature Belgian flags, in the centre of which was printed the coat-of-arms of the former burgh of Partick. … An open-air cinematograph display which was given in the evening in Maxwell Street was witnessed by a large crowd and good collections made.

In 1970 the *Sunday Mail* reported: 'The Red Cross should do well out of its Glasgow flag day as an Oxfam investigation has shown that the average Scot gives half as much again to charity as the English, Welsh or Irish.'

Advert for Glasgow Grand Fancy Dress Carnival, 1909.

WE NEED
YOUR HELP

to save our
War-Scarred
Horses

Wounded, Gassed,
and War-Worn !!

Thousands of horses are suffering and dying day by day—the work at the Front entails constant risk and heavy strain. These patient creatures are called to bear a noble part for our sakes—in turn we should do all we can to alleviate their pain and suffering.

£50,000
IS NEEDED TO HELP THEM NOW BY THE

R.S.P.C.A. FUND

For Sick and Wounded Horses—The only Fund authorised by the Army Council to assist the A.V.C.

Left: R.S.P.C.A. advert for funds for horses injured in the First World War, 1915

Right: Cover of Ygorra, RAG Week magazine, 1928

Above: Students at RAG Week, 1947.
  Cranhill Arts Project

Left: Glasgow RAG Week lorry float advertising the Grosvenor Cinema, 1964.
  British Film Institute

and eight bands'. While large crowds turned out to watch the 'picturesque' procession, the fact that the war had not ended by Christmas 1914 as had been predicted, and more men were being sent to France to fight, must have dampened the enthusiasm of many of the spectators.

The Fancy Dress Association of Glasgow disbanded in 1914, but a not dissimilar event was launched in 1922. Students at Glasgow University (and Manchester University) decided to revamp the traditional student 'carnival' that took place annually around Shrove Tuesday into an event to raise money for charitable causes. Possibly many Glasgow students remembered watching the Fancy Dress Association's pre-war parade as children, as when the students launched what they called RAG Week (Raising and Giving), it had much in common with the pre-war event. From 1922 through to the 1980s, RAG week comprised students dressed in all manner of bizarre fancy dress and a large cavalcade of decorated floats. Central to the event was the money made from selling the RAG week magazine, *Ygorra*. In Stanley Baxter's much-loved television pastiche 'language lesson' routine, *Parliamo Glasgow*, Ygorra was 'translated' as, 'You are required to.'

A different approach to selling a magazine for charity was launched in 1991 with homeless people being given the opportunity to sell *The Big Issue* to earn much needed money. More importantly for many it enabled them to gain confidence and turn their lives around. Daniel Collins who sold the magazine on Byres Road for seven years recounted how he enjoyed meeting people; some famous:

> The graphic novelist Mark Millar and I got talking when he was coming into Hillhead Library. I've been a big fan of the genre since I read *Daredevil* when I was about 12. I actually got Mark to sign a copy of his book *Jupiter's Children*. He's a very down-to-earth guy.'

In 2018 Daniel was able to move on from selling *The Big Issue* to working as a self-employed tour guide.

Daniel Collins selling *The Big Issue* outside Hillhead Library, 2015.
Mark Anderson (Big Issue)

Social Bite's Festival of Kindness, Vinicombe Street, 2022 supporting Christmas meals, food packs, gifts, and essential items for people affected by homelessness and food poverty.
Social Bite

Chapter Eleven

All Kinds of Folk

All the original residential accommodation in the road was built above the ground floor shops and consisted of tenement closes with flats sharing a common stair. The number of flats on a stair ranged from four to nine, depending on the number of rooms in the flat. Those towards the Partick Cross end were smaller. This chapter later looks in more depth at the occupants of two closes: No. 85, which was built with nine flats, each with just a room, kitchen and WC; and No. 313 that consisted of six flats, each with three rooms, kitchen and bathroom.

In Glasgow in the early 1900s two-room flats made up 50% of the total housing stock, while only 6% of flats in the city had four rooms. Although there were no single-room flats built in Byres Road, these made up 13% of Glasgow's housing stock and tended to be where the worst poverty existed. The different flat sizes in Byres Road did not reflect class distinction to any real extent, although there were those who lived at the Hillhead end who viewed themselves as superior to those at the Partick end, and, in early times, the children had their own class system, as Robert Service recalls from the 1890s when he lived in Roxburgh Street and attended Hillhead High School:

> There was a gang of about twenty boys in our street and we were very aggressive. On the hill beyond were boys of a superior breed. Their fathers were successful business men, and they went to private academies, not to plebeian board-schools like ourselves. We called them 'gentry pups' and sought fights with them. But down in Byars Road, which lay below us, was another class of small tradesmen, and their sons we called 'keelies'. With them, too, we were always at war. We were the middle-middle class, most bellicose of all, because we were better.

By the 1950s that antipathy of the past, often accentuated by which school the children attended, had disappeared. Among the author's friends in his early teens were boys from Kelvinside Academy, Hillhead High and Hyndland schools.

Generally, where people lived was more to do with what they could afford. Newly married couples might start life in an affordable small flat in what was considered a less salubrious address, and move on to a larger flat or house in a better-regarded area as their finances improved. As did the popular radio and TV fictional family, the McFlannels, who first 'lived' in a Partick tenement flat but later 'moved' to 'up-market' Knightswood. In earlier times, when almost all flats in Byres Road were rented out, people could move relatively

Advert for flats to let, 1895.

easily from one to another. Jock Mills, a popular Scottish comedian, who only stayed a few months at No. 1 in 1906, later became the landlord of Jock Mills' Variety Bar in Cowcaddens Street. It was not unknown for those whose financial situation was acute to do a quick 'flit' before the rent was due. Others rented their flats for years and almost certainly the longest tenant in Byres Road was Isabella Mackellar, who lived at No. 140 for eighty-years. Her parents rented the flat in 1894 when she was two years old. Her father was a sea-going marine draughtsman and her mother came from Orkney where Isabella and her sister Mary spent their holidays. Isabella recalled that in her childhood:

> Downstairs was a small shop where an old woman took in mangling, and her equally elderly husband made toffee balls, much relished by the local children. I also remember cows grazing round the corner in Highburgh Road that I think came from Ruthven Lane.

On leaving school Isabella became a corsetiere, but during the Second World War switched to work as a gas meter reader. She was still renting No. 140 into her mid-eighties, although she moved away a few years before her death in 1982, aged ninety.

Some flats were used for business and others for private work projects. Of the latter, the most extraordinary took place in the Kersland Street flat occupied by Percy and Ella Pilcher in 1891. They, along with their three siblings, were orphaned in their teens and the eldest, Thomas, joined the army to pay for his siblings' schooling. In 1887 Percy came to Glasgow when twenty years of age to work as an apprentice in the engineering department of a Glasgow shipyard and his slightly older sister Ella accompanied him as his companion and housekeeper. For the first two years they rented rooms in a flat in Byres Road but eventually were asked to leave as the landlady became unhappy at the birds they kept in their rooms. The reason they kept birds was that Percy had an obsession with the possibility of flying and wanted to study their flight. They moved to Kersland Street and it

Ella and Percy Pilcher with their Hawk glider, Kelvingrove Park, Glasgow, 1896.

was there that Percy and Ella began building a glider in five sections. Percy got a post as an assistant lecturer at Glasgow University and, needing more space, was lent a room at Glasgow University by its principal, the physicist Lord Kelvin, although the latter doubted the potential of aeronautics. In 1895 Percy tested his first glider, called *The Bat*. It could carry the occupant aloft for 30 seconds, double that if towed by a rope, and as Ella also flew in it, she became the first woman in Britain to fly. Test flights were carried out in Kelvingrove Park and longer flights at Cardross. Percy became the first person in the UK to show that flights could be made repeatedly and successfully in a heavier-than-air flying-machine. They then moved to London, where Percy began working on building a tri-plane to be powered by a 4hp engine, and he and Ella also built a new glider called *Hawk*. In it Percy broke the world distance record, flying 250 metres. Having built his tri-plane, Percy planned to demonstrate it on 30 September 1899 at Stanford Hall in Leicestershire. However, as the plane was not fully functional due to issues with the engine, Pilcher decided instead to fly his Hawk glider in front of the gathered crowd. The Hawk had risen to about 10 metres in the air when the tail broke and in the fall, Percy was seriously injured and died. Four years later, on 17 December 1903, Orville and Wilbur Wright made history when they flew their biplane from a North Carolina field. History could have been different, for in 2003 the School of Aeronautics at Cranfield University built a replica of Percy Pilcher's plane and it managed to carry out a flight of one minute

and 25 seconds in calm conditions, longer than the Wrights' 59 seconds at Kitty Hawk.

Today, the number of children living in Byres Road is far less than in the past, and few, if any, play outside. Yet, in the past, most children played in local closes, back courts, lanes and the street. It was there that football matches, cycle races, skipping games, etc., took place, and teenagers simply loitered, smoking a forbidden fag or chatting up the opposite sex. One recalled his childhood in Hillhead in the 1950s:

> We played in the street. The film *Ben Hur* had a great effect on us as we built bogies of various shape and sizes and raced them round the block pulling them with two or three bikes. What glorious smashes we had on these. There were not nearly so many cars then and we did not have anything more than scrapes.

Although the Botanic Gardens and Kelvingrove Park were fairly near, and there were private communal gardens such as Athole Gardens, children were not allowed to play in those spaces.

From the 1960s on, with the number of students at Glasgow University increasing, demand for short-term accommodation flats and bed-sits grew. In 1969, a correspondent to the *Glasgow Herald* wrote:

> If halls of residence met the accommodation demands there would not be the endless and ever-changing crowds of students standing at a newsagent's in Byres Road. looking for bedsitters and flats which are. advertised prolifically in its window. There the infamous bedsitter can fetch up to £5 per week, and a 'luxury flatlet', which is a euphemism for a single-end but costs

more, partly because of the name, and partly because all lets seem to be of the luxury sort, can cost £7.7s. per week. Sometimes three or four students will combine energies and resources to take over a whole four or five-room luxury flat that may cost £17.17s per week. Nor are these prices static; they rise inexorably year by year.

The newsagent being referred to was Bensons at No. 104 and for decades its window was almost completely covered by a wall of cards advertising flats or rooms to let or share alongside those offering meditation or guitar lessons, or seeking a lost pet. 'I got three flats over five years (Otago Street, Byres Road, Oakfield Avenue) via that window in the 1990s. The mind boggles at how things were pre-internet. I didn't even have a phone in one flat at the top of Byres Road.' Many an aspiring writer typed out their first offerings while shivering in a chilly, grotty West End bedsit, and the great chronicler of Glasgow, William McIlvanney, wrote about these bedsit dwellers:

> In my quite wilful map of the city, I tend to place them roughly around the Byres Road area, in Hyndland and behind the Botanic Gardens and off Great Western Road. They are dreamers of small, lonely dreams. I remember a conversation in a café in Byres Road with

a young man who had read something I had written and who recognised me. He came across and we talked for maybe half-an-hour. He was living in a bedsit with his girlfriend and doing, I think, translations from Spanish and wanting to be a writer. Our talk was for me a peephole into a fierce and private obsession sustained on meals that came pre-cooked in tinfoil and long talks into the night.

Still, for those who could afford it, more salubrious accommodation was on offer in 1973: 'Luxury flat over-looking Byres Road for 2-3 girls. Features include fitted-carpets, TV, fridge and cocktail bar.' Rent £15 a week.' By 2002, even without a cocktail bar, a double room in a shared flat 'one minute from Byres Road' was being advertised at '£300pm + bills. However, in the past, flats in Byres Road were lived in by families as the following detailed look at the two properties – Nos. 85 and 313 – illustrates.

Number 85 was part of a tenement block built around 1890 and owned by Andrew Paul, a solicitor. Like many he purchased the flats as an investment with his return coming from rents. On his death in 1905 the property passed to his son, also a lawyer. In the 1890s the tenants of the two room flats included a joiner, a riveter and a blacksmith. Two others were

Window of Bensons Newsagents, No. 104, 1982.   *Eric Watt*

occupied by local shop-keepers: William Smith, an upholsterer and bedding manufacturer with a workshop at No. 283, and David Dunlop, a dairyman at No. 152.

The 1901 census lists 36 people living in the nine flats. Thomas and Annie Walker had five children all under the age of seven, and Thomas worked as a fishmonger's assistant. John Shaw was a violinist and two of his five children, Violet and Annie, in their early twenties, are listed as professional vocalists, but sadly nothing has been traced of the family's musical careers. Another daughter worked as a waterproof machinist and the other two children were still at school. Denis and Elizabeth Sweeney and their two infant children shared their flat with Denis's brother, John. Both he and Denis worked as iron ship platers. They were fervent Irishmen and members of 'The Dawn of Freedom', a branch of the United Irish League. In 1916 they wrote from No. 85 to the MP John Redmond:

> We have been directed by members of the Dawn of Freedom to warmly congratulate you on your striking and candid speech at Waterford on the subject of compulsion for Ireland and reassure you that the Nationalists of Partick cherish undiminished and unbroken confidence in the work of the Irish Party at present withstanding so many attacks on all sides.

Redmond was a passionate advocate for All-Ireland Home Rule but earlier that year had seen the government decide to exclude Ulster from the plan, an act that caused Redmond to accuse the government of treachery.

Also living at No. 85 in 1901 were Jacky (John) and Elizabeth Robertson and their two young children. Jacky was a blacksmith by profession and had been a part-time professional footballer; playing for the local team, Partick Thistle, from 1892 to 1897. The year he stopped playing he was appointed the club's match secretary. That year was a significant

Letter from John Sweeney, 1916.

one for the club, as it won the Second Division championship so moved up to the First Division. Also, after 30 years without a permanent home, and thus having to play in different parks, including Kelvingrove, the club moved to a permanent ground in Partick, where they played until moving to the Firhill ground in Maryhill in 1908. Yet in spite of this success, Jacky as secretary had to deal with a number of negative issues, the most pressing being a threat to Thistle's future as other clubs were increasing the wages paid to their players, whereas Thistle's financial well-being depended on having part-time players who had other jobs. As the club was unable to afford the better players it struggled in the First Division. Supporters invaded the park at one match to vent their frustration and the match committee came in for intense criticism, and as a result, in 1899, Jacky resigned his post. However, two years later he was appointed the club's assistant

Partick Thistle football team, 1889.

manager. The other flats at this time housed a shipwright, a joiner, a railway guard, a coppersmith and an assurance manager.

The 1911 census records 43 people living in the nine two-room flats, of whom fifteen were children under the age of twelve. John Inglis, a plumber, and his wife, Mary, shared their two-room flat with six young children. The Sweeneys also now had six children and, unsurprisingly, Denis's brother had moved out. Elizabeth Sweeney had her sixth child at the age of 43 and thus for around fifteen years had been pregnant or looking after a recently-born baby, as well as the other children. It also is likely that a number of her pregnancies did not go to term. Infant deaths were common and two young children of Thomas and Annie Walker had died in the house in the previous ten years. Their surviving daughter, aged fifteen, was working as a clerkess for a boot manufacturer. Samuel and Mary Allison, who had two small children, shared their two-room flat with Samuel's brother and his wife. Both brothers worked as shipwrights. George Wallace, who worked as a chauffeur, and a shop assistant, a shipwright and a female telegraphist were the other tenants.

By the beginning of the First World War, George Weatherhead was renting one of the flats with his wife and son Adam (born 1896), who was working as a clerk for Glasgow University. The other son, James (born 1890) was an engineer and had left home in 1912 when he married Elizabeth McGregor; by the outbreak of the war they had two children. Both Adam and James signed up to fight in 1914. Adam joined the Highland Light Infantry and James

the Black Watch (Royal Highlanders). Both were in France by March 1915 and over the following years took part in the Battle of the Somme and other offensives. Adam survived but on 21 March, as part of the combined force defending the Western Front, from the Somme sector northwards to Flanders, James was one of 38,500 men wounded when 6,500 German guns and 3,500 heavy mortars opened up a terrifying five-hour barrage against the British armies. He died a few days later from his wounds and was buried in Cabaret-Rouge British Cemetery, Souchez. At the 1921 census Adam was unmarried and still living with his parents. Also still living at No. 85 in 1921 were the Sweeneys and the Wallaces. One of the Sweeney sons was working as a bookkeeper and another as an apprentice scientific instrument maker with Barr & Stroud at its Anniesland works. George Wallace still was working as a private chauffeur and his youngest son was now a driver for a wine & spirits firm. His eldest son, John, who also was working as a 'motor driver', had married and was living in one of the other flats with his wife and young son. Other tenants included Robert Forrest, a boiler foreman, and William Smith, a guillotine cutter at a printing firm.

When first opened, the shop below at No. 87 was an ice cream shop and café run by Massio di Petrio. In 1918 the business was taken over by Pasquale Verrecchia, who previously had worked as a ship's carpenter on the Clyde, and then named the University Café. Around 1925, Pasquale and his wife, Giuseppa moved into one of the flats at No. 85. Still living there in 1935 were the Wallace family, Robert Forrest, William Smith and Sarah Weatherhead,

now widowed. Other recent tenants included William Gaffney, an electrician; Robert Roberts, a salesman; and Alice O'Byrne, a typist. After the Second World War the Verrecchias purchased the two shops, Nos. 83 and 87 and expanded the café, and also purchased all the flats at No. 85. Alice O'Byrne was still renting her flat after almost 25 years, but over time all the flats became occupied by members of the Verrecchia family through to at least the 2000s.

Number 313 is part of the tenement block built around 1878 and initially

Pasquale & Giusepa Verrecchia outside the University Café, c.1925.

named Windsor Place. Unlike the other blocks between it and Loudon Terrace, it is four storeys and when built contained two flats on each of the three upper floors, all consisting of three rooms, kitchen and bathroom. Like other properties in Byres Road the block was bought as an investment by the recently-established Alliance Heritable Securities Association, which raised shares from small investors and bought property. In 1898 the block (then listed as 62-74 Byars Road) was offered for sale. No price was given but the income from rents was advertised as £583 annually. The block was purchased jointly by Carrick Howatt, an engineer, and Robert Macouat, a director of John Bilsland & Company, a bolt and rivet works in Cranstonhill. Macouat was a significant figure in Glasgow and served as a member of the Chamber of Commerce, Deacon of the Incorporation of Coopers, a Justice of Peace and Deputy-Lieutenant of the city's Territorial Force Association.

Over the years, a number of those who had businesses in the street rented flats in the close. In the 1880s, John McBride, a plumber, and Alexander Duff, a poulterer, who happened to have adjoining shops at Nos. 380 and 382, and William Hamilton, who had a fruit shop at No. 305, lived there. In that decade other occupants included Walter Wallace,

Highland Temperance League certificate, c.1890

the church officer of Hillhead Established Church in Observatory Road, which had opened in 1876, and George Ross, special deputy of the Highland Temperance League whose office was in Prince of Wales Terrace. The League was established in 1880 to promote temperance among the Gaelic-speaking population.

> The cause of temperance has long passed the stage of respectability, and is fast taking a high place in the world of fashion …and what with such powerful organisations as the good old Scottish Temperance League, the Highland Temperance League, and General Booth with his Salvation Army now invading the world – why, the whole framework of society seems moved to put and keep down this terrible and tremendous drink-disease, which is eating its way into the vitals of humanity.

Tenants in the 1890s included Henrietta Salkinson, a widow who taught German, her daughter Margaret who taught music and her son, Arthur, who worked in a chemist's; Francis Milne, the manager of the Hillhead branch of the Bank of Scotland in Great Western Road; James Todd, a cabinetmaker and upholsterer, who had his business at No. 327 through to the 1930s; Joseph Butters, who was a fishmonger at No. 378; and John Wilson, a butcher whose shop was in Argyle Street.

In 1908 Agnes Gentles moved here with her two sons, Robert and Archibald, and Archibald's wife, Catherine and their infant son. Agnes was recently widowed. She and her husband had run a stationers in South Woodside Road and following his death Agnes moved the business to No. 311, below the flat. She was described in 1908:

> In her widow's weeds and crumply black hat sat meek Mrs Gentles, seemingly resigned to life's tribulations, her sad eyes gazing. wistfully across *Aunt Kate's Dream*

Robert Macouat who jointly bought No. 313 in 1898.

Book, Home, Chat, Chuckles and *Lot o' Fun*, (magazines) as she shifted an evening paper nearer to you and took your halfpenny because that was the price of the paper.

Archibald and his family moved, but Agnes and Robert lived in the flat through to their deaths in the early 1950s. Robert had taken over running the shop where he was described as:

Being kept company by two cats. A trifle wizened, and of slight stature, he had a chirpy manner and a quizzical look in his eye that let you know you couldn't get the better of him. This he exemplified occasionally in recounting his war experiences. In the early 1920s he took to playing the banjo.

Catherine Davidson, another widow with five children all under the age of sixteen, rented two flats and at the 1911 census had four lodgers: a female teacher and three male clerks. Jessie and Violet Campbell, two unmarried sisters, also took in lodgers, although their advert in 1909 stipulated that they only let one room: 'Bed sitting room, hot bath, no other lodgers, terms moderate.' The room was taken by Edith Nunna, a teacher. Violet did not work but Jessie was a dress designer. In 1921 John and Evelyn Park were lodging with them; John was a master mariner and Evelyn worked as a cinema pianist.

Christopher and Margaret Sherry lived in one of the flats from 1903 with their three unmarried adult children. Christopher was born in Dublin and acquired his early horticultural training in Trinity College Gardens, and at this time was the senior botanist at the Botanic Gardens: 'His duties are to name the specimens of botanic interest, and to keep the collection in order. He is the highest paid member of the staff.' In 1901 he published *A guide to the Gardens. The Glasgow Botanic Gardens: Its Conservatories, Greenhouses, etc.* 'Mr Sherry's brief but sufficient guide cannot fail to be useful, especially at a time when so many visitors are flocking to the city.' Earlier, the family had had to move out of their flat in Alberta Terrace and Sherry applied to rent the curator's house in the gardens, which had been standing vacant for some time. The Botanic Gardens committee refused. Instead, they decided that the employee who was responsible for looking after the glasshouses should move into

The Glasgow Botanic Gardens by Christopher Sherry, published 1901.

Lewis Hutton collection

the property, explaining: 'He has to ensure they are kept at a proper temperature during the night as well as day, while Mr Sherry's duties do not necessitate his being in the Gardens before or after the ordinary working hours.' The 'snub' was raised at a Glasgow Council Meeting: 'Bailie O'Hare did not mince matters. He declared in good round terms that Mr Sherry was victimised because he was a Roman Catholic.' Sherry died in 1914. Two years after being widowed, Mrs Sherry heard that her oldest son, who had emigrated to Australia, had been killed while fighting with the Highland Light Infantry in France. Herbert Austin, a young Irish student, who lodged in one of the flats while at the university, also joined the Highland Light Infantry and he too died in the war.

Although the 1921 census records that five of the flats were rented by widows, only one may have been a war widow. However, daughters of three of the women – Ada and Hilda Davidson, Margaret Philips and Janet Law – were all unmarried and may have remained single, given the lack of eligible men following the carnage of the war. One positive note was that like many women by then, the war had opened up new employment possibilities to them: Ada (26) worked as clerkess bookkeeper; Hilda (23) as a 'Lady Tracer' at Harland & Wolff Shipyard; Margaret as a typist; and Janet (23) as a clerkess. Catherine Davidson was still taking in lodgers: 'Bed parlour, superior, front. 10s. suit two.' Four of the tenants from the 1920s were still living there at the start of the Second World War, and two into the 1950s. Robert, the son of Jessie Law who first moved in around 1912 with her husband, lived in his flat through to the 1970s.

Up until the 1950s all the flats had been rented but they began to be put up for sale. In 1955 one was on the market for £500 (in 2021 one sold for £285,555). In 1956 two were purchased by Keith and Helen Bovey, who had married in 1950. Both were lawyers and one flat was used as their home and the other for their law practice, Bovey & Bovey. In the war Keith had worked as an interpreter between the US occupying forces and Japanese POWs, and the use of the Atomic Bomb to end the war made him a pacifist; as a result he later became active in the Campaign for Nuclear Disarmament (CND). As a solicitor, Bovey was a founding father and early president of the Glasgow Bar Association, and during his long legal career gained a reputation for specialising in criminal cases linked to the misuse of drugs. Helen dealt with the conveyancing work while Keith focused on criminal defence. A friend recalled the couple driving around the West End of Glasgow in their Citroen 2CV, with, 'Keith's famous bowler hat stickin' oot through the rolled-back canvas top'. In 1959 the Boveys commissioned Byres Road's most famous artist, Alasdair Gray, to decorate the front door of their flat at No. 313.

Both Helen and Keith were members of the Scottish National Party (SNP) and for many years Keith was the SNP's president. In 1974 he stood for the SNP in the Hillhead constituency where Tam Galbraith, Conservative, was the sitting MP, but came fourth. Four years later he contested the Garscadden constituency. The SNP had high hopes of a victory there as it pitted the 'poshies' of Bearsden and Kelvindale against the working classes of Drumchapel and Maryhill. Standing for Labour was a fellow Glasgow lawyer, Donald Dewar and it was he who was victorious: a major setback for simmering Scottish nationalism, and personally for Keith. He and Helen moved to Edinburgh, but their daughter Jenny lived on in one of the flats until the 1990s.

A number of lecturers at Glasgow University bought flats through the 1980s and 1990s, including Richard Steiner, a lecturer in mathematics. He bought his flat in 1982 and resided there until 2000. Another to move in at that time was Alan Train, an architect who worked with Strathclyde Regional Council Central Design unit. Among his architectural projects was the award-winning Lorne Street Community Education Centre.

Front door of the Bovey's flat decorated by Alasdair Gray.
by permission of Alasdair Gray estate

The Bovey family at No. 313, *c.*1970

Chapter Twelve

Notable Buildings

The first public buildings erected in Byres Road were two churches: Partick East United Presbyterian Church, built at the bottom of the road in 1824, and Kelvinside Free Church, built at the top in 1863. Partick East United Presbyterian Church was built for a Secessionist congregation and was the first church built in Partick. Many of its congregation were weavers, whose radical viewpoint was reflected in their choosing not to be members of the established Church of Scotland. Until the church was built the Secessionist congregation worshipped in the Old Masonic Hall, while members of the Church of Scotland had to travel to churches in Anderston, or across the Clyde to Govan:

Partick East United Presbyterian Church, *c.*1850.

Dowanhill Church archives

> The crossing of the Clyde in all sorts of weather was a source of considerable danger, much discomfort, and continuous grumbling. After a dreich sermon it is not surprising that wild stampedes were regularly made for the ferry boat.

Rev John Skinner of Partick East United Presbyterian Church, *c.*1850

Dowanhill Church archives

Although Partick East Church was built with a ground floor and galleries on the first floor, the open space between the first-floor gallery was floored over and fitted up with pews, while the ground floor area below served partly as a joiner's shop, and partly as a hall for religious meetings and a Sabbath School. Around 1830, with the congregation growing, the building was restructured. 'We worshipped in that upper room for five or six years, but the place became too small for us, and we set about enlarging it. The floor of separation was removed, and the whole edifice converted into a church.'

At that time a hall for the Sabbath School was built behind the church. The first minister was Rev John Skinner, who was ordained on 10 April 1827. In 1866 the congregation moved to the newly-built Dowanhill Church in Hyndland Street and the building became home to the Third United Protestant Church of Partick (also known as Partick East United Free Church). They moved out about 1902 to a new building erected at the corner of Lawrence Street and Elie Street, and the church was demolished as part of the area's redevelopment linked to the building of the subway.

After many calls from Partick's members of the established church for a local church to be built to save them having to cross the river, eventually, in 1836, the Church of Scotland presbytery built a 'Chapel of Ease' – a subsidiary place of worship built for the convenience of parishioners who lived at a distance from the parish church – in Church Street. In 1869 it became Partick Parish Church (later known as Old Partick Parish Church). The building

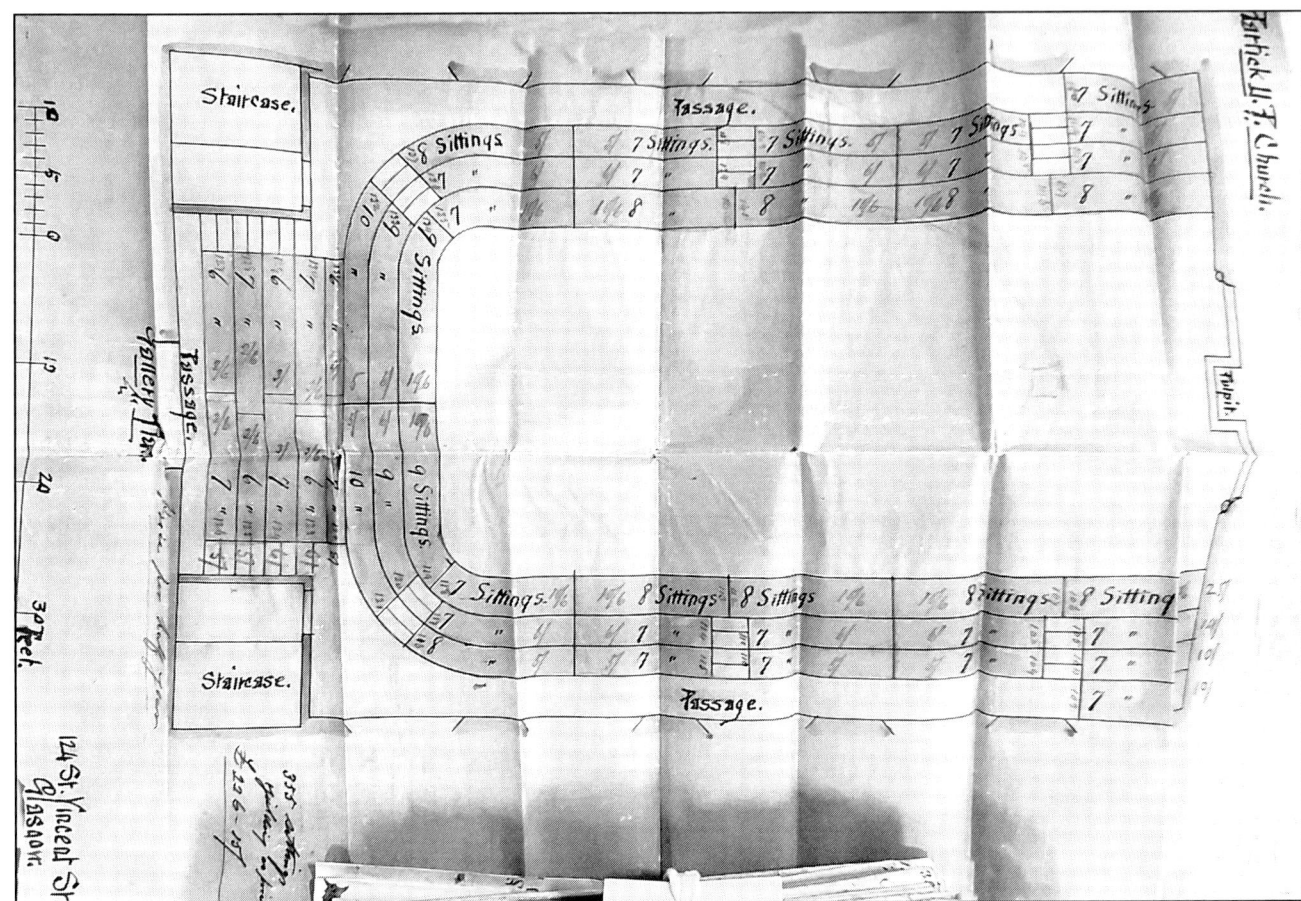

Drawing showing pew charges for Partick East United Presbyterian Church, 1828.   *Dowanhill Church archives*

was rebuilt in 1878 and expanded in 1895. The congregation of Old Partick worshipped there until 1990, when the building was sold for use as a furniture warehouse. After being badly damaged by fire in 2002 it was demolished. The minister of Old Partick Parish Church from 1928 to 1946 was John Macrae, Chief of the Clan Macrae. He was always open to new ideas and one he introduced in February 1939 was much reported:

> A religious service with talkie films, the first of its kind in Glasgow, was held last week in the Standard Picture House, Partick, under the direction of the Rev. John Macrae. For about an hour before the meeting was due to begin a queue began to form outside the kinema, and when the service opened there was an attendance of over 700 people. No restrictions were placed on the audience, many of whom smoked during the service. The films shown were *The Good Samaritan* and *Mastership*. There was no charge for admission to the kinema, but a collection was taken to defray expenses. The balance was for the Jewish Christian Refugee Fund.

In 1859 John Blackie, the noted publisher and writer, who lived in Kew Gardens, and other members of the Free Church, decided a church was required to serve the local residents of the new properties being built around Hillhead. Having purchased a site on the corner of Great Western Road and Byres Road they commissioned a design from the architect Campbell Douglas, and Blackie laid the foundation stone of Kelvinside Free Church on 4 September 1862. When building began it was discovered that the site stood over old coal workings:

> Several mining engineers advised that the foundations should be carried down below the waste, which was accomplished by making large bores through the rock and inserting eight iron columns, nearly ten feet long, which stand on the bottom the old coal pit, and are bound together by iron girders, bedded in concrete, on which rests the walls of the tower.

Kelvinside Free Church opened in September 1863: 'The design embraces numerous beautiful features which have not hitherto been introduced into any ecclesiastical edifices in the city. The style of the building is Venetian Gothic'. Following the First World War, Glasgow Academical school gifted eight bells that were erected in the spire dedicated to the memory, 'of the boys of Glasgow and Kelvinside

John Blackie, from *Memoirs and Portraits of 100 Glasgow Men.*

Kelvinside Free Church.

Academies, and of this church, who fell in the Great War, 1914-18.' Although no longer a church, the bells are still in situ, and are rung on 11 November each year.

The church's first minister was Dr William Trail and in 1864 he conducted one of the first marriages; Robert Arbuckle, another Free Church minister, to Marion McAdam. Weddings in Victorian times usually took place in the home of the bride or groom with a minister attending, rather than in church, and this wedding took place at 224 Great Western Road. In the 20th century church weddings became the norm and the author's parents, William and Margaret Price, were married in Kelvinside Church on 24 March 1939. On leaving the church a surprise awaited the newly-weds:

> The placidity of Great Western Road was considerably disturbed yesterday afternoon by the appearance of a young and blushing couple seated in a glazier's barrow, gaily decorated and being pulled by a team of bright young things. 'Twas a newly married pair and their barrow was provided by exuberant friends to carry the couple to a taxi lurking round the corner.

Although the church building is now Òran Mór, it continues to be a venue for weddings; in 2010 the then Deputy First Minister of Scotland, Nicola Sturgeon and Peter Murrell married there.

It was in Kelvinside Church that Jyoti Hazra and Helen Leatham first met in the mid-1950s. Jyoti came to Glasgow from Calcutta in 1952 to study at Glasgow University when aged twenty-two. He found Glasgow a daunting place as he felt the cold, had difficulty in understanding the Glaswegian accent and experienced discrimination. He and other Indian students at the university decided that to meet and socialise with Scottish people they should learn to dance, but at the dance halls almost all the women refused to dance with them.

> One day, I and three other Indian students decided to go to a church on the corner of Byres Road and Great Western Road (Kelvinside Free)', Hazra recounted, 'where we had discovered that free tea, coffee, cakes and sandwiches were served at an international evening. We were always looking for good food!' There was dancing and I asked one of the young women if she would partner me, but then discovered it was the Gay Gordons. I had no idea how to do it but she said, "just follow me".

He and Helen married in 1957. Jyoti later became a maths lecturer at Dundee College while Helen continued her musical career, including working as a pianist and repetiteur with Scottish Opera. The couple were married for 59 years. Helen died in 2016 and Jyoti five years later.

William & Margaret Price being wheeled along Great Western Road following their wedding in Kelvinside Church, 24 March 1939. The Kirklee Hotel at 19 Belhaven Terrace West is in the background.

Author's collection

Jyoti & Helen Hazra, *c.*1959.
Scottish Memories Immigration Stories

Hillhead Burgh Hall with police housing to the right. 1940s.

Henry Morton collection

Scottish Cocker Spaniel Show in Hillhead Burgh Hall, 1939.

Kelvinside Church Hall was often hired by the BBC for rehearsals and in 1959 the BBC TV show, *The White Heather Club* rehearsed there. For Andy Stewart, the show's presenter, one day was memorable:

> While rehearsing in Byres Road, a piece of music kept running through my head. It was an old traditional melody used by Rossini in *William Tell* and I learnt it on the mouth organ when I was six. As the tune kept churning round in my head I picked up an envelope and wrote on the back, 'There was a soldier, a Scottish soldier.'

His recording of the completed song, *A Scottish Soldier*, was an international hit, spending 36 weeks in the British Top Twenty.

By the late 1970s, Kelvinside's congregation had dwindled and in 1978 it merged with Hillhead Parish Church. The church became home to the Glasgow Bible College, one of the very first Bible Colleges in Britain when established in 1892. It offered training to workmen, shopkeepers, housemaids and many others who had been converted at the missions of the American evangelist D.L. Moody and wished to become missionaries, but were not welcomed by most of the established churches because of their lack of education. Many became missionaries in China, India, Russia and elsewhere. The college moved out in the 1990s and in 2004 the building was converted into the arts and leisure centre, Òran Mór.

The demolition of the Western Infirmary has brought into general view from Church Street the Infirmary's former chapel, the Alexander Elder Memorial Chapel. It was designed by Sir John James Burnet and built through a bequest of £50,000 from Alexander Elder whose family were shipbuilders. The chapel was dedicated to doctors who had lost their lives in the First World War and opened in 1925. Other churches built in the locality included St Peter's (RC) (later St Simon's), Partick Bridge Street, designed by Charles O'Neill, opened 1858 (destroyed by fire); Dowanhill United Presbyterian Church, Hyndland Street, designed by William Leiper, opened 1866; Hillhead Parish Church (later Kelvinside Hillhead Parish Church), Observatory Road, designed by James Sellars, opened 1876; Dowanvale Free Church, Dowanhill Street, designed by Alexander Petrie, opened 1881; Hillhead Baptist Church, Creswell Street, designed by Thomas Lennox Watson, opened 1883; Wellington Church, University Avenue, also designed by Thomas Lennox Watson, opened 1884; and St Peter's (RC), Hyndland Street, designed by Peter Paul Pugin, opened 1903.

Following Hillhead becoming a Police Burgh in 1869, architect George Bell, was commissioned to design Hillhead Burgh Hall. The building contained a public hall, Burgh Court, offices and police cells and behind were buildings for the police and fire services. At the laying of the foundation stone on 13 May 1871 there was a masonic parade from Botanic Gardens to the site by the Provincial Grand Lodge of Glasgow. The building opened in 1873:

> Last night, about 500 ladies and gentlemen, met together at the opening of Hillhead Burgh Hall to spend a pleasant hour or two. At the event the Burgh's first Provost, Robert Bruce spoke of the progress that had been made: 'Most of you will recollect the darkness which prevailed in the streets at night, the absence of pavements, the poor state of the streets and the absence of main sewers. Although from the state of the labour market and the extent of the work required, we have not been able to complete the whole of the works, yet a great deal has been achieved.'

Behind the main building was a yard that contained the ancillary buildings: 'The Police Station was a grim looking place with its entrance dark and foreboding, and its heavily barred dungeons at the back. The stables for the Cleaning Department housed the powerful Clydesdale horses that pulled the red panelled carts.'

Through to the early 1960s the Burgh Hall was used for a variety of events. In 1873 the hall housed, 'the first annual soiree and concert of the employees of the Partick, Hillhead & Maryhill Gas Company', and in 1884 one of the many musical concerts held there over the years took place:

> Some two hundred of what may be termed the inner circle of the musical society of Glasgow, who, notwithstanding the boisterous weather, were attracted by a lure which is but too seldom set for their enticement, namely the intimation of a concert of chamber music. Altogether, the couple of hours during which the recital lasted were spent most agreeably, and the audience, if numerically small, were certainly enthusiastic in the way of outward marks of appreciation.

In 1897 the Norwegian, Fridtjof Nansen, at the time famed for his polar explorations, was hosted in Glasgow by Lord and Lady Kelvin and a special entertainment was arranged in his honour in the hall:

> The delightful musical 'At Home' consisted of a programme of vocal and instrumental music contributed by Miss Crum and Miss Clench. Lady Kelvin was dressed in black silk enriched with jet, her becoming black bonnet being relieved with touches of white. Mrs. Nansen was very tastefully dressed in brown velvet with gold trimmings on gown and bonnet. She and Dr Nansen were most attentive listeners to the two hours' programme of delightful music.

In 1916, in honour of the Shakespearian tercentenary:

a charming performance was given on Thursday afternoon and evening in Hillhead Burgh Hall, when Miss Marjorie Gullan's dramatic class appeared in *Twelfth Night* in aid of the local charities supported by Laurel Bank School, of which the young ladies taking part in the entertainment were pupils.

The hall was also used for dance classes and Alison Downie, the *Glasgow Herald*'s Women's Editor, recalled attending these in the 1920s:

Then, dancing class meant wearing a party dress (second best, but still definitely festive), beneath the hooded cloak – velvet or velour cloth – which was our equivalent of the present-day duffel coat. Warm wool gaiters were pulled up over frilly underwear, and dancing sandals carried in a jug. After shedding cloaks, gaiters and outdoor shoes we joined the sprinkling of boys in kilts or sailor suits in the seemingly vast hall.

Partick was home to many Gaels and the various Gaelic groups regularly held ceilidhs and dances at the Burgh Hall. In 1930 the Uist & Barra Association Late Night Novelty Dance was held there and in 1947 the Clan Mackinnon Society Ceilidh. In 1921 Sir Daniel Stevenson, a Scottish businessman and politician, endowed a Chair of Citizenship at Glasgow University and spoke in the Burgh Hall on his reasons for so doing:

There is an apathy towards municipal government among certain sections of the community, and I believe

> **GLASGOW**
> **UIST AND BARRA ASSOCIATION**
> **LATE NIGHT NOVELTY**
> **D A N C E**
> (Spot Prizes)
> in
> **HILLHEAD BURGH HALLS**
> (Nr. Hillhead Subway)
> On FRIDAY, 10th MARCH, 1930
> 8 p.m. till 1.30 p.m.
> Admission Ticket • • • • • 3/-
> Hamilton Orr's Band and Association Pipers
> w1361   C. M. MacLellan, Hon. Secy.

Advert for a dance in Hillhead Burgh Hall, 1930.

there is a need for more education on the rights and privilege of citizenship. People ought to be proud of their own town and country, and take an interest in its affairs, and make their own town and country places to be proud of.

In fact, citizenship was often on show at the hall as it frequently was used for political meetings, including early suffragette events, and functioned as an election polling station. The establishment of today's Scottish National Party (SNP) arose from a meeting in the hall on 14 December 1933. At the time there were two nationalist groups – the left-of-centre National Party and The Scottish Party, a breakaway section of the Cathcart Conservative Association – and at that meeting the amalgamation of the two parties was agreed. The following year the new SNP came into being.

In the 1960s Glasgow council debated the future of Hillhead Burgh Hall. Some were of a mind to sell off the site while others proposed converting the building into a library or demolishing it to build a new library. One local resident bemoaned its possible loss to the community:

Already we have lost our own small police station on this site where before the Second World War we used to take our small problems of lost cats. Now we are to lose our last privilege of paying our gas and rates locally.

The new library idea was chosen, the halls demolished and the new library built on the site. The building to the

Demolition of Hillhead Burgh Hall, 1960s.   *Henry Morton*

left of the library – now the Six by Nico restaurant – was a South of Scotland Electricity Board showroom through the 1960s and 1970s, and the building next to it on the corner with Vinicombe Street remains an electricity sub-station. On the other side the police houses survived until the late 1990s when they too were demolished to make way for a block of flats with shops below. The building in Vinicombe Street, between it and Burgh Lane, probably was part of Hillhead's Cleaning Department's premises in the past.

Before the 1872 Education (Scotland) Act was passed parents wishing to have their children educated had three choices. For the better-off there were private schools or private tutors, while for poorer parents the only option was a church school that offered lower-cost schooling for younger children. However, many children did not receive any formal education.

The earliest school in Partick was a Subscription School dating from the 18th century financed by the local elders of the Church of Scotland. It stood in The Goat (Kelvin Street) that ran between Dumbarton Road and Castlebank (Beith) Street, and later became known as The Partick Mission School. In 1808 it advertised for a teacher:

Interior of Hillhead Library, 1970s. *Glasgow City Libraries*

> Partick School. Wanted a Schoolmaster, qualified to teach the reading of English, English Grammar, Writing, Arithmetic, and Book-keeping. There are attached to the appointment, a commodious well-aired school room, a convenient dwelling-house, and a neat small garden. The amount of emolument which arises from School Fees, will, in proportion to the teacher's exertions and success, run from £60 to £80 per annum. Candidates wishing to learn further particulars, and possessed of satisfactory attestations of ability and character, will be pleased to apply.

Partick Free Church School was opened in Anderston Street in 1846 by the Free Church of Scotland as a School of Industry for Girls, but by 1858 had been enlarged and become a public school for both sexes. There was a charge of a penny a week for each pupil. The first Roman Catholic school in Partick opened in 1864 as part of St Peter's Church in Bridge Street.

The Partick Academy, a private school, was built between Byres Road, Church Street and Torness Street, and opened in 1851: 'The foundation has been laid of an academy situated immediately to the west of Gilmorehill, and in a locality well adapted to afford the same advantages to the inhabitants of Hillhead, and to those in Partick itself.' It taught both boys and girls and along with the usual subjects, there were lessons in bookkeeping, and for the boys, fencing and gymnastics and for the girls, dancing and deportment. Five years earlier Glasgow Academy, another private school, had opened in Elmbank Street and John King, a pupil there in

Partick Mission School.

Church Street Public School, former Partick Academy, shortly before its demolition, *c.*1905. The halls that would house the workshops and swimming pool are under construction on the left. *Lewis Hutton collection*

the 1860s, recounted his walk from his house in Hillhead to the Academy:

> Hillhead was a rural suburb and in my daily tramp to and from the school I traversed what was largely open countryside, with hedges, trees and green fields on either hand. Woodlands Road justified its name and sauch (willow) trees bloomed in Sauchiehall Street.

In 1866 a government investigation found that of the 490,000 children in Scotland, 200,000 were being efficiently educated, 200,000 receiving schooling of doubtful quality and 90,000 receiving no education at all. Although Scotland's illiteracy rates of between 10% and 20% were on a par with the best-educated nations in Europe, it was decided that all children should receive a basic education and the 1872 Education (Scotland) Act was passed, introducing universal education for all children aged from five to thirteen, although it was not made free until later.

To deliver and oversee universal education the Act established local school boards; Partick and Hillhead came within the area of Govan School Board. Board members were elected every three years by voters who were owners or occupiers of property above £4 annual rental, and women were eligible to vote and to stand for election. However, the members of Govan School Board in its early years were all men, and the importance given to religious instruction in schools is reflected by the Govan Board having a large number of clergy – both Protestant and Roman

Catholic – as members. Many of its first meetings were spent arguing over whether or not meetings should commence with a prayer. All School Boards were faced with having to swiftly increase the number of available school places. To cope, Govan School Board took over the Partick Free Church School; rented the Partick Mission School and a wooden church in Merkland Street to serve as temporary schools; and purchased Partick Academy that they enlarged and re-opened as Church Street Public School. However, more schooling space was required and with funding available for building new schools the Govan Board commissioned four new schools in Partick and Govan to accommodate 4,600 pupils at a cost of over £40,000. In the board schools of the period, girls and boys were kept separate, and each had their own entrance, stairwell and playground. Parents whose children attended these were charged between two- and fourpence per pupil a week.

At this time the development of Byres Road was at an early stage, and the residents of the expanding West End suburbs mainly members of the professional and mercantile class population who chose to send their children to private schools. In 1874, 'a number of gentlemen in the West of Glasgow, feeling the necessity for a good education for their children organised a movement to build a new school… as to maintain our position as a great mercantile community we require young men of good ability in the common pursuits of life.' They established a company and sold shares to raise the funds, and Kelvinside Academy, a boys' school, opened in Kirklee Road in 1878. The year before, a school building was built on spec in Vinicombe Street and advertised:

The Academy is a most substantial building and planned with all modern improvements. The classrooms are large and well-lighted and ventilated. On the basement floor there is a gymnasium and covered playground. The school is capable of accommodating 300 pupils.

It became the Hillhead Academy for Young Ladies and operated until the early 1900s. In 1910 the building was demolished to make way for the Botanic Garage. The private girls' school, Laurel Bank School opened in 1905 at No. 1 Lilybank Terrace. In 1878 the Glasgow Academy moved to a new building in Colebrooke Street, off Great Western Road, and Glasgow High School, the city's oldest school (founded by 1460) moved into the Elmbank building.

By 1880 the mix of people living in Byres Road and the streets around became more diverse, and many parents were unable, or unwilling, to pay significant fees for their children's education. Thus, Govan School Board built new schools in the area: Hillhead in 1883, Hyndland in 1887 and Dowanhill in 1894.

The six daughters and one son of John and Morag Fisher. who lived at No. 26 Havelock Street, were educated at Hyndland School, and three of the

HILLHEAD ACADEMY
FOR YOUNG LADIES,
VINICOMBE STREET (NEAR BOTANIC GARDENS).
THIS ACADEMY WILL BE OPENED ON MONDAY,
2D FEBRUARY.

PRINCIPAL...................Mr JAMES LEITCH
(Late Rector of the Glasgow Normal School).
Author of ''Practical Educationists and their Systems of Teaching,'' ''Lessons in English Composition,'' &c., &c.
LADY SUPERINTENDENT......Miss EMILY A. LAMONT.
STAFF OF TEACHERS.

English, Grammar, History, Geography, Science, &c.... { Mr LEITCH, Miss LAMONT, Miss BARCLAY, and Miss A. LEITCH.

English Composition and Literature................... } Mr LEITCH.

Writing and Arithmetic...... { Mr LEITCH and Miss BARCLAY.

French...................... { Mons. A. L. GORECKI, Mr LEITCH, and Miss LAMONT.

German..................... { Herr JUSTUS WIDMAK, Mrs BOHMER, and Miss LAMONT

Drawing and Painting....... { Mr JAMES J. KING (School of Art).

Class Singing.............. { Mr DAVID B. JOHNSTONE (A.Mus., Trin. Coll., Lond.).

Pianoforte.................. { Misses LAMONT, BARCLAY, and GERRIE.

Pianoforte (Advanced)....... { Dr A. L. PEACE (Oxon). Mr JOHN K. SWANSTON (Conservatoire, Leipzig).

Elocution................... Mr W. BAYNHAM.
Needlework (Plain and Fancy), Cutting-Out, and Domestic Economy........ } Mrs LEITCH.

Fees from Half-a-Guinea to Three Guineas per Quarter inclusive.

Pupils are now being Enrolled.

Advert for Hillhead Academy in Vinicombe Street, 1880.

children later became significant figures in the revival of Scottish traditional music. Both parents were musical: John, a police inspector, sang with the Glasgow Police Choir, and Morag was a Gaelic speaker and singer. The first children to enter the musical scene were Archie and Ray, who formed a skiffle group, and later a folk duo. Both also had successful solo careers. Ray, who died in 2011, was described by *The Guardian* as, 'one of Britain's great interpreters of traditional song'. As well as his successful career as a folk singer and songwriter, Archie has produced other artists, including the first Clancy Brothers' albums, and for 25 years from 1983 presented the influential BBC Scotland radio programme *Travelling Folk*. Cilla married Artie Trezise and, in 1982, having previously performed as a folk duo, established The Singing Kettle, a popular

Dowanhill School from Dowanhill Park.   *Lewis Hutton collection*

Boy's class, Hillhead School, 1889

Traditional & New Songs from Scotland by The Fisher Family, Topic Records, 1966

St. Peter's School for Boys, *c.*1905.

Lewis Hutton Collection

Liz Cameron, Lord Provost of Glasgow 2003-07 and former pupil of Notre Dame School.

Girl's class, Notre Dame School, 1958.

theatre group that performs traditional children's songs. In 1966 all members of the Fisher family joined together to record *Traditional and New Songs from Scotland*. It was in the playground of Hyndland that Archie Fisher first became friends with Hamish Imlach, who had been born in Calcutta and whose parents recently had come back from India to live in Glasgow. The new pupil was hard to miss for Imlach wrote: 'I would go to school wearing a fez, a leather jacket and a Palm Beach shirt to attract the girls' attention. I had scant success.' Imlach also became a stalwart of the traditional folk scene. At one point his record *Cod Liver Oil and the Orange Juice* became the most requested song on British Forces Radio, although for a time it was banned by the BBC as the Corporation considered it scurrilous. Imlach was a great raconteur and influenced many other artists, including the musician and comedian, Billy Connolly.

Connolly attended the Roman Catholic school, St Peter's Boys in Stewartville Street, Partick. After leaving school he worked in various jobs until the mid-1960s, by which time he had already begun to perform at Glasgow folk clubs. With singer-guitarist Tam Harvey he formed the Humblebums and their first record was released in 1969. Gerry Rafferty joined the group and Harvey left, and the new duo recorded and performed until 1971. By then

Connolly's talent for parody had resulted in a theme song, *The Welly Boot Song*, a skit on the popular folk song *The Wark o' the Weavers*, and his song introductions had developed into drawn-out, comical monologues. Over the last 50 years Connolly, known affectionately as 'The Big Yin', has become one of Scotland's most successful performers, with a career that has encompassed music, comedy, acting and TV presenting.

St Peter's Boys School, originally Stewartville School for Boys, was opened by Govan School Board in 1891, since the religious divide in Glasgow required segregated schools. Notre Dame private girls' school opened in Observatory Road in 1897 and Govan Board opened St Peters' Girls' School in Victoria Crescent Road in 1905. Liz Cameron, who served as Glasgow's Lord Provost from 2003 to 2007 was born in Partick and attended St Peter's School for Girls, and then Notre Dame. It was there that her commitment to political reform began.

I absolutely loved Notre Dame and the teachers, both religious and lay, who gave me a super, well-rounded education. Indeed, I have had cause to recall, often, during my career, the words of my excellent history teacher, a young nun who passionately believed that public health and education reforms benefitted people more than any political revolution could do!

Billy & Iris Connolly with Jamie & Cara – James pointing to Connelly LP in the window of Echo Records, Byres Road, 1974. *Picture this Scotland website*

After teaching for a time, Liz served as a Labour member of the Glasgow District Council from 1992 and, from 1995, was councillor for the Knightswood South ward. While studying at Glasgow University she sang with the University of Glasgow Choral Society, and her passion for, and commitment to, the arts has seen her serve on a wide range of arts boards, including Glasgow Film Theatre, Scottish Baroque Ensemble and Scottish Opera, and as Chair of the Scottish International Piano Competition. For a few years in the early 1980s, she and her husband Duncan lived in Byres Road. 'It remains one of my favourite streets. It's so lively, colourful, diverse, arty,' Liz says, 'but being Glaswegian, it's also authentic.'

Although there were schools for Protestants and Roman Catholics, it was not until the 1960s that a Jewish school was

Jeremy Isaacs.

Horace Phillips was born in 1917, one of seven children born to Samuel and Frances. His father died when he was a teenager, leaving his mother almost penniless. After attending Hillhead School, Horace became a clerk with the Inland Revenue. After successfully completing the demanding Civil Service Examination he applied to join the Consular Service but was rebuffed due to his social background. During the Second World War he served in Iraq, India, Burma, Ceylon and Malaya, and was appointed a major in the Indian Army. After the war he was admitted to the Diplomatic Service and among the countries he served in were Afghanistan, Iran and Indonesia. In 1968 he was selected as the British ambassador to Saudi Arabia but the Saudi government withdrew permission due to his being Jewish. He then served as British High Commissioner to Tanzania and British ambassador to Turkey. Horace was the first British Jewish career ambassador and has a room in the Foreign Office's London HQ named in his memory.

At the Cresswell Street end of Cranworth Street, next to the Western Baths, is a large square building and as its façade appears to match that of the Salon Cinema at the other side of the baths, one might assume this was built at the same time as the cinema. In fact, it dates from the early 1990s and was erected as a sports hall for the Western Baths. Originally this corner site contained two houses: Elliot House, No. 40 Cresswell Street (formerly Elliot Street) and Cranworth House, No. 20 Cranworth Street, but both were demolished in 1973; this was unfortunate as each had a noteworthy past.

In 1910 Peter and Margaret (Skirving) Gibb moved from Hillhead Street to Elliot House with their six children. Five years earlier Margaret had founded the Glasgow Ladies Chess Club and was president of the Club until her death in 1918. Two of her daughters, Ellison and Margaret, who in 1910 were in their mid-20s, also were skilled chess players and Ellison took over as president of the Chess Club following her mother's death. More significantly both Ellison and Margaret were major Scottish figures in the Women's Suffrage movement that used art, debate, propaganda, and attacks on property to fight for the right to vote. Among the acts for which Ellison was arrested was a demonstration outside 10 Downing Street. Like other suffragettes, she refused to pay her fine and was sent to prison where she went on hunger strike. In 1914 Margaret was found guilty of striking a constable with a dog whip during a suffragette protest rally outside Holloway Prison and she was sentenced to two months in prison. On her release she made headlines when, in July 1914, she slashed John Everett Millais' portrait of

founded in Glasgow. This was mainly to do with numbers, as in 1901 there were 186,000 Roman Catholics in the city, but only 6,000 Jews; there was also some resistance to the idea of a Jewish school from other churches and local politicians. Thus, until the 1960s the majority of Jewish children attended public schools, while in England only a majority of Jewish children depended on state schools. A number of Jewish boys attended Hillhead Primary School; two of whom had notable careers later in life. Jeremy (Jeremiah) Isaacs was born in 1932, the eldest son of Isidore and Sara. Isidore was a jeweller whose father had immigrated to Kilmarnock and established a furniture business. Sara, who was a doctor, was the daughter of David Jacobs who had been born in Warsaw and served as rabbi of Garnethill Synagogue. Isidore and Sara married in 1928 and moved into a flat at No. 15 Roxburgh Street. Jeremy and his two brothers attended Hillhead School, and then moved to Glasgow Academy. Jeremy won a scholarship to Oxford, and while there was elected president of the Oxford Union. He then began a career in television, first at Granada Television, and later with the BBC and Thames Television, producing a number of outstanding programmes. He was the founding chief executive of Channel 4 that launched in 1981 and, later, general director of the Royal Opera House and president of the Royal Television Society.

Surveillance image of Margaret Gibb exercising in the yard of Holloway prison taken by an undercover police photographer from Scotland Yard to identify suffragettes, 1913

Mrs. STEVENSON, MRS. MICHELL, MISS F. H. STIRLING, MRS. RITCHIE, MISS FORBES, MISS E. GIBB, MISS GILCHRIST
MRS. ROE, MRS. SOLLAS, MRS. ANDERSON, MISS PRICE, MISS ABRAHAM.

Glasgow Ladies Chess Club. Ellison Gibb, back row, second from right, c.1920.

Thomas Carlyle in London's National Portrait Gallery with a butcher's cleaver. In January 1914 an attempt was made to blow up the Kibble Palace in the Botanic Gardens but, fortunately, only some panes of glass were broken. The newspapers blamed the suffragettes although there was no evidence this was their act, nor did they claim responsibility. (Yet one has to wonder, given that the Gibb daughters lived just down the road.) The outbreak of the First World War brought an end to the suffragettes' violent protests. In 1914 both sisters were presented with suffragette medals by the Women's Social & Political Union: 'in recognition of a gallant action whereby through endurance to the last extremity of hunger and hardship, a great principle of political justice was vindicated.' In 1918 the Representation of the People Act was passed which allowed women over the age of thirty who met a property qualification to vote. Although 8.5 million women met this criterion, that only represented 40 per cent of the total population of women in the UK.

From the late 1930s into the '40s, Cranworth House was the home and surgery of the veterinary surgeon, William Weipers. He was a pioneer in the field of surgery for small animals and was

William Weipers

instrumental in the creation of Glasgow University's veterinary school. In 1949 he was appointed its first Director of Veterinary Education and was knighted in 1966. When Weipers moved out at the end of the Second World War the house was converted into an events space with a ballroom and bar. It was advertised as, 'the house of successful functions', and events held there included wedding receptions, whist drives and dances. The venue closed in the early 1960s and in 1965 became Radio Scotland House, the land-based HQ for the pirate radio station that transmitted

Cranworth House.

Glasgow University Archives

from a former lightship off the coast of Scotland. One of the stations most popular disc jockeys was Stuart Henry, but he suffered from sea-sickness and became dubbed 'the seasick pirate'. Given his popularity, he was allowed to become a landlubber pirate DJ, recording his programmes from the calm waters of Cranworth Street.

Today's Grosvenor Hotel on the corner of Grosvenor Terrace and Byres Road opened in 1982 having been rebuilt after the previous hotel was destroyed in a spectacular fire. Grosvenor Terrace was designed by J. T. Rochead in the Venetian-style and when completed in 1858 was described as 'the finest range of buildings in Great Britain, being designed after the most palatial style of architecture.' The first hotel on the site was a conversion of two private residences, Nos. 1 and 2. The hotel opened in time for the 1938 Empire Exhibition at Bellahouston Park; a showcase for Scottish manufacturing, and a celebration of Empire trade and developments. Opened by King George VI and Queen Mary on 3 May, the exhibition had over twelve million visitors. In the early 1970s, the Glasgow-Cypriot businessman Reo Stakis acquired the hotel as well as purchasing the seven adjoining houses in the terrace and a row of one-storey shops (Nos. 383 – 391) in Byres Road, so as to greatly enlarge the hotel.

The most recent building erected in Byres Road is the Clarice Pears building, the new home for Glasgow University's School of Health & Wellbeing. Built on the corner of University Place and Church Street, it was designed by Atkins Architecture and opened in September 2023. The state-of-the-art building brings together researchers to work with third-sector organisations, local government and the NHS to support collaborative research to tackle some of the world's biggest health challenges and inequalities, both in Glasgow and around the globe. The ground floor of the building is home to the Byres Community Hub. The building is named in honour of Mrs Pears, whose family trust donated £5 million towards its construction.

Advert for Grosvenor Hotel, 1940s.

Chapter Thirteen

Mail, Money & Mortgages

In 1855 Partick and Hillhead had three mail deliveries a day, and in 1872 the first Hillhead Post Office opened at 61 Great Western Road. In 1881 another post office was opened, at No. 321 Byres Road, and was staffed by ladies; although as George Sheriff recounted, they were not the most efficient:

> The 'Female Assistants' as I believe their official status was at that time were a by-word for general snappishness to customers. An uncle of mine went in one day to get a penny stamp but the ladies were engaged in a private conversation which they continued without paying any attention to him. As Uncle Arthur was not the man to put up with this sort of thing from public servants, he raised his stick and rapped it soundly on the counter. At this one of the ladies turned and called out, "Well? What do you want?" "I want to send a telegram." "Can't you see the forms hanging up in front of your eyes?" retorted the lady. "Take one and write out your message." My uncle did so, but this time awaited the lady's pleasure without showing any further signs of impatience. When the lady eventually came over and took the form to count the words, she looked up with a startled expression and asked, "Do you want to send this?" "No, I don't," he replied, "but if I did, you would have to send it." The telegram read 'Postmaster General London – Lady Assistants Hillhead Post Office Glasgow too busy gossiping to attend to customers.'

Telegrams were an important form of communication in the days before telephones became widely available. When a telegram arrived at Hillhead Post Office it was printed out and then a 'telegram boy' was dispatched by bicycle to deliver it to the recipient's address. Telegram boys wore uniforms and were required to complete a daily drill. During the First World War people dreaded the arrival of a telegram boy at their door for War Office telegrams invariably brought distressing news of a relative injured or killed in the war. In 1934 the papers reported:

> In the Hillhead Post Office an experimental scheme of motor-cycle delivery of telegrams has been introduced.

Telegraph boys, *c.*1910.

Letter sent in 1836 by Mrs Ronald to Rev Skinner at Partick East United Presbyterian Church. This was before 1840 when postage stamps were first introduced. It is stamped with the Glasgow Penny Post mark, and a halfpenny added.
Dowanhill Church archives

> This enables 70 to 80 messages an hour to be handled as against 24 to 36 formerly. If successful the scheme will be extended to other parts of the city. In order to encourage the boys to ride carefully the Post Office is granting them a bounty if they succeed in driving for 10 months without an accident.

In 1883 the Post Office launched its first parcel post service:

> It would be foolhardy in the extreme to attempt to forecast the future of a system with such immense possibilities of development. The service is only put forward as an experiment and if it is not to be a success the fault will not lie in the lack of public patronage. In the burghs of Govan, Partick and Hillhead the postal officials did not experience much difficulty in coping with the extra work caused by the introduction of the

Hillhead Post Office, No. 314, late 1960s.

Guthrie Hutton

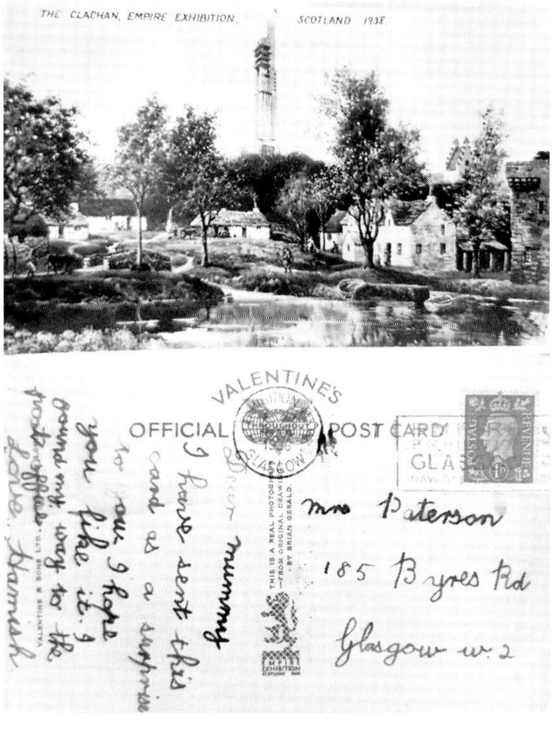

Glasgow postman, photo by William Carrick & John MacGregor, c.1860.
National Galleries Scotland

Postcard sent to Mrs Paterson at No. 185 by her son, Hamish who had gone to see the 1938 Empire Exhibition held at Glasgow's Bellahouston Park.
Author's collection

parcels post. Large numbers of stamps were, however, disposed of in the course of the day.

The post office moved across the road to Nos. 314/316 in 1905 and a sorting office was built behind, backing on Cresswell Lane. Its efficiency in 1986 was reported in the *Evening Times*:

> A colleague who has moved house posted a bundle of those "My new telephone number is…" cards just after 8am one morning this week at Hillhead Post Office. Just 90 minutes later his wife received a phone call from a girlfriend who had received one of the cards at her office in the city. I think a bouquet to the G.P.O would be in order for this example of speed and efficiency.

Byres Road Post Office closed in 2008. However, it is not too far a walk to Penny Black at No. 721 Great Western Road that as well as providing all the usual Post Office services, offers 'balloon services: 'all of our team are well trained in creating some stunning balloon centrepieces for your celebrations.'

In September 1877 some of the earliest phone calls were made from Glasgow University:

> Yesterday we had the opportunity to witness several experiments with the telephone made by Professor Graham Bell at present on a visit to this country. The first series of experiments were carried through in Sir William Thomson's laboratory at the University, Gilmorehill. The practical utility of the telephone consists in messages being electrically and articulately conveyed for hundreds or thousands of miles, and the principle is as beautiful as it is simple. In one series of experiments messages were exchanged over land lines – in one case of nearly two miles, in the other of upwards of ninety miles in length. With the short wire the most striking results were obtained. Conversation was carried on between persons at either end of the wire with the utmost freedom, and *Auld Lang Syne* and a number of other songs were sung. Both words and melody could be distinguished by large parties of privileged listeners with the utmost accuracy; and the applause which greeted the efforts of the singers was transmitted with equal distinctness by means of the instrument. Over the longer distance the sounds were considerably more faint.

By the 1890s, the National Telephone Company and other private telephone companies had opened phone services in Glasgow, although by 1900 only four businesses in Byres Road had telephone numbers: Colquhoun – bakers, Harvey – grocers, Colin Turner – plumbers and John Orr – decorators. As many found the services of the private phone companies to be inefficient and expensive, Glasgow Corporation decided to create its own municipal telephone enterprise and applied for a telephone licence in 1893. However, it was not until 1900, after the proposal had been discussed by two Select Committees of the House of Commons, that the city finally obtained a licence from the Postmaster-General to build and run its own telephone exchange and service, the first outside London. The telephone area covered parts of the counties of Lanark, Renfrew, Dumbarton and Stirling, as well as the city. The central exchange and offices were based in Renfield Street and a sub-exchange was opened at Hillhead. The telephone wires were laid underground in the centre of the city, and by 1904 almost 12,000 telephones had been installed in private and commercial properties. However, Glasgow's municipal telephone service was short-lived, as in 1906 it was transferred to the General Post Office.

In 1907 a new telephone exchange was built at 24 Highburgh Road, designed in the Arts & Crafts style by Leonard Stokes and Colin Menzies (now flats):

> The new exchange for the Hillhead and Partick districts that serves the 3,200 local subscribers is notable for the introduction of the central battery system. Signalling to the exchange is now done automatically by the simple act of lifting the receiver which lights a small lamp in front of the operator. An ordinary call is shown by a yellow light and a public call- in which the caller must deposit a penny before the connection – is given by a red light.

Hillhead Telephone Exchange, 1907.

While the better-off in Byres Road would have had a home telephone by the 1950s, many on lower incomes did not have a phone until the 1970s. Until then those without one in their house had to use one of the red public telephone boxes designed by Sir Giles Gilbert Scott that began to appear in the 1920s. Four were sited at the bottom of Great George Street and a familiar sight was people waiting outside in the cold, growing more and more irritated by the interminable phone conversations of those inside. In 1986 the *Evening Times* reported:

> Glasgow's Lord Provost has been asked to open all sorts of things in his long-distinguished career but today's appointment beats the lot. He will be opening a telephone box! Glasgow's first citizen will undertake this task today in Byres Road when he launches 'the new generation of public telephone kiosks in Scotland'.

Although these new boxes incorporated the novel phonecard technology and were modern in design, they were widely disliked. Many considered the red phone box to be a cultural icon and criticism of British Telecom's decision to replace them was widespread.

Shops in the road have reflected the swiftly changing phone technology. In the 1980s The Telephone Box had one of its three branches at No. 114 and advertised in 1987: 'If you're Christmas shopping for something completely different visit The Telephone Box. The choice is endless. Traditional and contemporary styles – onyx, gimmicky and nostalgic – and the popular cordless phone which is a favourite with gents.' By 1983 the first carphones – the forerunner of mobile phones – were being used by wealthy Glaswegians and as these became more affordable Carphone Warehouse opened at Nos.276/280. Today the once humble telephone is now 'a handheld electronic device' and Phone Geek at No. 53 offers repairs and new models.

The increasing move to close bank branches has seen the Bank of Scotland decide to leave Byres Road after 100 years, and while others may follow suit, at present the road is well endowed with banks. The oldest is the branch of the Clydesdale Bank (now rebranded Virgin Money) that opened at No.

Advert for a home phone, 1975.

324 in 1880, and later extended into No. 326. Next to open a branch was the Royal Bank of Scotland (RBS) at Nos. 187/189 in 1905. The National Bank of Scotland, with a branch at No. 257 from 1930 to 1959, was closed when it became part of RBS, and the RBS later moved to Nos. 187/189. The Union Bank of Scotland opened at No. 174 in 1925, but became part of the Bank of Scotland in 1955. The bank owned the property, including the flats above and the shop next door, and in the 1990s decided to expand. It wanted to extend into the flats upstairs but was refused planning permission, in spite of an appeal to the Secretary of State. Instead, the bank incorporated the next-door shop where the newsagents, Barretts, had traded for many years. Its owner, Fiona Barrett understandably was upset:

> Byres Road is becoming a desert of banks, building society offices, and TV rental shops. Our shop provides a valuable service to the community and now we'll have to close. The bank has given us time to find new premises. but there aren't any available and time is running out.

Notice for the opening of the Clydesdale Bank, 1880.

A type K6 telephone box, designed by Gilbery Scott.

New style of telephone box at bottom of Great George Street. *Author*

The Clydesdale Bank Nos. 324-6, looking very understated in the late 1960s. A painted 'Victoria' can just be made out above the name-plate for Byres Road, a relic of the unsuccesful renaming of the street. *Guthrie Hutton*

Fortunately, she was able to find new premises at No.267 and the shop continues today. A similar concern was raised in an article in the *Glasgow Herald* in 1977:

Many family firms have gone to be replaced by building societies and banks. Where Massey and Son, grocers once were established at the corner of Great George Street, the Bradford & Bingley Building Society now has imposing premises, and the Alliance Building Society has taken over from another grocery firm, William Kerr, on the corner of Roxburgh Street.

The opening of building society offices arose as tenement flats began to be sold off for private ownership. 'A particularly bright top flat on the corner of Byres Road and Havelock Street. Comprising three apartments, kitchenette and bathroom. The flat has been rewired and has a coloured bathroom suite. Up to 95% building society loan possible.' The history of No. 186 is typical of the shift in ownership. The block was first purchased by John Swan, an iron merchant and steamship owner, as an investment and all four flats rented out. By 1930 the block was owned jointly by Samuel McKinnon, a house factor & insurance agent, and Harris Finestone, a jeweller. In the 1950s they began to sell off the individual flats. In 1958 one on the first floor – 'excellent 4 rooms and kitchen flat, bathroom, etc.' – was on the market for £1,000 and purchased by Rikki Fulton, the actor and comedian. He had returned from London and at this time was working with Jimmy Logan and Stanley Baxter in the Five Past Eight shows and winter pantomimes. He sold the flat a few years later. In 2018 one of the flats sold for £335,000.

The shift to private ownership brought another group of businesses to the road as Val McDermid mentions in her 2012 thriller, *1979*: 'Byres Road was where the estate agents had pitched their tents.' One of the earliest to open was a branch of Slater Hogg & Howison at No. 153 (now at No. 146). The branch opened just a year after Mike Rutterford launched the firm and within ten years the firm had opened 30 branches and went on to be the biggest in Scotland.

Advert for TSB featuring 'old Hillhead boy', Gordon Jackson 1975.

Grocers Massey & Sons at No. 268, which became the Bradford & Bingley Building Society. Four telephone boxes stand in Great George Street, in this late 1960s photograph, predecessors of the pair on the previous page.   *Guthrie Hutton*

Chapter Fourteen

Your Country Expects

When the South African War (Boer War) broke out in October 1899 the Government was confident that the British Army was more than capable of defeating a 'bunch of farmers.' This did not prove to be the case and after a number of defeats the War Office decided to supplement the regular army with men who had joined the various volunteer forces since the 1850s; in the end over 100,000 of these volunteers went off to fight in Africa. They included James Colquhoun who was now running A. & A. Colquhoun Bakers, and brothers Alexander and Archibald Goodfellow who lived at No. 140. Those three survived but William Cameron, who lived at No. 249, did not and his is one of over 100 names listed on Glasgow's Boer War Memorial in Kelvingrove Park.

In spite of the early belief that the Boer War would end swiftly proving mistaken, there was similar confidence that Britain would quickly defeat Germany when war was declared on 4 August 1914. Within days thousands flocked to join the armed forces, including many husbands, brothers and sons living or working in Byres Road. James and Alexander, the sons of Frank Campbell, a chef and pastry cook, at No. 175, were early volunteers. Both were educated at Hillhead School and played for the school's rugby team. Now in their early twenties, James was working as a stockbroker's clerk and Alexander as an apprentice chemist. Later in the war brothers were not allowed to join the same battalion, but the Campbell brothers enlisted together in the 5th Battalion of the Queen's Own Cameron

South African War Memorial of the Highland Light Infantry, Kelvingrove Park, erected 1908. *Author*

Highlanders. In September 1915 their regiment attacked the German lines at Loos. The fighting was severe and bitter, and at the close of fighting on one day, James was reported missing. Early the next morning Alexander left the trenches to search the battlefield for his brother. A comrade later said that Alexander had found James seriously wounded and carried him on his back for a distance of two miles towards a dressing station. However, neither was seen again nor their bodies ever found.

William and Thomas Loudon who lived at No. 241 with their father, a postman, were below conscription age in 1914. William (seventeen) was working in a flour mill and Thomas (fifteen) was still at school. However, each was conscripted when they became eighteen. William joined the Royal Navy and served on H.M.S.

Private A. S. Campbell,
5th Batt. The Queen's Own Cameron Highlanders.

Private J. C. Campbell,
5th Batt. The Queen's Own Cameron Highlanders

Alexander & James Campbell.   *Hillhead High School War Memorial Volume*

JOIN THE
SEAFORTH HIGHLANDERS
ROSS-SHIRE BUFFS — THE DUKE OF ALBANY'S

Recruiting poster for the Seaforth
Highlanders, 1914

Lance-Corporal R. H. Arroll,
Seaforth Highlanders (Ross-shire Buffs, The
Duke of Albany's)

Richard Arroll.   *Hillhead High School
War Memorial Volume*

Postcard celebrating Women War Workers, 1915.   *Wellcome Collection*

Private Roy D. Harvey,
The Royal Scots (Lothian Regiment), attached The
Highland Light Infantry.

Roy Douglas Harvey.   *Hillhead High School
War Memorial Volume*

Hollyhock, a minesweeping sloop that was in action in the Mediterranean, while Thomas served as a private in the Black Watch. Both survived the war and returned to live in Byres Road. Richard Arroll, a house painter, who lived at No. 386, was exempted in 1914 as he was thirty-five-years-old and married with three young children. However, conscription was extended to older married men in May 1916 and Richard joined the 3/5th Seaforth Highlanders. In the capture and defence of Roeux in May 1917 he was wounded and repatriated to the Military Hospital in Hampstead, where he died three months later.

In 2018 the Commonwealth War Graves Commission marked National Poetry Day by publishing a specially-commissioned poem by Sir Andrew Motion, a former UK poet laureate, to mark the centenary of the Armistice. Motion drew on some of the most moving personal inscriptions found on the quarter of a million headstones of the First World War dead around the world, and to end his poem chose one from a headstone in Bouchoir New British Cemetery in France. Here is the final part of the poem:

> Soon rolling out plans from their corridors and offices
> highly efficient angels of the resurrection will descend
> to align with names they went by in their earthly lives
> nine million or thereabouts bodies and body-fragments.
>
> What is the duration of individual grieving they allow
> beyond an agreed upper limit of sixty-six characters.
>
> Think of Private Roy Douglas Harvey who was killed
> a reserved and thoughtful schoolboy from Hillhead
> leaving behind among other valuable relics a diary
> completed up to the evening before his dawn attack
> along with a much-thumbed Collins Gem dictionary
> from the pages of which rose and will continue rising
> these words as time and space maintain their relation
> *my task accomplished and the long day done.*

Roy Douglas Harvey was the son of James Harvey who opened a grocer's shop at No. 398 Byres Road in 1888. In 1890, James married Mary Haggerty and Roy was born in 1892, and later two daughters. The family lived first at No. 286 Byres Road, and then in Vinicombe Street and Roxburgh Street, before moving to Ancaster Drive in Anniesland. Roy attended Hillhead High School from 1898 to 1915, and as his father had died in 1912 took over managing the grocery shop on leaving school. He was not passed fit to enlist when war was declared but in the autumn of 1917 was conscripted into the 5th/6th Royal Scots when the urgent need for new soldiers reduced the physical requirements. He survived the Battle of Cambrai but soon after was invalided home with trench fever. Having recovered, he was sent back to France in the spring of 1918 and took part in the British advance that began with the Battle of Amiens on 8 August 1918. He was killed by a bullet three days later. He was found with a copy of his diary, written up to the previous day.

The large number of men going off to fight resulted in significant negative impacts on the city's businesses and services. By 1915, 132 firemen, almost two thirds of the Glasgow workforce, had enlisted, as had around 600 policemen, a third of that force. Of the fifteen doctors at the Western Infirmary, only two remained – and very much against their will – and students worked in their place. The shortage of men opened up new work opportunities for women. Glasgow Transport appointed the first women conductresses in 1915 and by 1916 also employed thirty-three women tram drivers, much to the astonishment of other British towns who still resisted employing women in such roles. It was not just men going off to war that caused problems for businesses. Alexander Colquhoun intimated to customers: 'owing to my horses having been requisitioned by the Military Authorities I am obliged to discontinue the delivery of bread'. By late 1917 official food rationing was phased in. The war scarred Britain for many years. Countless families lost loved-ones and many women were widowed; relatives had to cope with the return of severely disabled or mentally scarred soldiers; and numerous young women never had the chance to marry due to the huge loss of single men; in 1931 only about three-quarters of women aged 35-44 had ever married.

After the war the volunteer army force continued but was smaller than before, and relatively poorly resourced. In 1925 it was restructured as the Territorial Army and Air Force Association, as the training of pilots was included for the first time. At this time Glasgow's army reserve unit consisted of around 200 officers and 4,600 other ranks, with 17 officers and 155 other ranks in the Auxiliary Air Force unit. A small number of full-time army and air force personnel trained the men. In 1925 the Glasgow Territorial Association purchased all the flats at No. 133 to house the full-time company sergeant majors, who oversaw the training of the part-timers. The block was owned by the Association through to the Second World War.

In the months running up to the outbreak of the Second World War on 1 September 1939, the threat of bombing led to the issuing of gas-masks; barrage balloons being flown in the Botanic Gardens; air raid shelters erected – including one in the old railway tunnel under the Botanic Gardens; and the evacuation of children. Anne and Mary, the two youngest daughters of Percy and Harriett Huggins who lived at No. 229 Byres Road, were included in the list of children scheduled to be evacuated. So, in early September they mustered with other children at their local school. Each child was equipped with a gas-mask, a toothbrush, a change of underclothes, and a label with their name, school and the evacuation authority. Almost 120,000 youngsters were evacuated from Glasgow. Anne and Mary were taken to Kippen and spent a year or so with various hosts and Anne recalled one:

> One was a Mr T, a big, bluffly cheerful man who was the local gravedigger. He was kind and always in a good mood. We shared the living room with him, and Mary and I were in a double bed in a bedroom. It was the most spacious of our billets.

A local Aberdeenshire resident recalled the arrival of Glasgow evacuees when he was a boy:

> As the three hundred children from Dowanhill and Hyndland schools that had come scampering North settled into an alien community, culture shocks vibrated in all directions. They spoke of their flicks and fairgrounds, polis and Partick Thistle, their tramcars and subways. We gaped in disbelief as if their train might have come from Mars. Released from their bronchial back-streets and energised by the purity of our rural ozone, they ran riot in the new-found freedom, demolishing hay-stacks, tormenting bullocks and testing the elasticity of many a swinging udder.

Among the many pamphlets issued in the run-up to the declaration of war was *Advice to Animal Owners*: 'If at all possible, send or take your household animals into the country in advance of an emergency … If you cannot place them in the care of neighbours, it really is kindest to have them destroyed.' Although vets and animal protection organisations were incensed at this advice and made appeals to owners not to put down their pets, thousands were culled. Another unfortunate loss was many of the West End's stylish cast-iron railings – including those round the Western Infirmary – as in February 1941 Glasgow Corporation agreed to a large-scale plan of railing removal in order to recycle the metal for the war.

Percy Huggins was a foreman at Barr & Stroud's Anniesland factory. As the firm made range finders, torpedo depth recorders, periscope range finders and other equipment essential to the war, the firm's factory was a target for bombing. So a number of 'shadow factories' were set up, and Percy was in charge of one housed in a garage in Kirklee. His son, Alex, then working as golf correspondent of the *Evening Times*, volunteered to be a pilot in the RAF,

Advertising poster for the Territorial Army.

Anne & Alexander Huggins, c.1945

Diana Cranstoun collection

Air Raid Warden, *c.*1941.

Wartime rationing, c.1941.

Removal of railing as scrap metal, c.1942.

and although he muffed his interview got accepted because the interviewing officer turned out to be a fellow golf enthusiast. Alex flew more than seventy missions with 104 Squadron, and was awarded the DFC. After the war he became editor of *Golf World Scotland* magazine and in 1951 was the first golf writer based in Scotland to cover the Ryder Cup in America.

By the end of 1940, as the feared bombing of Glasgow had not occurred, many of the evacuated children returned to the city: unfortunately, just before the bombing began. Thus, Anne and Mary who were back living in Byres Road experienced the Clydebank Blitz of March 1941 as Anne recalled:

> My mother pulled all the mattresses into the hallway – well away from the windows – and we all slept there.

In the Clydebank Blitz fifty people were killed in an explosion in Partick's Peel Street, and bombs fell all around the West End. The comedian Stanley Baxter, who grew up in Fergus Drive, recalled going to the Grosvenor Cinema with his mother on the evening the Blitz began:

> When the film finished, we went to leave but were told Glasgow was being bombed, and to sit tight. We and the rest of the audience were there for hours until the all-clear was given. I was terrified. My dad was at home looking after my sister and we had no idea if they'd been bombed. We just had to sit there all night while the cinema played music, the same four songs on a loop.

Fortunately, the Baxters all survived. Although no bombs fell on Byres Road, nearby explosions shattered many windows, and a number of shops had their stock ruined. Many women served in the Civil Defence during the war, including Marion Macdougall who volunteered as an Air Raid Warden. She lived in Lawrence Street, although when younger and attending Hillhead High School, resided in Roxburgh Street. She studied chemistry at Glasgow University, and after graduating in 1915, trained as a science teacher, and through the 1920s and '30s taught at her former school, Hillhead. Marion was on duty in Queen Margaret Drive when the

Blitz began and on the second night of bombing was killed when two German land mines destroyed her warden's post.

A number of men from Byres Road who went to fight in the Second World War died. Willie Jones, who lived at No. 8 and worked in his father's pub at No. 4, joined the Royal Artillery and was killed in action in Italy on 17 February 1944. John Blyth, who had just completed his medical studies at Glasgow University, was still lodging at No. 18 when he signed up to be a Surgeon Lieutenant with the Royal Navy. He died in April 1945 while serving on H.M.S. *Philante*, a yacht converted as an armed escort for convoys across the Atlantic.

Throughout the war – and into the early 1950s – there was rationing because of food shortages. The window displays at Todd's fruiterers were hampered by a lack of bananas and other previously imported fruit. As shortages increased, long queues became commonplace and the rationing of petrol led to the reappearance of horse-drawn vehicles. Soon after the war ended Alex Huggins had home leave. As he had been transferred to the Azores on anti-submarine patrol he arrived home with a bunch of bananas. His sister recalled: 'Mother made sure their skins were put right on top of the rubbish bins so that when the lid was lifted the dustmen could wonder at them!' One end to rationing that took place on 5 February 1953 was widely reported:

> Careless of spoiling their dinners, and mortgaging their Saturday pennies for weeks ahead, children flocked into the sweet shops on their way home from school yesterday – the first day of unrationed confectionery.

Sugar rationing ends, 5 February 1953.

Chapter Fifteen

House Proud

In 1898 a journal wrote: 'The rapid growth of the west end of the city, has been quite phenomenal, and given an impetus to the building, painting, decorating and furnishing firms in the district.' One of the most notable was John Orr & Sons, ecclesiastical and house decorators. The business was established in Wellington Street by John Orr, who was particularly noted as a church decorator; he opened the Byres Road branch at No. 182 in 1870. He and his wife,

Stationery design for John Orr & Sons by Charles Rennie Mackintosh, c.1895.

Catherine, lived at No. 7 Ashton Place with their eight children, where they employed a cook and a nurse to assist. They later moved to Kelvinside Gardens. The firm was at the forefront of contemporary taste. The Byres Road's showroom displayed decorative fabrics – 'art hangings (English, French, and Japanese) are always in stock, and of the latest designs' – and in 1897 Orr commissioned Charles Rennie Mackintosh to design their stationery. The firm's work ranged in scale, from domestic interiors to churches, and in 1904 Orrs undertook the painting of the Central Station's new Argyle Street bridge, affectionately known as 'the Hielanman's Umbrella' as it was a meeting place out of the rain for Highlanders. Three of Orr's sons joined the business, which continued through to the late 1940s, although the Byres Road premises closed in the mid-1930s.

James Swan opened furniture and furnishing workshops and showrooms at Nos. 152/154 around 1890:

> The extensive premises have an attractive glass frontage, displaying to advantage many useful and artistically valuable articles of cabinet work and upholstery. Large and representative stocks of these goods are held in the well-appointed warehouse to the rear. The stocks include dining, drawing, and bed-room suites in great variety, carpets, oil cloth, linoleum, and other floor coverings of the latest and most attractive design, with beds and bedding in all sorts of materials. Throughout the show-rooms, too, will be found many highly artistic ornaments, and articles of archaeological interest, together with ancient and modern lamps, screens, &c.'

However, the business was short-lived and went into liquidation in 1898. The premises of Andrew Sadler's premises may have been similar to Swans, as he too was a cabinetmaker and upholsterer. He opened his shop at No. 345 in 1879 and also had a workshop in Great George Lane. By 1881 he employed sixteen men and was living with his family in Dumbarton Road. In 1889 he married Janet Proudfoot, the daughter of a farmer, and they moved into a flat at No. 14 Kersland Street. Tragedy struck in 1900 as Andrew died, leaving Jane widowed with two sons and two daughters under the age of nine, and pregnant with their fifth child. To assist, Janet's brother Adam came to live with her and helped manage the business, which continued to trade as A. Sadler.

Andrew Sadler's shop, No. 345. *Courtesy of Mrs Allison*

Janet suffered a second heartbreak four years later when the son she had given birth to following her husband's death died. By 1905 the firm also advertised as removal contractors and window blind makers, and by 1910 Janet and her children had moved to live at No. 2 Vinicombe Street. In the 1920s Janet's daughters, Lillias and Marion (now married, and Mrs Allison) began to trade in antiques. Alison Blood recalled visiting the shop when young:

> It was an upholsterer on one side of the double frontage and sold antiques on the other. That was rather an awesome shop to enter. It had a bell that rang automatically when you opened the door; and its sombre interior, with a half-seen hinterland of chairs and cabinets and bookcases piled roof-high, had a special smell compounded of sawn wood, varnish, and leather. Perhaps the slight distaste which we felt on entering was due mostly to the type of message we usually bore: 'Could you tell us, please, if the carpets have come back from the cleaning yet?' or 'Mother says the man still hasn't come about the stair-rods.'

When Mackinlay's decided to redevelop the row of shops that included No. 345, the Sadlers moved to No. 629 Great Western Road and focused solely on antiques.

> The premises consist of four large saloons and eleven smaller rooms and while Mrs Allison attends to sales, and ensures the making of a purchase is a leisurely business enlivened by talk about happenings in the neighbourhood, Miss Sadler who has an extensive knowledge of old furniture, silver and glass, is out and about seeking desirable objects d'art.

Another who began by opening a cabinetmaking and upholstering shop in Byres Road but swapped that trade for another was Alexander Kennedy. He opened at No. 3 Prince of Wales Terrace (now No. 404 Byres Road) in 1878 and like all budding business owners would have hoped for success. Yet it is doubtful that he could have conceived that his company would, some 120 years later, have a turnover of £95 million. Kennedy was born in 1857 in Ayrshire, where his father worked as a plumber and presumably Alexander apprenticed as a cabinetmaker and upholsterer before opening his own business. In 1880 he married Annie Wilson, whose father worked in a slaughter house, and they moved into a flat in Vinicombe Street. In 1889 Kennedy established a carpet-beating, dyeing and cleaning works in Castlebank Street in Partick, and within five years its success enabled him to move his business, now including a large laundry, to purpose-built premises in Anniesland, called Castlebank Laundry. By then Kennedy had given up working as

a cabinetmaker, although he retained No. 404 as a place customers could leave and collect their carpets and laundry.

At his Anniesland works, Kennedy introduced new cleaning techniques and established a research laboratory where his chemists developed new textile dyes. In 1915 the firm became a private limited company with Alexander as chairman and three of his sons joined the business. In 1930 the company introduced a scheme of co-ownership for the benefit of the principal employees and all employees who had worked for the firm for more than four years received a 'marriage dowry'. Alexander died in 1931, by which time the company employed around 700 people. Castlebank Laundry commissioned special bright yellow vans with an idiosyncratic shape, which were a common sight around the city, and a powerful form of advertising. The firm also made four advertising films in 1931. One, entitled *The Story of a Shabby Suit*, lasts nine minutes and begins with a man about to put on his jacket and

Advert for Castlebank Laundry, 1913.
Glasgow Post Office Directory

Castlebank Laundry, Anniesland, 1930s.

Model of 1930s Castlebank Laundry van.

Bowie, cleaners, dyers and launderers at No. 329 in
the late 1960s.   *Guthrie Hutton*

saying, 'By Jove! I'd no idea this suit had got so shabby! I'll take it to the Castlebank branch straight away!' The film then follows the jacket as it is collected, cleaned, repaired, pressed, carefully packed and delivered back to the satisfied customer who ends the film with the comment, 'What a transformation! My old suit has been made new – in four days – and only 3/6d.'

In the 1930s Castlebank Laundry merged with another laundry firm, Bowies, which had had a branch at No. 329 since 1906, becoming Bowie Castlebank. The combined company continued to expand, buying a number of companies including the national photo company, Klick Photopoint, which had a shop at No. 378. In the 1980s the Bowie Castlebank company moved its main offices to the upstairs of No. 227 Byres Road, where Colquhoun's tearoom and restaurant had once been. By 2008 the company was experiencing significant losses and closed.

John Rattray & Son, 'plumbers, gasfitters, bellhangers, heating and sanitary engineers', was established in Hope Street in the 1880s and in 1896 opened a branch at No. 359 and another in Hyndland Road. In 1913 the business was taken over by George McKinlay who lived in University Avenue. The Byres Road premises were in a small row of one-storey buildings, which Mackinlay purchased in 1931. He then redeveloped the site; erecting the elegant red-sandstone Grosvenor Mansions, and opening new premises on the corner, No. 339, that stocked the latest white goods and other kitchen equipment:

Spring is just around the corner we are led to believe and George McKinlay, 339 Byres Road, is preparing for

Advert for Rattray & Son, 1910.

it with a fine stock of refrigerators. A washing machine takes priority on most housewives' lists but once obtained a refrigerator is undoubtedly her cherished dream.

In 1958, at a dinner of the Scottish Federation of Plumbers and Domestic Engineers, George's son Harold Mackinlay, then President of the Federation, emphasised how the trade was meeting modern demands:

It seems to me there is a greater opportunity to-day for the plumber practising his art than has ever occurred before. I believe that it would be necessary to go back to the time of the Romans to find that plumbing had any importance in the community at all, but today our tradesmen haves advanced beyond the Romans. They have a wonderful choice of materials and the impulse and urge to use them in a more widespread way than the Romans ever had.

Mackinlays worked on major contracts and in 1959 were in charge of the project that was announced as being, 'most welcome news to the Scottish Rugby followers on the eve of a new season as the electrical wiring for Murrayfield's turf is being installed as a protection against frost this week.' The company also advertised 'work-saving electric home-helps' and demonstrations of new equipment were often given: 'Come and see the wonderful Kenwood electric-food-mixer'. As Mackinlay's had closed by the 1990s it was to Iceland's Byres Road branch that readers of the *Evening Times* were invited to hear, 'home economists Lisa Saxby and Hilary Reece answer all the questions you have ever wanted to ask about microwave cookery in a relaxed question and answer session. It will be an interesting night- and a fun one, too.' It is not known if the advice given included one unusual use for the microwave that some early users touted – using it to curl false eye lashes.

For all those DIY jobs about the house, and much more, ironmongers (later called hardware shops) have always been invaluable. John Fleming opened his at No. 374 in 1895, advertising as 'a furnishing ironmonger, cycle agent, blacksmith, tinsmith and gasfitter'. He had just married Christina Gerrard and they set up home in Wilton Gardens in Kelvinside, and had a son and daughter. Henry Morton recalled the shop:

Flemings was a household name to several generations. To the young it was the place to go to get your bicycle repaired. In its shop window was an attractive display of cycle accessories surrounding a splendid specimen of a Humber bicycle, its glistening black frame gold-lined.

John's son, Gerard, took over the running of the shop and traded until the late 1930s. Clearly there was sufficient demand for ironmongery in the area as James Russell set up in competition at No. 165 in 1904. Russell's shop was taken over by Henry Tully just after the First World War. Tully was born in Kelso in 1885, the son of a mason, and in 1919 married Agnes Turnbull. They began married life living in lodgings in the flat of two sisters, the Misses Teale, at 43 Lawrence Street. Tragically, the following year when giving birth there, Agnes died of puerperal fever and her baby son died soon after. Henry remarried Amelia Anderson in 1938 and they had a daughter who after Henry's death in 1947 continued the family ironmongery business. In 1977 she was concerned about the high rates and the state of the road, particularly the buildings opposite that had been scheduled for demolition; though later saved.

I think mine is now the longest-established family business in Byres Road,' said Mrs Hood (the daughter of Henry the ironmonger). 'My rates have risen to over £2,000 a year and are really a crippling burden on a business like mine. Nevertheless, I am determined to keep on as long as I can. I have a marvellous team of six assistants – two have been with me for more than thirty years and I'd like to go on giving our customers the sort of personal service they've been accustomed to, in spite of the difficulties.

Sadly, by the following year she had decided to cease trading and sold the business, and for its next ten years the ironmonger's was run by Brown & Faulds. There have been a number of shopkeepers in the road with unusual quirks. One was Sydney Sparrow who ran a hardware shop at No. 242 from 1938 through to the 1950s; he was well-known for sitting inside his shop in the gloom and only switching on the shop's lights if a customer entered.

Is yours a 'nice' house?

We know too many homes that you might think had been made out of blocks of ice.

True, the natives in them look a patriotic blue. But they *feel* blue, as well!

We'd rather *you* weren't left out in the cold.

Get Gas Central Heating. Let us wrap around you exactly the right kind of warmth, in as many rooms as you choose.

Gas Central Heating is automatic. Quick. Economical. Clean. Comforting.

And not as expensive as you thought. Call and ask about it at your Gas Showroom, today!

For Central Heating You can't beat Gas Heat

SCOTTISH GAS SHOWROOM
263 BYRES ROAD   GLASGOW, W.2

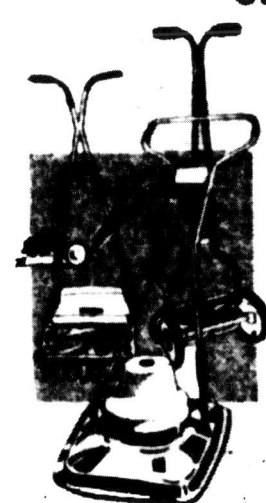

HENRY TULLY LTD.
General and Furnishing Ironmonger
The Shop with the Wonderful Stock

Chromium Ware : Locks

Stainless Cutlery : Oils and Paints

Electric Lamps

Locksmiths and Grinders

All Household Repairs

All Garden Equipment

Lawnmowers Set and Sharpened

165 BYRES ROAD

Telephone 041-339 4209

Advert for Tully, Ironmongers, No. 165, 1972.

Advert for Scottish Gas showroom, No. 263, 1971

City Bakeries took over the Colquhoun
Bakery in the early 1960s – original
Colquhoun sign still above

Advert for Barclay's tearoom and
restaurant, c.1950s.

BARCLAY'S

CAKE SHOP TEAROOM	RESTAURANT
at	at
205 BYRES ROAD GLASGOW, W.2	172 BYRES ROAD GLASGOW, W.2
	Telephone: WESTERN 7397
Telephone: KELVIN 3242	OPEN UNTIL 7 p.m.

Chapter Sixteen

Dining Out

The first restaurant in the road was opened in 1903 by Alexander Colquhoun above his bakery at Nos. 225/227. The stylishly designed restaurant served morning coffee, lunches, afternoon teas and high teas, which included breaded haddock with chips, buttered bread, and a selection of sweet cakes to accompany the pot of tea.

Colquhoun's restaurant was on the first floor but only the stylish windows remain..
Author

> With its mahogany walls, dazzling napery and shining cutlery, this was a great favourite both with regular local patrons not in search of alcohol, and distinguished visitors. I well remember the famous actress, Sybil Thorndike whom I had taken there for lunch enjoying the fare and having a pleasant chat with one of the waitresses, Miss Horn; obviously a favourite of hers.

It also was a venue for celebrations: 'A dinner in honour of George McNab who has retired from the rectorship of Bearsden Academy took place in Colquhouns Restaurant ... Members of the staff entertained the company with songs and pianoforte recitals.'

Entrance to Dowanhill House (now flats).
Author

When Colquhouns was taken over by City Bakeries in the early 1960s, the upstairs restaurant became a function suite called Dowanhill House. In 1970, twenty-two-year-old seaman Roger Williams and his fiancée, Mary Burns had fixed their wedding plans to include a reception there, but two days before the wedding all looked to be off as Roger's ship was delayed at sea. However, the Royal Navy had him airlifted from the frigate and after a 500-mile hectic dash from Portsmouth, Roger arrived on the morning of the big day. So, the relieved Roger and Mary were happily married and celebrated in the evening with the couple's fifty guests at Dowanhill House. In the 1980s, when City Bakeries moved out, the ground floor became a Wimpy Bar, the earliest UK chain serving hamburgers and hugely popular among young people who loved American TV programmes and music. Wimpey was different from the later hamburger-based fast-food eateries as it was only table service – quite different from Burger King that later took the premises.

In 1929 Bethia Barclay opened a small restaurant at No. 10 University Avenue offering morning coffee, afternoon tea and light snacks. Barclay's Restaurant became a firm favourite with locals and in 1934 her daughter, also Bethia (though known as Betty) who was then working as a secretary, agreed to give her mother a hand during a staff emergency for 'just a short time'. However, she ended up working there full-time and never returned to her typewriter. In 1936 the University took over the

Barclay's Restaurant, No. 10 University Avenue.   *Courtesy of Miss Davidson*

property and the restaurant moved to No. 205 Byres Road. When Mrs Barclay retired a third Bethia (a cousin) joined the business and in 1949 they opened larger premises at No. 172 that in its heyday employed fifty staff. Those lunching at Barclay's might enjoy steak-and-kidney pie, or, the diet conscious, a pineapple-and-cheese salad, although even the dieters usually found it hard to resist apple crumble to follow. In the early 1960s Barclay's restaurant began exhibiting the work of young artists as *The Scotsman* reported:

> There is one Glasgow tradition at least that continues undiminished and which the young Glaswegian seems in no hurry to reject: coffee drinking in carefully selected howffs, and if there happens to be pictures on the walls to glance at now and again so much the better. Today, one of the most efficient and consistent in this respect is Barclay's Restaurant in Byres Road. the proprietrix, Miss Barclay being herself an enthusiast for painting and a modest, unpretentious patron.

The Italians were the first to bring continental flair to eating in Byres Road, and while the Grosvenor Café always spurned chips, other Italians opened fish and chip restaurants. From the 1930s to 1950s, Pietro Giusti at No. 20 served his fish and chips on white tablecloths. The Savoy, which was opened at Nos. 285/7 by the Pieri brothers in the 1960s was a little less elegant, but its name conjured up fine dining – an image one local used to his advantage: 'I used to tell prospective dates that I'd take them to the Savoy for lunch. They thought I meant the hotel!' However, the Savoy's fish suppers and other menu items were of quality and popular. When it passed to the Simeone family, who had opened their first Glasgow café in Yoker in 1901, it was renamed Mario's Plaice, and then Simeone's.

In the 1950s the Curlers Tavern opened The Regency Restaurant in its upstairs. 'All the people from the BBC came to the Curlers restaurant. We had accounts that were so fabulous you couldn't believe it!' An advert for the restaurant at that time promised, 'Francois will cook in his own inimitable way your favourite meal'. Bill Nisbett, who worked there as barman, recounted an occasion when the soup course puzzled the diners: 'The cream of chicken soup and custard were both being prepared in the kitchen. For the soup course the cook lifted the custard by mistake and we'd ladled it out before we realised, and they'd started eating it.' Nisbett claims that the Tavern was the first in Glasgow to incorporate a small dance floor into a restaurant in the early sixties, offering dancing and dining, 'to the music of the Tommy McLaren Trio'. Nisbett recalled, 'You could hardly get a table on a Saturday night.'

Reo Stakis opened his first 'Reo Stakis Olde Worlde Inns' steakhouse at No. 116 in 1962 and, by the 1970s, there were fourteen Stakis steakhouses in Glasgow

Savoy Café, Nos. 285/7, 1983.

Courtesy of Stuart McKenna

Curlers Restaurant, 1957.

Advert for Curlers Restaurant Dinner Dance, 1980.

and others elsewhere in Scotland. Stakis was born in Cyprus and arrived in Scotland in 1928, aged fourteen. He began in business by selling his mother's handmade lace door-to-door. He settled in Glasgow and in the 1940s opened his first restaurant, The Victory, and by focusing on inexpensive prices began to change the way Scottish people dined out. His steakhouses offered a limited menu of main courses – fish and chips, gammon steak, half-chicken, rump or sirloin steak of different weights – and the price of each main course included a starter and pudding. On offer to start were farmhouse broth, egg

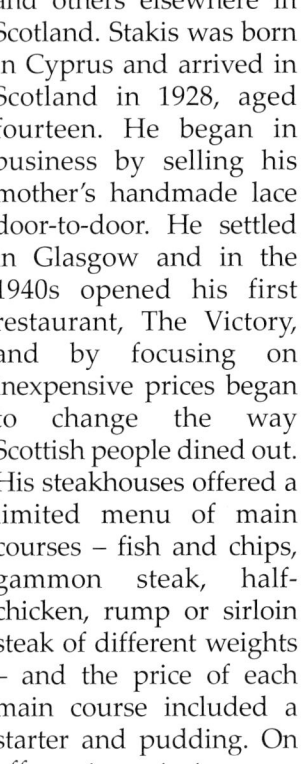

Busy Businessmen.... *Famished Families....* *Leisurely Lovers....* *Marvellous Models....* *Shrewd Shoppers....*

.....everyone! eats inn style

delicious prime steaks at

REO STAKIS OLDE WORLDE INNS

GLASGOW AREA

Alfa, 111 St. Vincent Street.
Avion Hotel, Thornliebank.
Blenheim, 241 Sauchiehall Street.
Bombardier, 36 Kelvingrove Street.

Burnside Hotel, Burnside.
Byre, 116 Byres Road.
Charing Cross Hotel, 528 Sauchiehall Street.
Doune Castle, 61 Kilmarnock Road.
Georgic, George Street.
Glassford Hotel, Glassford Street
Grosvenor Hotel, Botanic Gardens.

Jamaica Inn, 18 Jamaica Street.
Knightswood OWI, Knightswood Shopping Centre.
Pond Hotel, Great Western Road.
Poseidon, 18 Bothwell Street.
Regency, 15 Waterloo Street.
Saddle, 240 Buchanan Street.
Vega, 15 Union Street.

REO STAKIS OLDE WORLDE INNS THROUGHOUT SCOTLAND.

Advert for Rio Stakis steakhouses, 1970s.

mayonnaise, pâté or prawn cocktail, and of these all but the soup were exotic for the time. The puddings were served from a 'sweet trolley' that was wheeled round the tables, offering fruit salad, trifle, apple pie or forest gateau. One happy diner recalled: 'In the mid-60's the Stakis Byre Restaurant in Byres Road was my end-of-school-term treat with my mother. Providing you stayed off the steaks, two people could eat for just under £1.' Stakis later bought the Grosvenor Hotel at the top of Byres Road. He had to rebuild it after a fire in 1978 but in 1999 he sold his empire to the Hilton Group for £1.2 billion.

Following the British Nationality Act 1948, which offered nationality to people in British colonies, many took the opportunity to move to Britain. Those who settled in Glasgow mostly came from India, Pakistan and Hong Kong. Some opened restaurants and, from the 1960s on, Glasgow's diners were introduced to a range of new cuisines. In 1967 Andy Chung opened Amber, the first Chinese restaurant in Byres Road at Nos. 130/132, premises that previously had been The Berkeley restaurant serving 'British and Continental delicacies'. Chung is reputed to have been the first to bring authentic Cantonese food to Glasgow, and was particularly known for seafood dishes. In 2017 his restaurant moved to the Merchant City.

An early Indian restaurant, The Hot Spot, was opened in Vinicombe Street in 1972 by Sagli Ram Sharma. He came to Glasgow to study in 1950 but

AMBER CHINESE RESTAURANT
130/2 Byres Road, Glasgow
041-339 6121/8970
NOW OPEN
LICENSED TILL 1.30 a.m.
We are proud to have satisfied many of you with our menu and service, and our chef looks forward to cooking for you traditional Peking and Cantonese Cuisine.
BUSINESS LUNCH (Choice of 45 Dishes) **90p**

Advert for Amber Chinese Restaurant, No. 130/2, 1971.

The Hot Spot
GLASGOW'S INDIAN ★ RESTAURANT ★
Voted Second in the Glasgow University's 1974 Handbook with a ★★★★ Rating. We offer you the fullest range of Eastern and Western Dishes in elegant surroundings.
THE HOT SPOT
28 VINICOMBE STREET
(Off. BYRES ROAD)
GLASGOW
Telephone 041-334 4483 for Reservations

Advert for The Hot Spot Indian restaurant, Vinicombe Street, 1974

after a short time decided to try to earn enough to set up his own business, so took a job at the Singers sewing machine factory in Clydebank. After working long hours for a year, he had enough cash to open a grocery shop in Maryhill. Later, he and his wife opened a dry-cleaning shop and in 1972 decided to add a restaurant to their small commercial empire. Sagli also bought a house in Great George Street and converted it into one of the first Hindu temples in the city. Like other Indian restaurants, The Hot Spot offered take-away food, although in the early years customers had to take their own dishes as tin foil containers had not yet been invented. Around the same time, Shabana restaurant opened at No. 124 offering 'delicious Pakistani Tandoori dishes with an extensive European menu.' Since then, restaurants offering a diversity of foods from around the world have opened, and closed; including Mexican, Japanese, Greek, Thai and Vietnamese, although traditional Scottish fare remains popular at Old Salty's at No. 337.

In the 1970s a number of chefs began to revitalise Scottish cuisine and one of the earliest was Ronald Clydesdale, who along with Ian Brydon opened the Ubiquitous Chip in 1971. With little resources they converted a rundown property in Ruthven Lane:

With the help of friends, they have carried out the conversion themselves. The result is a tastefully simple L-shaped room, with white and orange brick walls and

Old Salty's, No. 337   *Author*

dark beams, seating about 50 persons. The food arrives by way of a rickety little lift from the upstairs kitchen. The menu contains a lot of Scottish things. Mr Clydesdale says they would rather use the food of the country than not, although they are broadminded in this respect. There is no licence, but customers are encouraged to bring their own bottle, although due to the ridiculous anomalies of the law, you must stop drinking your own drink by 10.10pm.

The Chip soon became lauded and in 1975 moved to its current premises in Ashton Lane, by which

Ubiquitous Chip, Ruthven Lane, interior,1974.

Ubiquitous Chip, Ashton Lane, 2010. *Author*

time it had, 'a wine list to rival the best and that can be enjoyed until 1am'. One evening The Stranglers (punk band) arrived to dine wearing gasmasks on their foreheads and leather waistcoats without shirts. They lounged about drinking beer until they saw the wine list, at which point they took off their masks and started asking intelligent questions about the wine and the food. The Ubiquitous Chip became a must for many visiting Glasgow; Mick Jagger, Princess Margaret and Kylie Minogue are just a few of the celebrities who have dined there. In a 2017 review *The Guardian* food critic, Marina O'Loughlin wrote:

> I waft upstairs past *vaut-le-detour* murals of former staff by eccentric local genius Alasdair Gray to find a poster for "a selection of suitably unhealthy snacks" such as Scotch pie and Forfar bridie. I kind of love this: evidence of Glasgow's ability to laugh at itself. The Chip may have relented on its commitment to actual chip-dodging – they're now on the brasserie menu – but it's still flying the flag for Scotland's finest.

The Chip continues, as does No. Sixteen at the bottom of Byres Road, which has delighted diners since opening in 1999. Other restaurants, such as both The Puppet Theatre and The Poachers that opened in Ruthven Lane (now The Bothy), have come and gone. The newest, that opened in 2023, is a branch of Nico Simone's Six by Nico restaurants at No. 358.

The oft-recounted story is that the influx of Italians into Glasgow around the 1890s happened

No. Sixteen restaurant, at No. 16! *Author*

John Tobia of The Garden's Café.   *Weir Studio.*

Advert for The Gardens Café, No. 294, *c.*1960.

because many who had set sail for New York disembarked in Glasgow, where transatlantic ships often temporarily stopped off, believing they had arrived in the Big Apple; alas, this is a myth. What is true is that at that time a large number of Italians travelled to find a new life as drought and famine in Italy had brought widespread poverty. Most of those who chose to come to Scotland were joining relations already living here, and often the Italian men planned to find jobs as miners or manual labourers. However, those jobs had been taken by the earlier influx of destitute Irish men, and instead, luckily for Byres Road and other places in Scotland, many of the Italians turned their hands to businesses that drew on the Italian love of coffee and ice cream. The first Italian café in Byres Road was The Garden's Café established at No. 322 in 1870 by Giovanni (John) Tobia, that later moved to No. 294. Although there are glowing reports of the cafe's ice cream, one child in the 1900s was less taken by the confectionery:

It was the only shop in all the Byres Road that was open on Sundays. Here, I, stifling my conscience, broke the

Sabbath and bought tuppence worth of sweets. I shared them with us lesser fry, but never have chocolates tasted so untoothsome. They were as dust in the mouths, and our upbringing had been such that I believe every one of us attributed the dustiness entirely to the fact that they had been bought on a Sunday. We had never heard the phrase; 'old stock'.

Tobia's sons, Harry and Alfred took over the running of the café through to the 1950s. In 1905 Angelo Rossi, whose family had other ice cream shops in the city, opened a confectioners and ice cream shop at No. 230. In 1911 he sold the business to Louis Marzaroli who already had a café in Argyle Street. His grandson, Oscar Marzaroli, became one of Glasgow's most notable documentary photographers. In 1929 Marzaroli sold the business to Renato and Odilia Zanotti who paid £1,000 for the goodwill. Renato and Odilia had four children: Enrico, Clara, Liliana and Renato, Tragically, Renato senior died when the children still were young, so three of the four children had to be sent to Italy to live with relations while Odilia ran the café with Clara's help. After the end of the Second World War the three children, now in their twenties, returned to

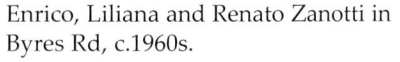
Gardens Café, No. 294, c.1950.

Right upper: Enrico & Renato Zanotti in the original Grosvenor Café, No. 230, 1949.

> *Glasgow Family Album*

Right lower: Grosvenor Café, Ashton Lane, *c.*1980s

> *Courtesy of Zanotti family*

Enrico, Liliana and Renato Zanotti in Byres Rd, c.1960s.

> *Courtesy of Zanotti family*

help their mother and sister run what was by then called The Grosvenor Café. The family lived across the road in a flat at No.249.

The Grosvenor Café became a Byres Road institution. Renato recalled that their lemonade from Dunns was still delivered by horse and cart in the early 1950s until. eventually, the police objected as the horse and cart blocked the traffic. Unlike many other Italian cafes, the Zanottis did not introduce a juke box but instead had a large radio:

> I and my three teenage friends would go to the café every Saturday morning in the early 1960s and while nursing an ice cream float, listen to the Saturday Morning Club, one of the earliest BBC radio pop music programmes. Like so many others who whiled away an hour or two in the café, spending little, the Zanottis never complained nor nudged us to buy more or leave.

Around 1970 the café expanded into the next-door shop and opened a small restaurant. In 1977 came the disturbing news that the city planned to modernise the underground system and expand Hillhead Station, and that this would involve demolishing a number of properties, including the café. As tenants, the Zanottis were offered no compensation by the city. Fortunately, an old property that had once been a coach-house and stable with accommodation above for the coachman – by then a derelict workshop – was available in Ashton Lane and with borrowed money the family revamped it, and relaunched the Grosvenor Café, with a restaurant on the top floor. Their dedicated customers were happy to follow.

The proximity of the university, Western Infirmary and the BBC Scotland studios brought a diversity of customers. 'The politician Donald Dewar was a regular,' recounted Renato. 'He did like to talk.' Stuart Murdoch recalled how in the early 1990s he was looking to find people to form his new band, Belle and Sebastian: 'I plonked myself down in the Grosvenor Café and corralled the first seven people who came along. I ended up with a failed professional snooker player, a music student, a writer and others.' Alan Clements and Hamish Barbour, who were studying at the University, were regulars; they later became TV moguls.

> I was an aspiring musician, says Barbour, so I was in there hoping for glimpses of the successful folk like Skin

from Hipsway and Del Amitri's Justin Currie. I'm sure that the Grosvenor's vegetable soup – homemade in a big galvanised bucket – was the one thing that kept me alive at university.

Clements recalls going there the day his wife, the broadcaster Kirsty Wark, was in labour.

> I remember being sent away from the maternity hospital where Kirsty was suffering a terribly long labour. It was very early in the morning, so I went to the Grosvenor, where I told one of the matronly Italian waitresses the whole awful story of what Kirsty had been going through, and currently still was. She was very sympathetic, and ended up by asking me what I wanted – meaning did I want a son or a daughter but I replied, 'a roll and bacon'.

The Zanottis sold the business in 1991. While one past customer's view that, 'no coffee ever tasted as good as the Grosvenor coffee,' may be disputed by afficionados of other coffee spots, the fact is that it was the Italians that introduced many in Glasgow to quality coffee. One was Matthew Algieri, who in the 1860s set up his own tea and coffee wholesale business. He later changed his surname to Algie and his firm, Matthew Algie, provided the roasted coffee to cafes and other shops all across Glasgow, continuing to be a major coffee supplier today. David Williamson who opened Tinderbox at No. 189 in 1998 was a descendent of Matthew Algieri.

While the Grosvenor Café has gone, the University Café continues at No. 87 with its

University Café, No. 87, 2023.   *Author*

evocative exterior dating back to the 1940s, and has been run by the Verrechia family for over 100 years as Gino Verrechia recounted:

> Pasquale, my grandfather who opened the café in 1918, previously was a ship carpenter on the Clyde. These booths, you see the chisel marks on the wood, they were shaped by hand, that's why we don't touch it, that's the way it will stay.

It too launched careers. Johnny Beattie, the popular Scottish actor and comedian, recounted how his theatrical career began there in the 1940s:

> I know that everyone likes to say that they always wanted to be on the stage, but, in my case, it really was by accident. I was sitting in the café with friends, admiring the female talent, and I discovered that they were all in the local amateur dramatic society, so I joined.

As well as his many theatre appearances, for thirteen years Beattie played the kind hearted and loveable family man, Malcolm Hamilton in the BBC soap, *River City*. However, as he recounted, not everyone thought this his best role:

> I go walking up Byres Road in Glasgow several times a week. The old wifies come up to me and say 'Aye, I see you in that *River City*, Johnny. I've seen you a lot funnier, though. Mind we used to see you in the pantomime, dressed as a wummin? Can ye no dae that again?'

In 2015 Anthony Bourdain, the American celebrity chef, revisited the University Café as part of his television series, *Anthony Bourdain, Parts Unknown*: 'A

Cosy Neuk Café, No. 327 in the late 1960s.   *Guthrie Hutton*

happy place from my past, where once I frolicked young and carefree in the field of frialated arts. The University Cafe, where I learned at the foot of the masters the *dao* of hot fat and crispy batter.'

During the Second World War Italy allied itself to Germany, and the café, like a number of other Italian businesses, was attacked, and its windows smashed. Ironically as one of the family, Alfredo was a British national and serving with the RAF. Vincent Pignatelli who opened the Cosy Neuk café at No. 327 in the 1930s boarded up his shop at the outbreak of the war and moved to the safer countryside, but returned in 1945 and ran the café until the late 1970s.

Fortunately, in spite of competition from the big coffee shop chains such as Starbucks at No. 254, distinctive coffee places continue to thrive, including Kember & Jones at No. 134, opened in 2004 by Phil Kember and Claire Jones, and the more recent Alchemy Experiment at No. 157 that serves art with its coffee.

Anthony Bourdain enjoying a fry-up and Irn-Bru at the University Café, 2015.
CNN TV

Chapter Seventeen

A Pint, a Fag and a Newspaper

Curlers public house, 1960s.

Curlers Tavern mural portraying bar regulars as historical figures, including the poet, Hugh McDiarmid (centre,) and writer and broadcaster, Jack House (left front), *c.*1950.

The originally-named Curlers' Tavern (now the Curlers Rest) was built in the mid-1840s and first run by Mrs Sinclair. When the worthy residents of Hillhead established their burgh one disappointment was that the dubious Curlers Tavern fell just inside its boundary, as the pub's rough clientele were not thought to be in keeping with the vision for the new burgh. So the new police force paid an early visit to the tavern and warned Mrs Sinclair to keep a respectable house. Originally the Curlers was one of two adjoining properties, with a small passageway between that led through to a small Lanarkshire County Police office. The other building was a small house and shop. Until around 1900 it was lived in by an old woman, Mrs Gow: 'She kept a shop called "Jenny a Things" which had two signs above the door; "Lyons Tea sold here" and "Mangling done here."' In 1919 Henry Murray took over the small shop and ran it as a newsagent until around 1960, at which point it and the passageway were incorporated into the pub.

Mrs Sinclair and her husband had run an earlier pub in Partick but it is not known where. It may have been at the bottom of Byres Road, where No. 4 is today as in 1864 its then owner, John Purvis, was being fined for 'contravention of the laws for the regulation of public houses.' By 1880 the pub was managed by William and Jane Tweedie, who had married in 1866 and first ran a pub in Green Street in

James Wilson public house, No.4 (site of earlier 19th century. pub), 1960s.

Advert for James Wilson, 1970 public house.

the Merchant City. When they moved to run the Byres Road pub they lived in Clarendon (now Chancellor) Street with their four children. William died in 1882 leaving Jane a widow with four children under the age of fifteen. She remarried Andrew Mitchell in 1886 and after being widowed for a second time in 1895, ran the pub with her family until 1920. Around 1900 the buildings that included the pub were redeveloped and a new tenement erected, with the pub reinstated at its old address, No. 4. From 1920 it had various owners and in 1969 was bought by Robert Wilson who ran Wilson's Bar on Maryhill Road at the corner of North Woodside Road. It was later run by his son, James who advertised the pub as a 'sumptuous cocktail lounge with star entertainers.' It closed in the 1990s and became a restaurant.

While nothing could be done about the Curlers Tavern, Hillhead Burgh ensured that the Lanark magistrates did not grant any further pub licences in its section of Byres Road. At a meeting of Lanark licensing magistrates in 1881 one early application to open a public house at the bottom of Great George Street was debated. Hillhead's objectors pointed out that Partick had thirty-three pubs and argued that to grant a new pub licence in Byers Road would be, 'to bring up the most disorderly portion of Partick a little nearer the West End of Glasgow'. Objections were again raised in 1886 when Hugh Tennent, a relation of the family who owned Tennents Brewery, applied for a spirits licence for a planned pub on the newly built corner block at Highburgh Road (No. 191). Among the objectors were Glasgow University:

In the opinion of the University's Principal and Professors, the granting of a licence in the road would be fraught with danger to the students. We are entrusted with the welfare and discipline of the students and that would be seriously menaced if the licence was granted. There are two thousand students and there is no ground for a showy public house within a few minutes' walk from Gilmorehill. This is to cast no reflection on the students, but some are sure to be found easily led away. The students are at a time of their life when they are especially exposed to temptations.

That the many existing Partick pubs were easily within reach of the University, and no doubt some well frequented by students, was glossed over. However, in spite of the University's concern, the licence was granted by just one vote: 'The result was received with applause and

Tennents public house, No. 191.   *Author*

hisses. The indignation afterwards of the Hillhead people as they left the court was loud and deep.' Even by 1983 it was reported:

> Respectable citizens in Hillhead are 'seething with discontent' over the number of licensed premises in their area and are objecting to an application for a real ale and wine bar to be opened in the foyer of the former Grosvenor cinema.

Thus, the opening of the bar and entertainment venue, Òran Mór in 2004, must have incensed some residents and, given the bar was a conversion of the former Kelvinside Church, caused many past Hillhead Protestant worthies to turn in their graves.

While many Hillhead residents objected to pubs opening in the upper part of Byres Road, few, apart from teetotallers, complained about grocers in Byres Road being given licences to sell wine and spirits. This may reflect the fact that it has been shown that in the past many members of the middle and upper classes consumed four times as much wine and spirits in their lifetimes, as members of the working class. A photograph of the exterior of the grocer, James and George Hunter, around 1910 shows in the

Advert for Agnew Stores off-licence featuring Rikki Fulton and Greg Fisher.

Advert in window of Hunter, grocer.

window adverts for their own Victoria Blend Old Scotch Whisky and Yarra Australian Wine, indicating that there were many who lived around Byres Road at that time who enjoyed an alcoholic tipple. And continue to do so. A report of sales at the Byres Road branch of Agnews off-licence at Nos. 147/149 in the weeks running up to Hogmanay in 1971 reported: 'The store sells 100 cases of whisky a day, 1,500 dozen cans of beer and an enormous assortment of liqueurs and table wines which vary from Chinese Chefoo to wines from Chile, Turkey and Greece'. Agnews was one of a number of off-licences owned by Ricky Agnew, who opened his first in Uddingston in the 1960s when just eighteen-years-old, and within twenty years owned fifty-two across Scotland. Hogmanay was not the only occasion on which sales boomed:

> Cash registers were ringing at every off-licence as the Tartan Army began the big count-down to Scotland's World Cup zero-hour. Agnew in Byres Road said, 'There has been a big upturn in the sale of beers. Lots of people are buying it in cases.

This was June 1978. The Scottish football team had qualified for the World Cup in Argentina and their matches were eagerly awaited as many pundits tipped Scotland to do well. However, for the Scottish fans watching the matches on television, their carry-outs had to drown sorrows rather than celebrate success, as Scotland failed to make it through the opening round.

Almost ninety years on from the objections to the opening of Tennents, the pub came under fire again; this time for its long-standing policy of banning women. Shelley Russell, an American student, organised a 'sit-in' in protest and in response the pub removed the ban, and a small cleaning cupboard was turned into the ladies' toilet. Other pubs in Byres Road were more welcoming to

Rubaiyat public house, No. 94, 1970s.

Advert for the Rubaiyat, 1964.

The Aragon public house, No. 131, 2023.

'A rabbit goes into a public house…'

women, including the exotically named Rubaiyat at No. 94 on the corner with University Place. When it opened in the early 1950s it described itself as an 'oasis of refreshment' and its stylish bar included mirrors with quotations from the Rubaiyat of Omar Khayyam, and included a small circular cocktail bar named 'The Bowl of Night.' There are many jokes that begin with an unusual animal going into a bar and ordering a drink, and when the *Evening News* reported in 1964 that Robert Gill, who lived at No. 102, regularly took his pet rabbit, Harvey, with him to the Rubaiyat, the paper could not resist closing with one: 'Harvey never buys a drink. He's got no doe.' Harvey was long gone by 14 December 1979 when drinkers in the Rubaiyat, and in pubs across Scotland, enjoyed an extra hour's drinking time on the day that Scotland's long-standing 10pm drinking curfew ended.

> A happy nursing sister, Elizabeth McKenzie said, 'As a young highland woman I think it's disgraceful, all this extra drinking. But seriously,' she added. 'I think at first people are going to treat the extra hour as an excuse for a booze-up. After a while it will settle down and people will get used to slower drinking habits.

Two years earlier, on Sunday 23 October 1977, another significant loosening of Scotland's licensing laws occurred when the Sunday ban on pub opening was lifted. A *Scotsman* journalist went to Byres Road for his first official Sunday tipple but found every pub in the road shuttered: 'Eventually the word went round that The Dolphin in Dumbarton Road was open and dozens of men crammed in to be greeted by a free drink to celebrate the new civil drinking hours.'

The Rubaiyat is long gone. Nos. 71-77 that opened as The Chancellor in the 1960s is still a licensed bar,

but has found it hard to forge a lasting identity as its many name changes have included Russell's Bar, Embargo and Rumbongo. The Aragon at No. 131, which opened around 1970, retains its original name. Some like to believe that it is named after the French Communist surrealist poet, Louis Aragon as that would be very West End, but as the pub's sign shows a monk scribbling with a feather quill, it clearly is named after James of Aragon, the eldest child of King James II, who renounced the throne to become a monk. If so, the bald head is artistic licence, as James died when only thirty-eight years old, and his portrait shows him with long hair that would not have been out of place in the Aragon in the late 1960s when Billy Connolly and Tam Harvey, the original Humblebums, signed their first professional contract there.

New bars are always looking for innovative ways to gain press coverage but none in Byres Road – nor elsewhere in Glasgow – have rivalled BoBar's launch event'; 'Naked At Bobar'. Before opening at No. 385 in July 2006, the bar advertised that it was looking for, 'nudes of every shape and size for a project celebrating the eclectic, bohemian and artistic spirit of Glasgow's west end'. The project was the idea of photographer, Alistair Devine who devised it as a homage to Spencer Tunick who has photographed hundreds of naked people in cities around the world. On the day, around thirty volunteers turned up and stripped off. The group included a bank clerk, a dental nurse, an American tourist, a radio presenter and a book publisher, and of all ages, shapes and sizes, and posed naked in a variety of bar-room scenes for a series of photographs.

For over a hundred years from the 1740s, Glasgow was the centre of the tobacco trade, importing the leaf from American plantations

Advert for Mackenzie & Co, tobacconist & cigarette manufacturer, No. 252, 1905.

worked by enslaved labour, and thus it was the slave trade that funded Glasgow's rapid development. Although cigars were smoked by the wealthy, most people smoked pipes until the 1880s when factories producing cigarettes opened, many of the largest in Glasgow. The availability of mass-produced cigarettes, allied to mass-marketing, led to smoking becoming common among both men and women. By 1950 it was reported nationally that 80% of men and 40% of women in Britain smoked, and that percentage certainly was higher in Glasgow. One of the earliest tobacconists in the road was a branch of Mackenzie & Co. at No. 252, who also operated as a small cigarette manufacturer. Shops required a licence to sell tobacco and in 1930 Antonio Cocozza who had a confectionery at No. 108 sold cigarettes illegally

Murray, newsagent, No. 260, *c.*1922.

from his ice cream van. One customer turned out to be a Customs & Excise Officer and Cocozza was fined £3.

Negative views on smoking date back centuries: in 1604 King James V1 of Scotland called it, 'a custom loathsome to the eye'. Yet for decades offices, pubs, transport, entertainment venues and many homes stank of cigarette smoke. In 1925 a Scottish newspaper wrote: 'Nothing is more characteristic of our civilisation than the abandon with which one section of mankind blows its tobacco smoke in the face of the other.' Through the 1950s and 60s, the link between smoking and cancer became clear and by 1960 Government research showed that 98% of people in Scotland knew of the possible connection. Yet large numbers continued to puff away. In 1978 the *Glasgow Herald* reported that seven Byres Road shops were competing on cigarette prices. Even by 2006, when the Scottish Government introduced the ban on smoking in enclosed public spaces, many smokers attacked the legislation as an affront to their liberty.

Tobacconist shops have always been a target for criminals. In 1946, a young man entered Fraser's tobacconist at No. 142, pulled out a gun, and demanded money from the young shop assistant, Bridie Coyle. At that moment a customer began to enter the shop and the robber warned Coyle he would shoot her if she alerted the customer. He then crouched below the counter with the revolver pointing at the terrified shop assistant who managed to serve the customer. The gunman then fled, having only managed to steal a few pounds from Coyle's purse who, fortunately, was unharmed, though shaken.

A similar incident took place in 1960. When ten-year-old Craig Leroy went into a

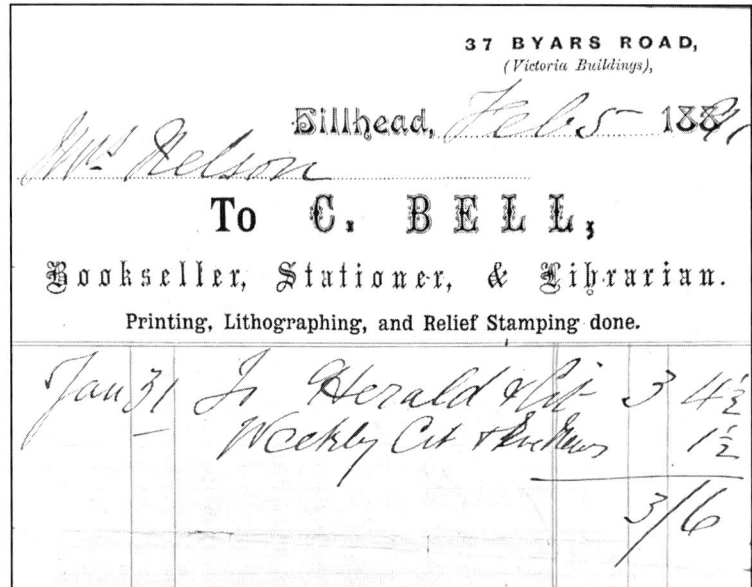

Receipt for weekly newspapers, Feb 1889 from C. Bell, stationers and librarians. At this point the shop's address was No. 9 Victoria Buildings – now No. 314 ,

Byres Road shop to buy tea he was confronted by a young man standing over the female shop assistant, Mary Milliken, spreadeagled on the floor. The man said, 'This is a hold-up. You'd better go home.' However, brave Craig stood his ground and it was the thief who rushed out. The police were called and Mary was helped into a chair. Unfazed, or in a state of shock, she immediately got up again, and asked Craig what he had come for. 'She got up, and gave me the quarter of tea and threepence change,' Craig said. It is not known if the robber was caught but if he was, undoubtedly the police would have delivered some initial rough punishment for Mary Milliken's father was one of Hillhead's police constables.

Many of the shops that sold tobacco also were newsagents where adults bought their copies of the *Glasgow Herald* or *Daily Record* and youngsters their *Beano* or *Bunty*. Pilfering youngsters are usually the main criminal threat to newsagents but, in 2009, MK & Co. Newsagents at No.104 had £2,000 of goods stolen by two seventy-year-old pensioners; believed to be Scotland's oldest robbers. One distracted the shop assistant while the other plundered cash, stamps and mobile phone top-up cards. In 1919 Henry Murray opened a newsagents in the small shop that later became incorporated into the Curlers pub and around 1960 moved to No. 196, later demolished when the subway station was restructured. Early each morning local schoolchildren would gather there to start their paper-rounds; a popular way to eke out pocket-money:

> My round was one of those organised by Murray Newsagents and around 6.30am I would join the other bleary-eyed boys and collect my stack of papers. The most sought-after paper-rounds were to main door houses – the most likely to give a good tip at Christmas – while tenements were unpopular, especially those where the papers had to be delivered to the top floor.

Until well into the 20th century purchasers of daily newspapers were largely confined to the better off, but local weekly newspapers were read by all social classes. The shops that later became termed 'newsagents', previously were called 'stationers' and often rented out periodicals as well as books. When Augusta Bryson began in business in the 1890s in Great Western Road, she described herself as 'a stationer and librarian'. She moved her business to No. 178 about 1910 and by the 1930s sold: 'toys, games, books, cigarettes and smoker's requisites.' She lived in one of the flats above the shop at No. 176. After her death in 1944 the shop continued to trade as Brysons, stationers and newsagents, through to the 1970s. It later became Barretts, which now trades from No. 267. It is one of a number of independent newsagents in the West End that is included in a series of drawings by Will Knight, an architectural illustrator, that celebrate the significance of newsagents' shops in our everyday lives. As Knight comments: 'They are often the place where as children we engage in our first monetary transaction, buying sweets or comics ....as we grow older, so might our purchases change, buying lottery tickets, cigarettes or alcohol.' Over the decades the stationers have transformed into newsagents, and continue to evolve: Barretts now advertises as, 'the West End's first choice for news, stationery and bouncy balls.'

Barretts newsagents by Will Knight.   ©*Will Knight*

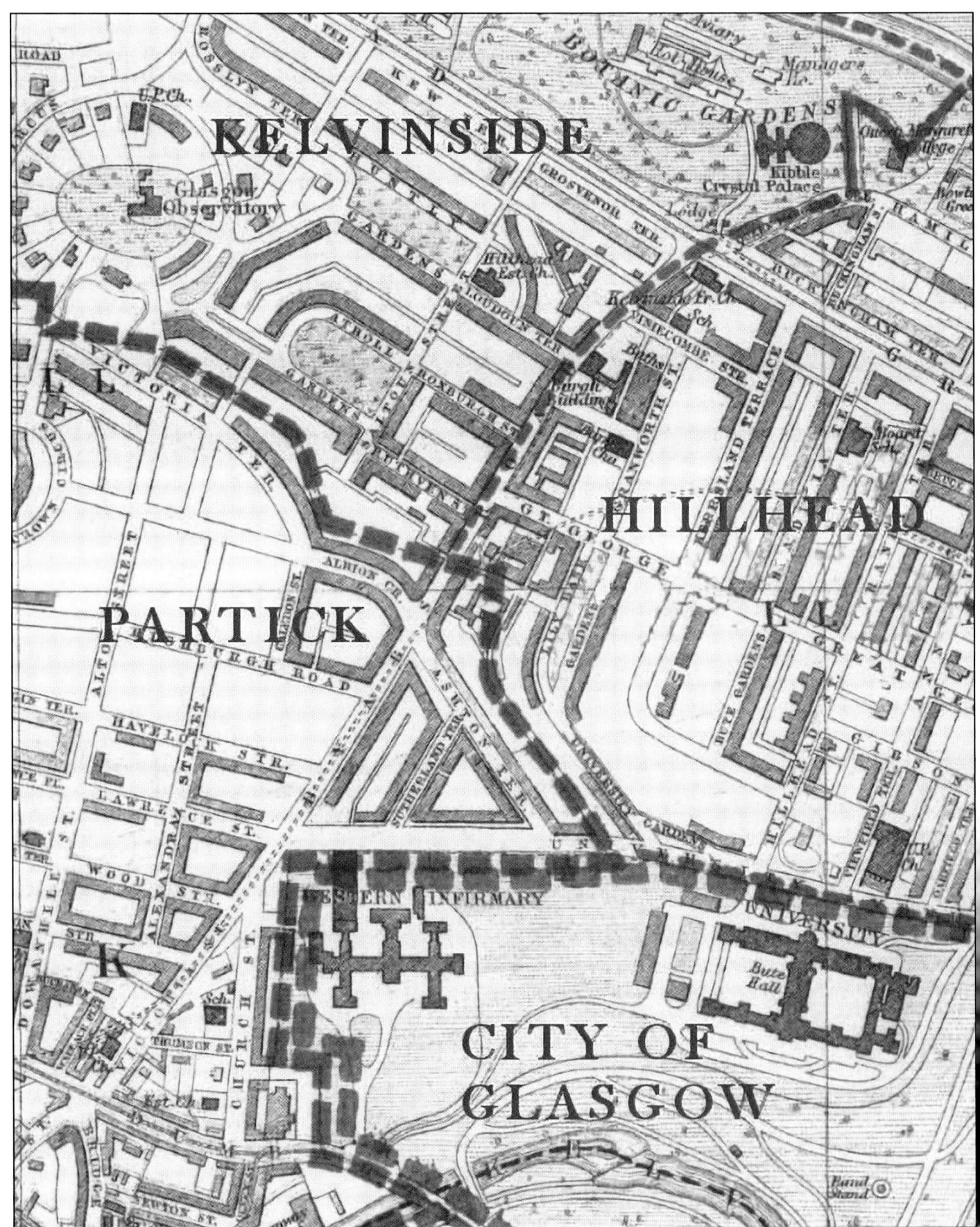

Boundaries from 1870 until the three areas were amalgamated into Glasgow. Kelvinside never became a burgh.

Chapter Eighteen

Tussles for Power

Partick Burgh coat of arms.

Byres Road voters have often been at the centre of significant political moments. In 1982 the *Sunday Times* called the Hillhead Parliamentary election, 'the most important by-election since the Second World War,' and just over 100 years earlier, in 1890, the Partick election similarly was seen as nationally important:

> That the eyes of the country are on the Partick election is becoming increasingly evident, for even the London newspapers cannot keep away from it but are pouring forth advices every day to the supporter of both candidates.

At this time, both Partick and Hillhead still were independent police burghs. By 1852 Partick was beginning to expand as a centre of shipbuilding and heavy industry, and its population was around 6,500; that year it successfully applied for police burgh status. The section of Ashton Lane that leads into Byres Road was the boundary with what later would become Hillhead Burgh, and the boundary dividing it from Kelvinside ran along Dowanside Lane. The required twelve commissioners were appointed and David Todd, a shipbuilder, was elected the burgh's first provost. A burgh hall was opened in Anderson Street, and police and firemen were employed. A new burgh hall designed by William Leiper was built in Burgh Hall Street in 1872.

The new Partick Burgh Hall c.1910.

Lewis Hutton collection

Hillhead became a police burgh in 1869 and its first provost was Robert Bruce, a papermaker. Although its area included the top section of Byres Road, the properties on the east side were not, as the boundary with Kelvingrove ran up the middle of the road. This odd state of affairs was jokily commented on in 1892 by the *Glasgow Evening Post*:

> A rather peculiar state of affairs exists. The title at the top end on the west side is Byres Road, Kelvinside, while on the east side it is Victoria Street, Hillhead. Thus, a ratepayer giving dinner would order the waiters to come to Victoria Street, Hillhead (so that they would not charge too high) and address the invitations from Byres Road, Kelvinside (in order to impress).

Hillhead appointed its commissioners and employed small fire and police forces, and within a few years built its burgh hall in Byres Road containing police and fire stations, and a cleansing department.

From the 1870s on, Glasgow tried on numerous occasions to have the neighbouring areas to the west, including the burghs of Hillhead and Partick, incorporated into the city. In 1886 a number of Kelvinside's wealthier residents succeeded in having legislation passed in the House of Commons that empowered Glasgow to annex both Kelvinside and Hillhead, but as this was done against the wishes of Hillhead Burgh the House of Lords overturned the decision. Then Hillhead tried

Hillhead Burgh crest on Kelvin Bridge, Great Western Road.

unsuccessfully to annex Kelvinside and Dowanhill into its burgh. Clearly for a time the upper section of Byres Road was a tricky border! At another time the Burghs of Maryhill, Hillhead and Partick considered merging into a 'super-Burgh' but that did not progress. Glasgow City continued to push for annexation. In 1887, Partick's commissioners responded to a Parliamentary review into Glasgow's proposals:

> The village of Partick is believed to have had an existence so far back as about the second century, and it is certain that it was known as a village several hundred years ago. Upwards of a century ago it was possessed of several public works and a number of famed mills, affording employment to the people resident in the village, which was distant about two miles from Glasgow. It was thus a separate and distinct community from Glasgow, and in no sense owed its origin to proximity to that city.

Glasgow City's approach became more conciliatory, focusing on the benefits of being part of a larger municipality, and there were conflicting views on amalgamation among residents in both Hillhead and Partick. Eventually in 1891 the political factions in Hillhead agreed to become part of the city, as did Kelvinside and Maryhill, but it was not until 1912 that Partick and Govan agreed to be assimilated.

Until 1918, the Partick constituency took in a large swathe of the area to the west of Glasgow, including all of Byres Road. The reason for the national

Bruce, first Provost of Hillhead Burgh, 1869.

interest in the 1890 Partick election was because the outcome was seen to have implications for an issue that would remain hotly debated for decades after: Scottish Home Rule. In 1886, when the Liberal Prime Minister William Gladstone proposed the restoration of an Irish Parliament – Irish Home Rule, there was an acrimonious debate, with one of the main bones of contention being the right of Irish MPs to sit and vote in the House of Commons. Those who favoured Home Rule for Scotland used the moment to convince Gladstone that the so-called 'Home Rule All Round' would be 'logically and practically the only solution'. Gladstone agreed. Thus, the Partick election was, to a large extent, fought on whether or not Scotland should have Home Rule, with the Liberal candidate, Charles Tennant in favour and the Liberal Unionist candidate, James Parker Smith, opposed. Tennant was owner of the large Glasgow firm, St Rollex Chemical Works, and Smith the only son of James Smith, owner of the Jordanhill estate. Gladstone spoke about the importance of the outcome of the Partick election at various meetings around Britain. 'I am confident that the Partick electors will throw off the Coercionist yoke. As by extraction a Scotchman, I am proud to think that Scotland has often led England in the path of progress.'

As this was before the wider enfranchisement introduced in 1918, only 9,429 men, out of a population of around 60,000, were eligible to vote. On 11 February 1890 they cast their votes and Parker Smith won by just 219. Small as the majority was, many claimed it represented the death-knell for Scottish Home Rule, a view expressed by London's *Standard* newspaper:

> Partick is not only Scotch, it is about as representative a district as could be found in the United Kingdom for it contains a considerable sprinkling of the 'classes'. It also includes a fair percentage of Glasgow's country shopkeepers and a good many thousands of shrewd hard-headed, well-educated artisans of the Lanarkshire factories and shipyards. If an electorate of this kind and, what is more, a Scottish electorate, is not permeated through and through by Home Rule, where is the advance to be discerned?

In fact, Scottish Home Rule did not die. In 1895, the Commons voted in favour of a resolution for Home Rule, but it ran out of Parliamentary time. Then, in 1914, Parliament voted 204 to 159 to bring in federalisation for Scotland and only the outbreak of the First World War prevented the Bill from progressing. Scotland had to wait until 1999 for Devolution.

The 1918 Representation of the People Act did away with most of the threshold of property ownership and residential requirements for voters, and gave women over the age of thirty a vote (men could vote from the age of twenty-one). Thus, the size of the British electorate tripled from 7.7 million to 21.4 million, with women accounting for about 43% of the electorate. In 1928 the voting age for women was equalised with that of men. A restructuring of Parliamentary boundaries also took place in 1918 with Byres Road split between two constituencies: Glasgow Partick and Glasgow Hillhead. At the 1918 general election the Prime Minister, David Lloyd George, a Liberal politician, advocated that the wartime governing coalition should continue. Thus Robert Horne who was elected for Hillhead, although a Unionist (the Scottish arm of the Conservative Party), served under Lloyd George as Minister of Labour and later as Chancellor of the Exchequer. Horne was a Scottish advocate and businessman, and a bachelor well-known for his womanising. He served as the Hillhead MP until 1937.

The successful candidate for Partick was Robert Balfour, a Liberal, who had won the seat in 1906. Although he grew up in Scotland, his commercial career before becoming a MP was spent in America and England.

Scenes of great enthusiasm were witnessed in the Cecil Skating Rink, Byres Road (No. 17 – later a snooker hall), where a crowd that packed the building congregated to hear the result of the election. When it was declared

Election poster for Robert Balfour, 1915.

that Mr. Balfour was elected the audience rose from their seats in a body, and for some minutes the building rang with boisterous cheering and the blowing of whistles.

There was similar elation in Partick at the result of the 1929 election, but this time it was Labour Party supporters cheering as their candidate, Adam McKinlay, won; beating the incumbent MP, Major George Humphrey Maurice Broun-Lindsay, a Unionist, by just 409 votes out of the 28,786 votes cast. McKinlay was a joiner and active in the Trade Union movement. Winning the seat helped Ramsay MacDonald's Labour Party gain the most seats in Parliament. However, it was a hung parliament and at the election called just two years later, a Unionist candidate was reinstated. From 1935 until 1950 the MP was Arthur Young, a Unionist, who on leaving Parliament was created 1st Baronet of Partick.

Following Horne, Hillhead was represented by another Unionist, James Reid, Baron Reid, who held the seat through to 1948. He was a judge and in government served as Solicitor General for Scotland and Lord Advocate. Further Parliamentary

Baron Reid, MP for Hillhead.

constituency boundary changes meant that from the 1950s to the 1970s Byres Road was split between Hillhead and Woodside, and, bizarrely, Hillhead Burgh Hall, Hillhead Post Office, Hillhead School and other parts to the east of Byres Road were placed in the Woodside constituency. That constituency was held by the Unionist Conservatives until 1962, when Neil Carmichael won it for the Labour Party. An engineer by trade, he was the grandson of George Carmichael, a founder member of the Independent Labour Party. Carmichael served in Harold Wilson's governments in various positions, including as Parliamentary Secretary for Transport, and held the seat until 1974 when amalgamation brought all of Byres Road into the Hillhead constituency.

In 1950 Hillhead elected another Scottish Unionist, Thomas (Tam) Galbraith. The *Glasgow Herald* said of his win: 'a notable achievement by a young candidate. succeeding one of the outstanding Unionist members of recent years.' Galbraith went on to defend the seat at the next ten elections, and when he died in 1982, while still a Member of Parliament, he was Scotland's longest-serving MP. He held a number of government posts, including Civil Lord of the Admiralty and Under-Secretary of State for Scotland. For decades Hillhead remained one of two safe Conservative Party seats in Glasgow, although Labour's share of the vote increased over time. Within days of Galbraith's death in 1982 the election was being trailed as 'one of the most fiercely contested in Scotland this century', and it became widely covered in the national press. Its significance was due to the Social Democratic Party (SDP) deciding to mount a candidate. The year before there had been a split in the Labour Party and a small number who left formed the SDP. To the surprise of many, Roy Jenkins who had left politics to become President of the European Commission from 1977 to 1981, joined the new SDP, and it was decided that he should fight the Hillhead seat. Jenkins was the son of a Welsh coal-miner, although often mocked in the media as a 'claret drinker', and had served as an MP from 1948 to 1976, holding many ministerial posts, including Chancellor of the Exchequer and Home Secretary. The SDP's choice of Jenkins to fight the seat had nothing to do with his knowledge of Hillhead, for as he himself admitted on seeing the University's tower for the first time: 'the view was as mysterious to me as the minarets of Constantinople were to Russian troops during the Russo-Turkish War.' Rather, the choice was made in recognition that none of the other candidates had his wealth of political experience and gravitas.

One of the many young people who canvassed for the SNP candidate, John Leslie, at that election was

EVENING TIMES   PAGE 7
Wednesday, May 11, 1955

Housewife V Bachelor - It's going to be exciting

In one corner is Mrs Jane Davidson, of Campbeltown, who says she has been a member of the Labour Party for 22 years—"since I grew up and had sense."

And in the other corner is Mr T. G. D. Galbraith, 38-year-old bachelor son of Commander T. D. Galbraith (who has now become Lord Strathclyde of Barskimming on his elevation to the House of Lords).

Mr Galbraith has been the sitting member for Hillhead for six years, and was last declared winner with a thumping majority of 11,295.

DAVID and GOLIATH on the heights of Hillhead —but is Mrs Davidson's stone big enough to damage Goliath Galbraith?

Evening Times cartoon on 1955 Hillhead election.

Tam Galbraith, Hillhead MP.

Roy Jenkins campaigning in Hillhead, 1982.

the satirist Armando Iannucci, at that time nineteen-years-old and living at No. 286 Byres Road. 'I mainly was interested in seeing the process from the inside. It was a kind of political Glastonbury, there was every chance that Ted Heath would lumber past while you were waiting for a bus.' All parties were determined to win as a light-hearted article by Alison Downie in the *Glasgow Herald* noted:

> The douce housewife tripping out to the bakers in Hyndland Road to buy four cookies and two crumpets for tea runs the constant risk of being waylaid by a pollster armed with a clipboard and asking meaningful questions like, 'Can you tell me which party you are going to vote for?' Back home, she has scarcely time to put cookies and crumpets on a plate before she is summoned by the front door bell to confront another pollster armed with clipboard and asking meaningful questions like: 'Can you tell me which party you are going to vote for?' As she closes the door the phone rings. This time it's a pollster from the Telephone Survey Research Unit, asking meaningful questions like: 'Can you tell me which party ...' Unexpected passengers are hopping on the political bandwagon by virtue of alleged local connections, like Mrs Mary Whitehouse (known for her campaigning against what she saw as a permissive culture) who has caused a communication to be pushed through every Hillhead

resident's letterbox, commencing: 'Dear Friends, As a lover of Glasgow – my father was a Glaswegian – and a descendant of the Hutcheson Brothers – who founded Hutchie's – I care very much what happens in your city'. Taxi-drivers, naturally, are getting in on the act. 'See and not vote for yon Jenkins — he'll just be in the front door and oot the back, wipe his feet on the mat and then b—r off!; advised one such as he dropped me within the Hillhead battle zone before reversing and setting forth for neutral territory around Central Station.'

Within days of it being announced he would stand, Jenkins swiftly set forth to address his ignorance of Hillhead, by buying a flat in Kirklee Terrace, into which he and his wife moved, and walking the streets, getting to know the locality and its residents. Jenkins won the seat and proved a hard-working constituency MP, holding weekly surgeries and taking up the problems of many residents as Iain Mann recounted, 'When I raised an obscure point about a family member's pension he wrote directly to the UK Chancellor and argued the case so persuasively that the rule was changed in the next year's Budget speech.' However, Jenkins lost at the next election in 1987 and was given a peerage; choosing to become Baron Jenkins of Hillhead.

The man who defeated him in 1987 was the charismatic George Galloway who, like Horne, was also renowned for his womanising. Six years earlier, Galloway had been chosen as the youngest ever chairman of the Scottish Labour Party and prior to becoming Hillhead's MP, had been general secretary of the charity, War on Want. In 1989 his controversial views led to half of Hillhead's Labour Party executive resigning, stating that they had no confidence in the Labour MP's integrity. Galloway's response on hearing the news was, 'Bloody hell!' He survived and continued to serve as Hillhead's MP. In 1997, when the Hillhead constituency was abolished, Galloway won the seat of Glasgow Kelvin and held it until resigning in 2005. In 2001 Melanie Ried wrote in the *Herald*:

> There is a peculiar sense of romance about Mr Galloway, and it is nothing to do with his undeniable charm or the tabloidisation of his private life. It's because he has that delicious sense of the outlaw, the arrogance of the untouchable, which makes a day in his company feel like playing truant with the bad boy at school.

Donald Dewar, who lived all of his life in the West End and regularly was to be seen in Byres Road, was elected as a Labour MP for the Glasgow Anniesland seat (formerly Garscadden) in 1978. In that year the Labour government put forward a law to create a Scottish Assembly but the Act stipulated that it would be repealed if less than 40% of the total electorate voted in favour. Dewar was one of the leading campaigners for the Assembly but in the referendum of 1 March 1979, although the devolution scheme was supported by 52% of those voting, this only amounted to 33% of the electorate so devolution did not go ahead. Undeterred, Dewar continued to campaign for Scottish devolution and in 1997 the Labour Party included the establishment of a Scottish Parliament in its election manifesto. Labour won by a landslide and Dewar was appointed Secretary of State for Scotland, and spearheaded the devolution process. This time the decision was to be by a simple majority and on 11 September 1997 almost three-quarters of those who voted backed the creation of a Scottish Parliament. In January 1998 Dewar announced that he would stand for a seat in the new Scottish Parliament and on 6 May 1999 was elected as the Member of the Scottish Parliament (MSP) for Glasgow Anniesland, having the unusual distinction of being both an MP and MSP for the same constituency. He was chosen by the Scottish Parliament to be the First Minister of Scotland and officially sworn in on 17 May 1999. At the opening of Scotland's first Parliament in almost 300 years Dewar said:

> This mace is a symbol of the great democratic traditions from which we

George Galloway. Hillhead MP 1987.

Donald Dewar campaigning for a Yes vote in the first, unsuccessful, Scottish devolution referendum in 1979.

A charity shop in Byres Road avoids political bias with Yes and No displays, 2014.

draw our inspiration and our strength. At its head are inscribed the opening words of our founding statute: 'There shall be a Scottish Parliament' Through long years, those words were first a hope, then a belief, then a promise. Now they are a reality. This is a moment anchored in our history. Today, we reach back through the long haul to win this Parliament, through the struggles of those who brought democracy to Scotland, to that other Parliament dissolved in controversy nearly three centuries ago.

On 18 September 2014, Scotland went to the polls to vote in a referendum on whether Scotland should become an independent nation. On the day many in the media headed to Byres Road, including *The Independent*:

At Glasgow's busiest polling station off Byres Road in the city's West End, located between the student population of Glasgow University, middle-class

Hyndland and the once traditional Labour voting of Partick, almost forty percent of registered voters had marked their ballot papers before 3pm. Brothers Ben and Leon, one a freelance journalist, the other a would-be music sound engineer, held opposing views but nevertheless marched to the poll together and still smiling. Ben was voting Yes because 'this might be a one-off opportunity' while Leon described the Yes campaign as 'idealistic and over-optimistic'. Outside the polling station a CNN camera crew were broadcasting the views of this part of Glasgow to the world. One elderly woman, who said she'd lived in Partick all her life said, 'It's about time the world learned what I think. My wisdom's been ignored for too long.' Her pals were laughing through her joke.

Although the majority of those who went to the polls in Glasgow voted in favour, the overall outcome was 55% against Scottish independence.

Birrell confectioners, 1933.

Building our Past

Birrell's Special Theatre Box of Choice Sweets, *c.*1930s

Robert S. McColl featured on Ogden's Footballers Cigarette Card, 1902.

Advert for R.S. McColl confectioners, 1925.

Chapter Nineteen

Treats

Given Glasgow's sweet tooth, it is hardly surprising that Byres Road has long been home to confectionery shops and the first was opened in 1878 at No. 319 by John Walker. In 1905 John Stewart Birrell opened his first shop at 352 Dumbarton Road and four years later opened a branch at No. 271 – later No.190, one of a number of the firm's shops that began to spring up across Glasgow. He and his two sons also opened a confectionery factory in Thornwood Avenue. Around the same time, Robert Smyth McColl, a successful professional footballer whose hobby was making sweets – earning him the nickname of 'Toffee Bob' – decided to invest the large £100 signing-on fee he received from Newcastle United FC to start a confectionery business with his brother, Tom. The McColl brothers went on to establish a chain of 150 shops, including one at No. 316 that opened in 1915. Robert founded the R.S. McColl cup junior football competition – a trophy still played for today. Both firms invested in commissioning stylish shopfronts and interiors to entice customers.

In Birrells, the glowing display of shaded lights on its toothsome products nestled amid cascaded folds of silky pink was a constant lure for romantic generosity to respond to the bewitching spells of the deepening night by buying a 2lb box of Milady Chocolates instead of a quarter pound of vanilla toffees.

They often sited shops near places of entertainment as for many, a night out at the theatre or cinema was not complete without a supply of sweeties:

R. S. McColl's Theatre Box of delicious chocolates will make you the most popular member of your theatre party. It holds an ample store to beguile the longest play. You cannot always be sure of enjoying the show, but the sustaining delight of fresh creamy chocolates never fails.

Although never advertised for another long sit, sweets – particularly those with a long suck – were considered essential by many worshippers to sustain them through lengthy church sermons. The Birrell firm eventually was taken over by McColls – and Birrell's factory in Anniesland became the group's headquarters – but the company's shops traded under their original names through to the 1970s, by which time there were a combined 420 McColl and Birrell shops. The Birrell name later was dropped while the R. S. McColl brand continued.

A competitor to the existing sweetie shops in the road arrived in the late 1950s when Woolworths opened at Nos. 300/304. Its famous 'pick and mix' counter displayed a tempting array of dozens of different sweets, from Fizzy Cola Bottles to Pear Drops, and customers' filled bags were priced by weight. The incursion of outlets such as Woolworths threatened independent shops and in 1966 things got even more difficult as Glasgow City Council significantly increased the rates of Byres Road properties. For Elizabeth Lattimer who had a

Pick 'n' Mix, Woolworths, 1950s.

GENERAL VIEW   BUTLIN'S HOLIDAY CAMP • AYR   A.107

Butlin's Heads of Ayr Holiday Camp.

Stenlake Publishing

tobacconist and confectionery shop at No. 142 this was the last straw and her shop closed. Unsurprisingly, given that recent research showed that two out of every five Scots admitted to eating sweets once a day, there is no lack of Byres Road's shops selling confectionery today.

Although holidays sometimes do not turn out to be as pleasurable or relaxing as anticipated, they are usually looked forward to as a treat. It was not until 1938 that the act entitling all workers to one week's paid holiday per year was passed. Before then many firms in Glasgow closed for a period as part of the July Glasgow Fair, a traditional workers' holiday, but before 1938 only most had two- or three-days off. When a one week's holiday became standard, most Glasgow businesses closed over the same 'Fair Holiday' week in July and 'Fair Friday' saw an exodus of people heading for their chosen holiday destination. For many that was 'doon the watter', travelling by train or bus to Greenock to catch the ferry to Dunoon or Rothesay. The better off stayed in hotels while those with less money crammed into boarding houses, on occasion three families in one room. There was a well-known Rothesay joke: 'How do you get more people into a Rothesay boarding house room during the Glasgow Fair? Take off the wallpaper.' By the 1950s, the destinations and types of holidays began to expand. Butlin's Holiday Camps were popular and many from Glasgow headed for the company's Heads of Ayr holiday

HALLEY CARAVAN SHOW

AT

7 Dalcross St., Glasgow

(600 yds. WEST OF KELVIN HALL)

•

During the Scottish Motor Show

YOU ARE INVITED TO A SHOW OF 1958 MODELS

OPEN 9 A.M. TILL 10 P.M. (Except Sunday)

•

HALLEY   CARAVAN CO.
       GLASGOW RD.
MILNGAVIE   MIL 1088

Advert for Halley Caravan Co., No. 7 Dalcross Street, 1958

Clyde Chandlers, No. 7 Dalcross Street, *c.*1970.

camp. Staffed by the famous Butlin's Redcoats, adults enjoyed regular meals, the pub, the theatre entertainments and the ballroom, while the kids delighted in the funfair, indoor and outdoor swimming pools, amusement arcade and miniature railway. Caravan holidays grew in popularity, and in the 1950s premises on the south side of Dalcross Street (now derelict ground) housed Halley Caravan Company:

> Unfortunately there will be no caravans at this year's Scottish Motor Show. But within a few miles of the Kelvin Hall the enthusiast will be able to see displays of almost as many as were shown at Earls Court last month as the Halley Caravan Company will have a special show at their Dalcross Street garage.

Through the 1970s and 80s the premises housed a different form of holiday transport and was described in the *Evening Times* as, 'Hemmed in by tenements, this boatyard in the heart of Partick brings a whiff of the sea to city dwellers'. This was the showroom of Clyde Chandlers that advertised themselves as, 'Britain's biggest boat showroom with over 300 boats, outboards and trailers'.

For those who had grown weary of chilly days at the Scottish seaside or being cooped up inside a caravan on wet days while the Calor gas heater struggled to bring sufficient warmth, the opening in 1965 of A. T. Mays on the corner of Byres Road and Havelock Street offering package holidays to exotic sunny climes was a godsend. This was one of Mays' earliest branches outside of Kilmarnock, where Jim and Margaret Moffat first launched their travel business. Jim had been running a pet shop and being an authority on budgies was asked to judge a bird show in the US. Finding a reasonable flight and hotel package proved so hard that Margaret spotted an opportunity, and it was her enthusiasm and energy that got their travel business established. The firm took advantage of the inexpensive charter flights initiated by Freddie Laker to Spain, and such was the firm's success that by 1989, when it was sold to Thomas Cook, A. T. Mays had 290 shops across Britain. Package holidays gave people a taste for overseas travel and for those seeking a more adventurous holiday, especially back-packing students, the STA Travel branch at No. 284 was the place to go: 'Want to get away but don't know where to start? Come and join us for our "Big Trip" travel talk on Thursday 27th February, 7pm at the Byres Road branch. Experts will be on hand to get you on your way!' Unfortunately, the company, privately owned by a Swiss family, went bust in 2020 in large part due to the Coronavirus pandemic wiping out travel.

When the comedian Wal Butler and his wife

A.T. Mays Travel Agents

advertised for lodgers in the 1940s, they highlighted that their flat at No. 73 had 'easy access to all theatres'. They were targeting fellow entertainers who needed digs while appearing on a Glasgow stage. Today's AirBnB adverts offering lodgings in Byres Road as, 'ideal for the night life and restaurants', instead are aimed at people holidaying in the city. The idea that Byres Road would one day be a holiday destination would never have crossed Wal Butler's mind, or if it had, only as the basis for an incredulous joke.

For children, October into November was an exciting time as Alison Blood recalled from her childhood around 1900:

> The real party season began with Hallowe'en. To this day the smell of apples makes me think of it. The false-faces and Chinese lanterns that appeared in the toy shop windows, and apples and nuts in the greengrocers towards the middle of October, and about that time some child was bound to appear at school with an excited face and a bundle of addressed envelopes which were handed round with due empressement. 'We are giving a little party on October 30.' It was considered rather chic to give your party the day before Hallowe'en in defiance of the idea that you must be bound by a definite date. It probably meant that you wouldn't get any guisers at the door, but there were lots of other amusements, and it was better to keep the guisers for the real Hallowe'en when there might not be a party.

Guising at Hallowe'en (now usually called 'trick or treat') has had a long tradition in Scotland and involves children dressing up and knocking on the

Christine Collins (bottom right – dressed as 'Wee Willie Winkie'), her sister and friends ready to go out guising, 1960s.
Courtesy Christine Collins

doors of their neighbours. In exchange for the children performing a burst of song or a short spoken ditty, sweets, fruit or, better still, cash, is given. The Byres Road closes are handy for guising as children can visit all the flats easily and are known to their neighbours so likely to be welcomed. However, in the past, children who lived in closes with less well-off neighbours often would strike out into the dark, and head for the posh Hillhead and Kelvinside houses in the hope of better takings.

Only a week later came the next exciting event – though one dreaded by all pets – the 5th of November. In the weeks running up to Guy Fawkes Night fireworks were widely on sale. Joel Sneader at No.117 advertised: 'Fireworks – Scotland's largest selection'. In the week or two before the actual night, many children participated in a tradition that mainly has fallen away: 'penny for the guy'. Children made dummies, often just by stuffing a pillow case with old clothes to roughly resemble a person, which they then wheeled around in an old pram or cart, asking passers-by for money. In 1976 the *Evening Times* surveyed the city's guys and reported that Glasgow children were netting £1 an hour.

> At the Botanic Gardens church on Byres Road four youngsters claimed that they had made £21 in fifteen hours spread over five days. 'The secret', said one, 'is to ask for ANYTHING for the guy, not just a penny.' Said another, 'One lady gave us 50p – and she wasn't even drunk.'

Twopenny bangers, *c.*1950s.

While the main fireworks were kept for the actual night, and their setting-off usually overseen by parents, for days before mischievous children would delight in setting off exploding 'bangers' – especially inside closes where their boom particularly reverberated – or 'jumping jacks' that often were tossed at the feet of their chums who had to avoid the exploding fireworks that hopped about in an erratic way. Accidents due to fireworks were not uncommon. The author was one of those who had the embarrassment of going to school the following day with his fingers in a bandage, having stupidly picked up a rocket he thought had failed – only for it then to ignite!

After these two excitements came the long dark weeks waiting for Christmas. While Roman Catholics had always celebrated Christmas as a religious festival, for centuries following the Scottish Parliament's law in 1640 making 'Yule vacations' illegal, Protestant Scotland mainly frowned on marking the day. It was not until 1958 that Christmas Day became a public holiday in Scotland – and Boxing Day not until 1974. Thus, for many families in Scotland, it was not until the 1950s that celebrating Christmas started to become the festivity it is today. Yet, an article in the *Glasgow Herald* in 1884 shows that by that time, for the middle- and upper- class Protestants at least, Christmas had already started to become a significant date in the calendar of festivities, and its observance remarkably similar to today.

In Scotland, Christmas is both a modern institution and an ancient one. We know not whether John Knox

Advert for Bell's Toy Shop, No. 320, *c*.1960s.

regarded it, but our grandfathers would assuredly have ranked going to church on Christmas Day as nothing less than 'Papacy.' The change which has come over the religious world of Scotland in respect of Christmas observances is very marked. The number of services held in Presbyterian churches last evening, and which will be held to-day, has probably never been equalled in the history of the Church. The truth seems to be that the desire, smothered by generations of Puritanic severity, to commemorate both by praise and by feasting the birth of Christ has never been killed in the Scottish character. ... There is something about mince-pies quite inseparable from Christmas. Roast beef all of us eat almost every week of our lives; geese are not unknown at many times between Michaelmas and Candlemas; turkeys most of us will, in a week or two, desire never to set eyes, or forks, on again. But mince-pies are just for Christmas ...While past songs and such tell of a merry Christmas, alas, how often in this world has fact an unpleasant habit of contradicting theory. This is an age which is peculiarly addicted to analyses of all kinds and were a quantitative analysis of Christmas to be made by some expert the results might be something like this (in percentage terms): Eating 25.00%, Drinking 25.00%, Jollity 0.20%, charity 0.50%, religion 0.10%, unpaid bills 39.00%, headache 9.60%, indigestion 9.60% and traces of irritation.

Already by that time many sent Christmas cards, although usually these were not posted until Christmas Eve, and in 1894 it was reported that the sending of Christmas parcels had increased: 'The establishment of a temporary sorting office in Byres Road has

Bell's Toy Shop, No. 320, 1929.

been of great facility in the delivery in the Hillhead and Partick districts.'

For children Christmas has long been synonymous with toys, and Catherine Bell's shop at No. 320, which opened around 1880, offered many temptations:

> What a vista opened before us when we entered that stationer's-cum-fancy goods-cum-toy-shop door! There was simply nothing that you could want that was not to be had there. On the left-hand side was a three-tier stand with the more expensive toys, tea-sets, dolls, trains, all tastefully set out, and on the floor such super toys as rocking-horses and tricycles. But at the far end of the shop, tucked well out of the main thoroughfare, were the penny and twopenny and threepenny shelves; and thither we found our way and spent the best part of every Saturday morning. How patient a being must the proprietor be of a shop that sells goods to children. It took us hours of gazing and touching and testing to make up our minds about something that cost, at the very most, threepence. And many a time have we spent a smaller sum, and then, after going outside, have talked it all over again and finally taken our purchase back to be exchanged!'

Partridge's Childrens Annual, c.1920

The Beano Book, 1942

at 175 Great George Street opened in the 1980s and on one occasion advertised: 'New stock in! Starlight projectors, chatter teeth, marbles, racing gliders, rainbow springs, super magnets, glow in the dark stars, magic sets, Jack straws, tiddly winks, binoculars and more!' When Claire Kilmurry opened the shop she asked a young artist, Vin Deighan to design the shop's logo. He later, under his alias, Frank Quitely, gained international fame, illustrating comics such as Batman and Superman. Kilmurry always fought against gender stereotyping of toys so she steered away from 'pinks and blues'. As she said, 'Why shouldn't girls play with tools and hammers?' When she closed the shop in 2017, she explained it was due to, 'a perfect storm of factors' including the loss of the BBC on Queen Margaret Drive, the closure of the Western Infirmary and Sick Children's Hospital at Yorkhill.' The shop's closure was much mourned, as even those who did not shop there enjoyed its enticing seasonal window displays.

A common Christmas present for many children is a children's annual, and in the early 1900s that

The shop traded for decades and became known locally as Bell's Toys. Matthew Brown opened another toy shop at No. 13 in 1945 and ran it until his retirement in 1978. He advertised: 'Hornby high speed train set £29.75 for £23.95; Tank Battle £6.50 now £4.75; Evil Knievel stunt cycle £10.85 now £8.85; Sindy Doll with horse £7.99 now £6.50.' For budding magicians in the 1950s Joel Sneader's shop at No.117 offered: 'Conjurors marked cards, Double Head Penny, £1 Note Making machine and numerous other mystifying tricks. Explosives (harmless) for cigarettes, etc. Card tricks from 6d. All kinds of novelties.' Sentry Box Toys

Sentry Box Toys, No. 175 Great George Street, c.1990.

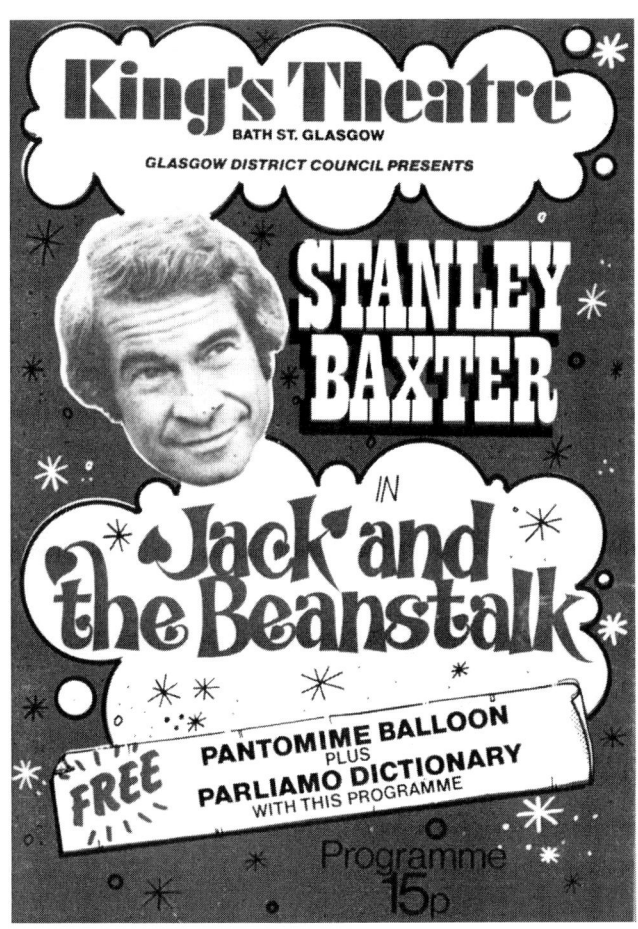

Poster for *Jack and the Beanstalk* at King's Theatre, starring Stanley Baxter, 1976.

Cinderella 2, Christmas pantomime at A Play, A Pie, and A Pint, 2021.   *A Play, A Pie, and A Pint*

might have been *Partridge's Children's Annual* for daughters and *The Boy's Own Annual* for sons, but from the 1940s on most Byres Road children asked Santa for *The Beano* or *Bunty* annuals. While the number and scale of presents children received depended on their parents' economic situation, almost all would pin up a sock or stocking before going to bed in the certain anticipation that it would be filled with goodies when they awoke, and always with the traditional tangerine at the bottom.

From 1924 until 1985 for many living in and around Byres Road a visit to the Kelvin Hall Circus and Funfair was essential:

> While the teenagers headed for the waltzers, chairoplanes and sticky wall, younger siblings could try to win a goldfish by hooking a plastic duck or throwing a ping-pong ball into a jam-jar. … Today's SECC carnival with its hi-tech, thrill rides and computer-generated fun may now be one of the biggest indoor events of its kind in Europe, but memories of the sounds, tastes and animal smells of the old Kelvin Hall Circus and Carnival can still make some Glaswegians go misty eyed.

Outings to the theatre have always thrilled children at Christmas time, although it was as much the parents who enjoyed the famed Kings Theatre ones starring local boy, Stanley Baxter as the raucous ugly sister, Big Natalie. On occasion, festive outings do not go as planned. In the late 1930s, a young Lois de Banzie, who was brought up in Hillhead, and later became a successful theatre and film actress in America, was taken to a Glasgow production of *Peter Pan*. To save the dying Tinkerbell the children were encouraged to yell out, 'I believe in fairies', but

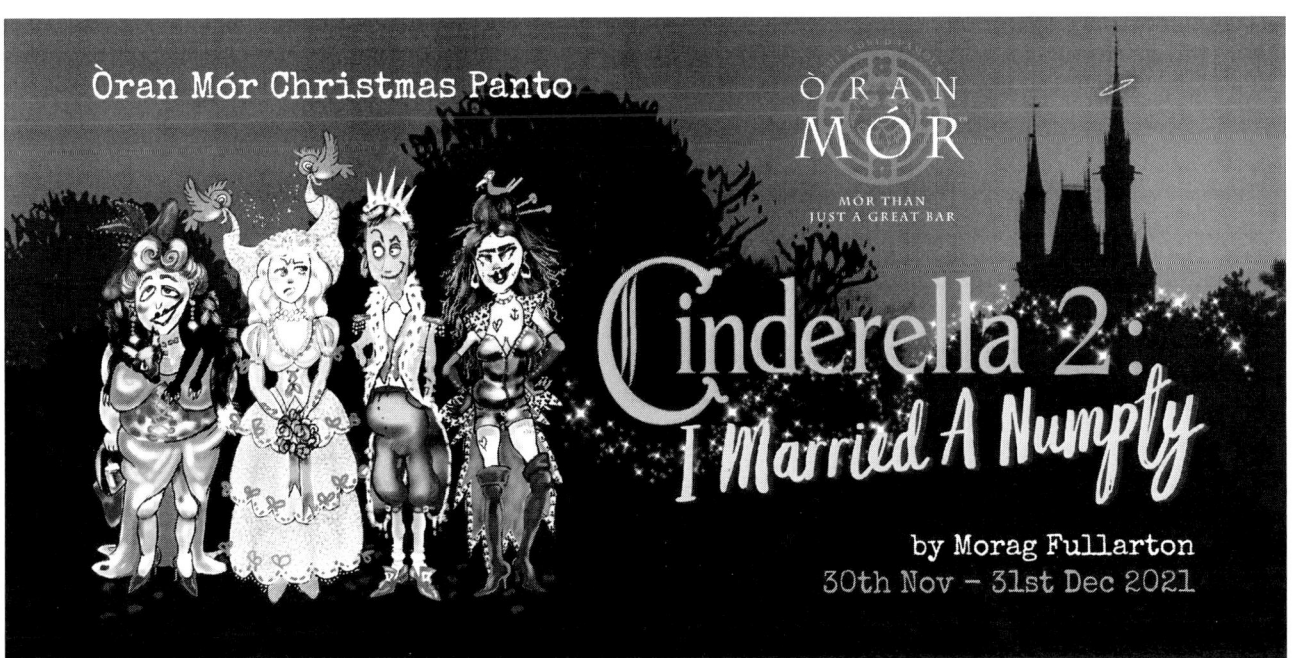

Lois was unimpressed and, in a very loud voice, instead bellowed, 'Baloney!' Much better behaved are those attending the popular annual pantomimes mounted by A Play, A Pie and A Pint at Òran Mór, although the great majority of the 'children' have balding heads or grey hair.

Both Christmas and Hogmanay are festive times for adults today, but in the past Hogmanay was the main celebration. Women – and perhaps a few superstitious bachelors – spent part of the 31st cleaning the house, clearing the old ashes from the fire and setting a new one. As midnight approached many Byres Road residents would open their windows to listen out for the Clydeside ships' horns celebrating the arrival of the New Year, before setting off First Footing or welcoming their first guest – preferably a tall, dark man bearing gifts: a piece of coal or a piece of shortbread. In exchange the visitor would be given a dram, although the partaking of drink by most adults in celebration was not unknown! When TV sets became common, the traditional television New Year's programme formed a focal point, particularly *The White Heather Club* presented by Andy Stewart. Hogmanay has always brought out partygoers into Byres Road, although in the past these would have been few compared with the 3,000 that now attend the annual Ashton Lane party:

> Revellers at the Ashton Lane Hogmanay Street Party will be able to spend the night under the Lane's twinkling canopy of fairy lights and enjoy live entertainment, DJs, street performers and hopping around their favourite bars and restaurants during the event.

The White Heather Club cast singing *Haste ye Back*, 1960s.
BBC Scotland

One wonders if below those revellers' there still is an equivalent to James Kelly who was featured in the *Evening Times* in 1979:

> When the bells chime and the corks pop to welcome in the New Year, James Kelly of 128 Byres Road will be on his own, away from the crowds, A few yards above his head will be happy gatherings with music and laughter. But for James, only silence.

James volunteered each Hogmanay to patrol the underground system as even on that special night someone was required to check the tunnels when the trains had finished running. Being a bachelor James regularly volunteered: 'I'll join the nightshift workers who come on at 3am and celebrate then.'

Ashton Lane Hogmanay Party, 2022.

Chapter Twenty

In Sickness and in Health

In the past, Glasgow had a higher that average percentage of people suffering from bronchitis, pneumonia, and pleurisy, but as these respiratory diseases tended to be linked to poor working conditions and relatively few Byres Road residents worked in hazardous industries, the health of Byres Road residents generally was good. The risk of disease was lower because most flats and closes in the road were kept clean, although there were reported instances of unsanitary conditions in a few of the two room flats at the Partick end. In the 1870s the burgh medical officer reported that Hillhead had a lower death rate as a percentage of the population than average, although in Partick and Hillhead, 'the deaths of children under five years were 273, 45% of all deaths in the localities'. However, as the medical officer explained, the high rate of infant mortality was skewed for the two burghs, 'as Partick has nearly the highest birth-rate of any populous place in Scotland.'

The frequent death of infants was, in part, the reason for many couples in past times having larger families. Large families took their toll on wives, many of whom experienced a decade or more in which their physical and emotional energy was absorbed by child-rearing. Even by the 1950s, half of all births took place in the home, usually attended by a midwife. In 1890 there were two midwives living just off Byres Road: Mrs Anderson at No. 16 Great George Street and Mrs Donald at 23 Dowanhill Street. Both also advertised as a 'ladies nurse' and in that role would have supported a mother for a week or so after birth, taking care of household chores and looking after any other children. Midwives were also valued by women in the community as they could be consulted on reproduction and other confidential matters relating to the female body. In earlier times pregnancy was a period of considerable vulnerability. Few were the pregnant women who did not live with fear of injury during the delivery or of dying in childbirth. In 1920, Agnes, the wife of Henry Tully, a Byres Road ironmonger, died while giving birth in their lodgings at 43 Lawrence Street from puerperal fever, a highly contagious disease that affected women within the first three days after childbirth.

For many decades hospitals concentrated on surgical rather than medical cases, so the majority who were sick had to be cared for at home. For those who could afford it, private nurses, were available. Annie and Christina Grieg who lived at No. 125, advertised as private nurses, and in 1890 Miss John established the Hillhead Nursing Institution at 46 Sardinia Terrace. In 1895, one of the Institution's nurses, Annie Deane, was living temporarily at No. 52 Sardinia Terrace, the house of Alexander Wellwood Rattray, a well-regarded landscape artist, who had employed her to care for his wife, Jemima Rattray. Sometime after the employment ended, Deane was called as a witness in a 'sensational divorce case' in which Alexander sued Jemima for divorce on the grounds of adultery with a stockbroker, Robert Anderson. Deane told the court, 'Mr Anderson called and Mrs Rattray asked me to go to the baker for some cakes, and not to hurry back. I was away about a quarter of an hour. There were no servants in the house and I had no key. When I rang the door was opened by Mr Anderson. He looked very flushed.' The divorce was granted.

However, most ill people were cared for by relations and most deaths took place in the home. In cases of ageing parents who needed on going care it often was a single female relative who had to give up work to take on the responsibility. In the late 1930s a government enquiry expressed concern about the number of women left in poverty after caring for elderly relatives. When George Burrell became infirm, he moved to live with his son,

Elizabeth Clark Neil worked at the Hillhead Nursing Institution, 46 Sardinia Terrace, around 1908 and later served with the Territorial Force Nursing Service in Salonika during the First World War.

Scottish Women's Hospitals / Surgeons Hall

In 1892 the Glasgow and West of Scotland Co-operation of Trained Nurses was established to help trained nurses, with contacts and opportunities for work in the Glasgow area so they could easily find employment. The following year they acquired the house at 18 Sardinia Terrace which served as their headquarters and provided accommodation for members that needed it.
Lewis Hutton collection

Alexander who lived at No. 1 Dunkeld Place, on the corner of Byres Road and the south side of University Avenue (now demolished). Alexander was wealthy enough to employ a servant to help look after his father George who died from a stroke at 1am on 27 August 1881, a year or so after moving there. George had begun life as a clerk, but later established the shipping and forwarding agent firm, Burrell & Son. Two of his sons joined the firm and when George retired took over the running of the business. His grandson, William, joined the firm in 1875 and over the following decades it grew to become one of Britain's largest cargo shipping companies. The firm's vast profits enabled William to amass his outstanding art collection that forms Glasgow's Burrell Collection.

On occasion, those who took in lodgers had to deal with a boarder's death as was the case in 1923:

Joseph Densdale (45), a film photographer, who lodged at 266 Byres Road was found unconscious in his bed by his landlady, Mrs MacColl, yesterday morning. The doctor who was called ordered his removal to the Western Infirmary, where Dr Wilson found him to be suffering from poisoning, possibly caused by opium. Densdale died a few hours after being admitted to the infirmary. When spoken to by his landlady on Sunday night he appeared to be all right, and asked to be roused at nine, o'clock yesterday morning.

In recent times deaths have more commonly taken place in hospitals, hospices and nursing homes: 'Peacefully at Huntershill Nursing Home on 10 March 1984, Matthew Brown (retired toy retailer, Byres Road)'. Brown's toy shop, and his book lending library, called the Embassy Library, was at No.13 from 1945 to 1978.

While the better-off bought life assurance policies and others paid into Friendly Societies which provided some death benefit, the unexpected death of a husband resulted in financial hardship for many widows, especially those with young children. It was not until the late 1920s that all widows received a state pension, and allowances for children under the age of fourteen, although an earlier pension and dependents' allowance had been introduced for those who had lost their husbands in the First World War. The potential hardship faced by one widow in 1903 was averted by extraordinary good fortune. In July that year, a train carrying holidaymakers back to Glasgow from the Isle of Man, crashed into the steel buffers at the end of the platform at St Enoch's Railway Station and fifteen people died. One was

Pearson's Weekly, 20 August 1903.

The Western Infirmary opened next to the University in November 1874, and within two days the 150 beds in the two surgical and two medical wards were full. The capacity was increased to 350 in 1881 and 630 in 1906. At that time hospitals were financed by charitable donations and annual subscriptions, mostly from factories, shipyards and warehouses that deducted a small amount from employees' wages to pay for access to the hospital's services. Until much later the hospital concentrated on surgical rather than medical cases, and apart from those admitted due to an accident, a patient would only be admitted if recommended by a subscriber or if their illness was of interest for medical teaching.

Edward Darroch who lived at No. 97 Byres Road. He was forty-two-years old and left a widow and infant. It transpired that he was a regular reader of *Pearson's Weekly* that included a weekly coupon offering £2,000 insurance for anyone killed in a train accident who was carrying a copy of the current issue and had signed a form on the back page. Remarkably, Darroch had with him the current issue of the magazine and had signed the claim section, and so *Pearson's Weekly* paid out £2,000 (at least £250,000 today). The following week the magazine carried a large page spread on the payout: 'The sum of £2,000 has never before been paid by any weekly publication in the world in respect of a railway or other accident, and perhaps the least sad part of this terrible calamity is the fact that Mrs. Darroch and her child are placed beyond any risk of poverty.'

In March 1918 the flu pandemic – which probably originated in America but was known as Spanish Flu because the pandemic was being reported in Spain, whereas elsewhere the information was being suppressed – reached Britain, and it is thought it arrived first in Glasgow via a ship. It was the second wave from September to November that was the most serious and it is estimated that around one million Scots contracted the flu and 70,000 died, and died swiftly. Previously healthy people could become ill on the way to work and be dead by nightfall. One of the flu's victims was fifteen-year-old Jenny Maclean who died at No. 163. Her father was a teacher, and he and his wife had already experienced tragic loss as Jenny's funeral notice stated that she was their 'only surviving child'. In 2020, the Coronavirus pandemic struck, and on this occasion the majority who died were older people. One was Margaret Kerrigan who had worked as the bar manager in the Curlers pub in the 1960s, and there met and married one of the pub's regulars. Joe and Margaret, who both died in 2020, were married for fifty years.

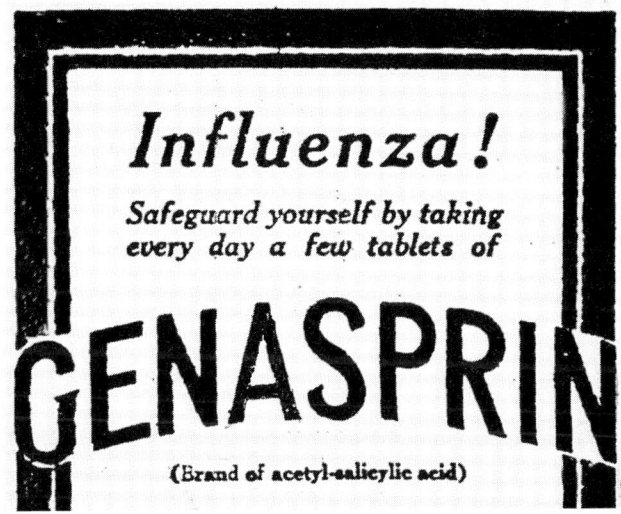

Advert for Genaspirin during the Spanish Flu epidemic, 1918.

'Be kind poster' during Covid pandemic in Byres Road, 2021.

Western Infirmary in the 1880s.   *Lewis Hutton collection*

Western Infirmary Outdoor Dispensary, Church Street, 2003.
Author

In 1877 Hillhead experienced a significant typhoid epidemic in which eleven people died, including five Glasgow University students. A report by Dr James Russell, the medical officer for Glasgow, into the outbreak concluded that the cause was contaminated milk, and although this had been known for some time to be a frequent factor, it took his report to stir the government into introducing The Contagious Diseases (Animals) Act 1878, which improved the inspection of dairy farms and shops. The Western Infirmary did not deal with contagious diseases, so in the late 1870s the Burghs of Hillhead, Partick and Maryhill jointly built The Knightswood Fever Hospital in Jordanhill where patients with such diseases as measles, whooping cough, diphtheria and smallpox were cared for. It had two wards for the different fevers and a pavilion, quite separate from the others, for cases of smallpox, and could accommodate 100 patients. In 1912 the hospital was taken over by Glasgow Corporation and expanded.

Until the National Insurance Act of 1911 all workers not covered by a union medical scheme or equivalent had to pay for health care, and even then the 1911 Act excluded wives and children, or anyone not in work. This meant that there was significant disparity in health care until the introduction of the National Health Service after the Second World War. The better-off residents of Byres Road would have had a family doctor while those with little money would have called a doctor only in extreme cases of illness. As doctors survived on their fees, their priority was their better-off clients and the level of care they provided was often proportional to the status of their patent. The working class had little choice but to accept pain and discomfort as part of life to be endured with stoicism.

For many, the primary source of medical help was the local druggist, who offered advice and was literate in the kinds of drugs needed to treat minor ailments. The Pharmacy Acts of 1852 and 1868 helped create uniform standards, and druggists and chemists (shops that sell items other than medicines) generally were well-regarded professionals and had status within the community. In 1877 William Currie, 'family and dispensing chemist', opened at No. 223. He was secretary of the Edinburgh District Chemists' Trade Association: 'Photographs of the last picnic group of the Association taken at Tarbet may be had for 1s 3d from Mr W. L. Currie.' In the same year that Currie opened his shop, Charles Flint opened his at No. 211: 'Exantaline, the positive cure for corns and warts in a few days. Only from Charles B, Flint, Hillhead, Glasgow. Price 1s'. In 1886 Flint sold the business to John Miller who lived in Queen Margaret Drive, and had three other chemist shops in Glasgow. In 1984 the shop became a branch of Scotts Pharmacies. In 1880 the regulations changed to allow companies as well as individuals to operate pharmacy businesses and Francis Spite's company, at that time a grocery business based in St. Enoch Square, began to trade in medications:

> Spite's premises in St. Enoch Square are known as the 'Economic Supply Store' and comprise a stately and strikingly handsome block of six ample floors. The stock of groceries, provisions, tea, coffee, and other specialities on sale is one of the most select and valuable in the city. The drug department was added in 1887 and under its present conditions the company are prepared to supply genuine drugs and chemicals, patent medicines and proprietary articles of the best

reputation, invalids' specialities and infants' foods, perfumery, fancy soap, toilet requisites, homoeopathic medicines, aerated and mineral waters, ships', yachts' and family medicine chests, trusses, air and water beds and all kinds of surgical appliances. The company

Advert for Ivy Leaf Corn Cure, Spite & Co., 1905.
Wellcome Collection

Looking towards Partick past Boots the Chemists shop at No. 277.

Guthrie Hutton

issues a bulky catalogue, which is not only a complete handbook and cash price-list to a stock of exceptional magnitude, but also possesses a special value as a practical medical adviser, being replete with valuable and effective information.

The company opened four chemists shops in Glasgow, including at No. 276 in 1897. It moved to Nos. 333/335 in the 1920s and traded through to the late 1930s.

Askit powder was a medication that was stocked in cafes, sweet shops and even from ice cream vans, and often displayed next to bottles of Barr's Irn-Bru, as the combination was widely regarded by Glaswegians as a cure for a nasty hang over, a belief encouraged by Askit's simple and effective TV advertising campaign, 'Askit Fights the Miseries'. In the early 1900s a Glasgow-based apothecary, Adam Laidlaw, began to sell 'Mr Laidlaw's Powders', a mix of aspirin, phenacetin and caffeine. It was rebranded in 1920 and the new name allegedly derived from Mrs Laidlaw overhearing two girls who had entered the shop saying, 'If it's the lady chemist I'll ask it – if it is the man chemist you ask it'. Mrs Laidlaw suggested to her husband that 'Ask for Askit' would be a catchy logo. By the 1960s the packets of powder were being produced in millions and sold across most of the British Commonwealth. However, questions began to be raised about its negative health effects and these eventually led to the product being discontinued in 2012.

The first dentist in Byres Road was Frederick Parson, who set up his surgery at No. 186 in 1894. In 1899 he sued Miss Colquhoun for £9.16s, claiming she had not paid for a set of false teeth he had supplied. In her defence Miss Colquhoun alleged

Advert for Askit in Ygorra RAG week magazine, 1934.

the teeth did not fit, a claim supported by another Glasgow dentist whom she called in her defence. He told the court: 'I have seen the teeth in the mouth and out of the mouth and my opinion is that they have been bungled, and that the defect is not one which could easily be repaired.' Parson lost the case and the widespread newspaper reporting can hardly have helped his practice. In 1918, the more successful Robert Dodds opened his dentist's surgery at No. 175 and in the 1930s took on Henry McCall as a partner. Henry served in the dental branch of the Royal Air Force during the Second World War and returned to Byres Road to run the practice. It continues today as the Byres Road Dental Practice.

There was a time when wearing spectacles was regarded by many as a necessary evil, and vain individuals would prefer to squint rather than succumb. For many such self-conscious individuals, the arrival of contact lenses in the early 1960s was a boon, and John McElvanney advertised these when he opened his opticians at No.

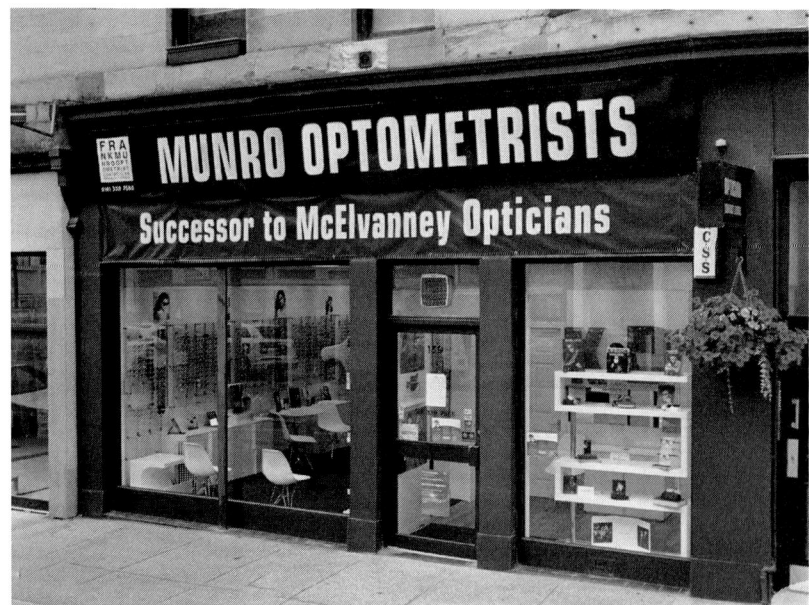

Munro Optometrists, Nos. 137-139.

139 in 1963. The shop is now one of six branches of Munro Optometrists. In recent times, to try to break down resistance to wearing glasses, spectacles began to be marketed as 'eyewear'. Marc de Lange, founder of the Dutch chain Ace & Tate that recently opened at No. 221, proposed that, 'glasses should be thought of as a lifestyle accessory'.

Sports, such as swimming in the Western Baths, helped many people remain healthy, while others have kept fit by participating in team games or running. In the 1980s, Jim Spalding opened a specialist sports shoe shop, Runsport, in Ruthven Lane, but advised: 'Spending £200 on expensive running shoes won't make bad feet run well'. An observation with which some of the participants in the first Glasgow Marathon run in 1983 might have agreed. A guide to that marathon route counselled:

> Three miles gone and there is a welcome break as the route plunges downhill to Byres Road. You can snatch a brief rest by leaning forward and letting your body weight carry you down. You will need all the rest you can get because the next three miles through the West End and Maryhill is undulating and uphill.

Glasgow Marathon runners in Byres Road, 1983.
Courtesy of Stuart McKenna

For many women organised sport has never appealed and some have turned to other ways of keeping fit. In 1947 it was announced: 'The Women's League of Health and Beauty classes resume in the Hillhead Burgh Hall on Thursday 4 September.' Founded by Mollie Bagot Stack in 1930, the Women's League of Health & Beauty was the first, and most significant, mass keep-fit system, with classes that included dance, callisthenics and rhythmical exercise to music. By 1937 it had 166,000 members and regular classes in Hillhead Burgh Hall were held through to the 1960s. At the same time that Spalding's shop in Ruthven Lane was fitting out runners, Butterfly, a shop also based in the lane, offered, 'all the attire you will need for aerobics or dance. Look good while keeping fit in a gorgeous leotard. 'While some of those attending zumba, ballet, street dance and other classes offered by Dance Glasgow at its studios in Ruthven Lane since 2010 might not feel a leotard flattering, Dance Glasgow makes clear that

Women's League of Health & Beauty badge, 1930

Dance Glasgow, Ruthven Lane.

Courtesy of Dance Glasgow

Advert for Joel Sneader's Sun Lamps.

its classes are, 'accessible to everyone, irrelevant of their age, body shape or ability.'

Many have sought out alternative health therapies. Joel Sneader, who first had a shop at No. 117 selling magic tricks, began to advertise, 'chiropody knives, nippers and Sun Ray Pads to relieve pain'. He then closed the shop to focus on offering alternative health treatments. He first promoted himself as the Principal of the Royal College of Massage, Queens Drive, although this college appears to have been of his own invention. In the 1960s he advertised as a hypnotist who could help overcome, 'blushing, stammer, lack of confidence, etc'. One person recalled his adverts on the Glasgow Underground: 'He had a quarto ad at each of the 15 stations on the circle. What was different, was he changed his middle initial – it was Joel A. Sneader at St Enoch, Joel B. Sneader at Bridge Street and so on. I assume if customers saw his advert, he'd enquire which name so he could gauge which stations worked best!' Sneader claimed to be able to help people give up

cigarettes and Cliff Hanley, in an article about hypnotism in his regular column in the *Evening Times*, mentioned Sneader's skill:

> I had a friend called Eddie Campbell who was a sub-editor and tamed lions as a hobby, so I took him along to Joel to be hypnotised became he seemed the least likely candidate for mind-bending. Actually, he went into a trance in ten seconds, and never smoked since.

Today, residents in Byres Road have a range of options for keeping healthy, from gymnasiums to the Western Baths, and the significance of health and wellbeing is now enshrined in the Clarice Pears building, opened by Glasgow University on the corner of University Place. Yet, just across from the new building lies temptation as the University Café continues to offers battered fish, sausage haggis and black pudding chip suppers, washed down with Irn-Bru.

University of Glasgow School of Health & Wellbeing, 90 Byres Road.

Chapter Twenty-One

Images and Words

William Ralston.

Peter Ralston, who trained as a pattern designer for calico printers in Glasgow, set up as a portrait photographer in Argyle Street in 1856, but as the medium was still in its infancy and people still wary, his business struggled. His eldest son, William, left school aged twelve to work in the studio, but his health was poor and he was sent to Australia as it was thought the climate would be beneficial. By the time he returned his father's business was beginning to find success and William joined the business again. William's younger brother, John, became an artist and gained recognition as an illustrator: his work was praised by Vincent Van Gogh. In 1879 Ralston opened a second studio at No. 311 Byres Road, managed by William, and the family moved to live at No. 2 Kersland Street. The mainstay of the studios' photographic business was portraits. William was keen to emulate his artist brother and while working in the family business, produced designs for book-covers and humorous illustrations. These were commercially successful, appearing in London magazines, such as *Punch*. The most enduring of his works is his illustrations for the 1886 children's book, *Tippoo: A Tale of a Tiger* that he created with the writer, C. W. Cole.

In 1905 the Ralstons sold the Byres Road studio to John and William Weir, who traded as the Weir Brothers or Weir Studios, although sometimes their photographic prints carry just John Weir's name. The Weirs previously had a photographic studio in Dalmarnock Road. In the firm's early portrait photos, the sitters appear in their best apparel and often are set amid fittings, such as a chair or table, as was the convention of the day. The firm traded in Byres Road until the late 1950s. William was a skilled photographer. He often acted as a judge at photographic competitions, was elected a fellow of the Royal Photographic Society and president of the Partick Camera Club, and exhibited his work in exhibitions. His photo of Kilchurn Castle is in the collection of the National Galleries Scotland. In 1954, six child portraits by the Weir Studios were accepted in a national competition organised by the Institute of British Photographers to find, 'the most charming child in Britain'. Although the Weirs had more entries accepted than any other Scottish studio, sadly none of the Glasgow children were deemed the 'most charming,'

While at Hyndland School in the late 1970s, Alan Dimmick co-founded the school's first photographic society and went on to study photography at Glasgow College of Building and Printing. In 1984, when he was beginning to develop his freelance photographic career, he lived at No. 2 Byres Road. He was a founding member of Glasgow Photography Group and exhibited at their inaugural exhibition in Hillhead Library in 1988. Since the mid-1990s Dimmick has documented the lively

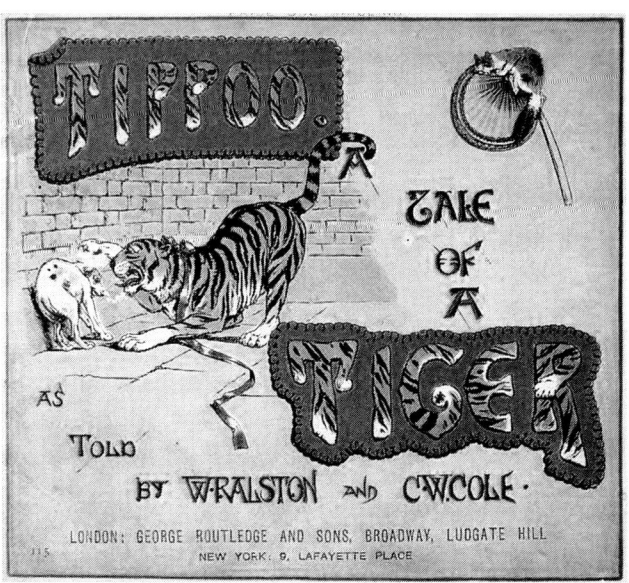

Tippoo, Tale of a Tiger by William Cole, illustrated by William Ralston, published 1886 .

Ralston & Sons, Cabinet
Portrait *c.*1890

James Walker & Charlie Ramsay, photographed by Weir
Studios, *c.*1910.

Stephen Pastel, Bearsden, photo by Alan Dimmick, 1982.
Courtesy of ©Alan Dimmick

Byres of Partick by David Young Cameron 1894.
Boston Library

Hervert Whone working on his painting, *Tram and Figures in rain, Byres Road*, 1960

contemporary art scene of Glasgow, capturing many of the events that have shaped a significant period in Scottish culture. In 2022, an outdoor exhibition of his work was displayed on poster sites across Glasgow, including Byres Road.

David Young Cameron grew up in Sardinia Terrace in Cecil Street and after attending Glasgow Academy, studied art at both Glasgow and Edinburgh Art Schools in the 1880s. He became an internationally regarded etcher and served as the King's Painter and Limner in Scotland from 1933. Working around the same time was Muirhead Bone, although he had a tougher route to artistic success. Born in Peel Street, Partick he attended the local board school and aged fourteen left to take up an apprenticeship as a painter of porcelain. Although he did not attend Glasgow School of Art, he took evening classes there, and he too became a highly regarded etcher, and watercolourist. He is best known for depictions of industrial and architectural subjects, and for his work as a war artist in both the First and Second World Wars. Both he and Cameron received knighthoods. Herbert Whone, who was born in West Yorkshire, began his art career by taking photographs, but then trained as a violinist, and in the 1950s was deputy leader of the Scottish National Orchestra. During that time he lived in Partick and inspired by Glasgow's changing cityscape produced many notable paintings, particularly of shipbuilding and trams. In 2021 his work, *Tram & Figures in Rain, Byres Road* sold for £18,000.

The artist, and writer, most closely linked to Byres Road is Alasdair Gray, who lived in Kersland Street for much of his life. In Gray's major novel, *Lanark*, published in 1981, the character Duncan Thaw says: 'Imaginatively Glasgow exists as a music-hall song and a few bad novels. That's all we've given to the world outside. It's all we've given to ourselves.' If that was once true, it was radically changed by Gray who *The Guardian's* obituary termed, 'the father figure of the renaissance in Scottish literature and art which began in the penultimate decade of the 20th century.' Gray, who died in 2019, was born in 1934 in the east end of Glasgow and studied at the

Detail of Hillhead Underground Station mural by Alasdair Gray, created 2012.
By permission of Alasdair Gray estate

mural-making department at the Glasgow School of Art in the 1950s. In later life, in spite of gaining an international reputation as an author, illustrator and artist, he often wryly referred to himself as 'an increasingly fat Glasgow pedestrian'. However, the novelist Will Self called him 'a little grey deity.'

Four of the area's most notable buildings contain remarkable murals by Gray, created in collaboration with the artist Nichol Wheatley and others. The first was commissioned in 1979 by the then owner of The Ubiquitous Chip restaurant in Ashton Lane, Ronnie Clydesdale. Gray created artworks in the main restaurant and back staircase, mostly being paid in food and drink, and the murals feature many of The Chip's regulars at the time, including Clydesdale. It was there in the restaurant's bar that Gray worked on the final edits of *Lanark*. When Colin Beattie bought Kelvinside Church in 2002 to create the entertainment centre Òran Mór he commissioned Gray to create a number of artworks to complement the church's stylish interior, and in 2010 Strathclyde Partnership commissioned murals from Gray for the revamped Hillhead Underground station. Gray created a large tiled mural depicting a panoramic view of Hillhead and a number of its denizens. It contains the adage: 'Do not let daily to-ing and fro-ing, to earn what we need to keep going, prevent what you once felt when wee, hopeful and free.' At its unveiling in 2012, Gray said: 'Such a mural is in a tradition of civic art that once flourished in several Italian city states, between the 14th and 16th centuries, where public buildings were decorated

with views of the city.' Side panels in Gray's quirky mischievous style illustrate Lucky Dogs, Hard Workers, Hopeful Children, Wise Old Owls, Ardent Lovers and more. The fourth of his artworks is in the Western Baths, and was created by Gray while working there as artist in residence between 2011 and 2013. The mosaic, seven feet by seven, is on the theme of 'Refresh Mind, Refresh Body, Refresh Land and Refresh Love', and includes images of swimmers, some using the pool's rings and trapeze equipment.

In the days before public libraries, and at a time when books were expensive to buy, book lovers headed for one of the stationers that operated small subscription libraries. There patrons could borrow books and periodicals for a fee. At Alexander Mackenzie's West End Library at Nos. 205/207, which opened in 1886, borrowers could either pay an annual subscription or hire a book for 2d a week, but, for whatever reason, his business closed within a few years. From 1908 until 1920 Agnes Gentles had a lending library in the back of her stationers shop at No. 313, though from a description of it the library may not have been widely patronised: 'In the back of the shop was a large cavernous recess which housed the remains of what had been sometime in Britain's historic past a lending library but had little current appeal.' For many years Brysons at No. 178 also offered a library service that included periodicals: 'For magazines such as The Tatler and Strand customers would pay a few coppers to read them.' The Grosvenor Book Club opened at No. 182 in 1943 and was successful as it stocked the latest titles, although the newest books cost double to rent and

Advert for West End Library, Nos. 205/207, 1892.

Byres Road and Hillhead Parish Church Byres Road by Sir Muirhead Bone, from his book, *Glasgow; Fifty Drawings*, 1911

Detail of Hillhead Underground Station mural by Alasdair Gray, created 2012.

By permission of Alasdair Gray estate

Alasdair Gray in Dowanside Lane, photo by Alan Dimmick, 1985.
Courtesy of ©Alan Dimmick

Interior of Hillhead Library, 1979. *Glasgow Library Service*

could only be hired for a shorter period. 'In the early 1960s I'd be sent to collect the latest romance by Georgette Heyer for my mother, and seek out a Denis Wheatley thriller for myself.'

Private lending libraries in the area did good business as Hillhead lacked a public library, a deficiency that for years was a bone of contention. In 1960 there was a proposal that the then unused Hillhead Burgh Hall should be converted into a local library and one *Glasgow Herald* correspondent applauded the proposal:

> The idea of establishing a public library in Hillhead Burgh Hall would be welcome and long overdue. As children at the beginning of the century we willingly tramped to and from the Woodside Library when asked by our parents. Now, in the eventide of life, the perilous journey thither and back demands from us, each fortnight, no little courage.

A Hillhead library had been planned in 1901 but never materialised. That year the Dunfermline-born American philanthropist Andrew Carnegie, who funded over 2,000 free public libraries around the world, gave Glasgow £10,000 to build a number of neighbourhood libraries. The Glasgow Libraries'

Committee decided the money should fund, 'five first grade, six second-grade, three third-grade libraries, and three reading-rooms throughout the city.' To finance the running costs and buying of books, the Corporation imposed an extra halfpenny in the pound on the rates, one-half payable by owners and one half by tenants. Partick, still an independent burgh, did not take up the offer of a library as it was unwilling to increase its rates. Hillhead was scheduled to have a third-grade library but as a suitable site could not be found it never materialised.

In 1962 it was announced that instead of converting Hillhead Burgh Hall into a library, the building would be demolished and a new library built on the site. However, there was a lengthy delay, apparently caused by problems in relocating the Cleansing Department that was part of the Burgh Hall site, and it was not until 1975 that Hillhead Library opened, but it was worth the wait. Designed by Rogerson and Spence and costing £450,000, it was at the time the largest branch library built after the Second World War in Scotland, and the first Glasgow library to have, 'listening points for records and tapes', and air-conditioning. The library was opened by Richard Buchanan, MP, Honorary President of the Scottish Library Association:

> In carefully chosen words Mr Buchanan eloquently illuminated for us all his concept of what the systematic storing of books in accessible places had contributed to the intellectual and moral progress of mankind. Libraries, he stressed, as he lightly covered the ground between Rome and Hillhead, banked the richness of the human mind throughout the ages, and they were to be accounted high among earth's treasuries.

Hillhead Library certainly was thought so by residents, as it immediately became the busiest branch library in the city, and has remained so ever since. Since its opening, Hillhead Library regularly has run talks and events to promote writers. The successful Byres Road Book Festival is run by the library in partnership with Waterstones, the Oxfam bookshop and the Byres Road & Lanes Business Improvement District. In 1986 the library mounted an exhibition called 'Writers Writing' that included a selection of manuscripts, press cuttings, letters and photographs from over thirty Scottish writers, the majority of whom lived within walking distance of the library.

The Grant Educational Company, a publisher and owner of 'Glasgow's premiere bookshop', which had been in Union Street since the 1900s, opened a branch at No. 100 in 1961. Ten years later the Byres Road shop had to relocate as the property was scheduled for demolition – although that never happened – and it moved into what had been a grocery shop at No. 6 Havelock Street, almost directly across the road from its previous site. Its manager said of the new premises: 'The shop caters for family needs, with the emphasis on weekend reading and children's books.' The scheduled demolition that never happened also forced Daniel Lee to close his antiquarian bookshop at No. 162 in 1966. Unfortunately, he was unable to find alternative premises and the business closed. John Smith & Son, whose main bookshop was in St Vincent Street, opened a branch at No. 254 in the 1980s next to the underground station. The firm was founded in 1751 and alongside books, sold snuff and coffee, and was much patronised by Glasgow's tobacco lords. The closure in 2000 of the St Vincent Street shop, and the Byres Road branch, was much bemoaned as at that time the firm was the oldest bookseller in the world: 'Customers were bursting into tears amid the tall shelves. Newswires round the world flashed headlines like 'World's Oldest Bookseller Killed By Internet'. The closure of the Byres Road shop was equally lamented by many local writers; music lovers were equally distressed as upstairs was a renowned record shop.

Other bookshops have come and gone. In the late 1990s, before publishing her successful first novel, Louise Welsh bought and sold second-hand books from a stall in Ruthven Lane, and many local writers such as James Kelman and Liz Lochhead would visit

Barrett Newsagents. At this time it also had a bookshop next door, Nos. 263/267, c.1984.   *Courtesy of Stuart McKenna*

to scour her stock. Fans of comic books enjoyed rummaging through the chaos of Glasgow's first comic shop, Future Shock, run by Neil Craig at No. 89. To encourage buyers, he placed 'magic tickets' into some of his back issues that might win the buyer another fifty issues. Today, books can still be bought at Waterstones at Nos. 351-355, and second-hand ones from the Oxfam bookshop at No. 330. When it was relocated, it was opened by Bernard MacLaverty, who expressed delight for, as he explained, it would give him a new window to look in during his regular rambles down Byres Road with his dog.

Gilbert Highet and Helen McInnes, who married in 1932, are two writers with Byres Road connections who, in spite of glittering careers, are little known today. Both were born in Glasgow in 1907 and studied at Glasgow University where it is said they met. However, it is possible their romance began earlier, for in the 1920s Gilbert, whose father worked for the telegraph office of Glasgow Post Office, was living at No. 136, and Helen helped in her father's tobacconists shop at No. 280. After graduating from Glasgow University, Gilbert won a scholarship to Oxford, where he gained a double first and was regarded as one of the most brilliant classicist of the day, while Helen got a job in the Glasgow University Library. After marrying they set up home in Bowmont Gardens where their son was born. In 1932 Gilbert wrote a radio play in 'robust Scots verse' about witch-hunting in 17th century Scotland that was broadcast by the BBC. A year or so later, the family moved to Oxford when Gilbert was appointed to teach Classics at St John's College. There Helen performed as an amateur actress and Gilbert was recruited to join the British intelligence service. In 1937, although still only thirty, Gilbert was appointed to the prestigious post of Professor of Classics at Columbia University and they moved to America.

Gilbert Highet and Helen McInnes, 1970s.

Martha Holmes

Gilbert continued to work for MI6 during the war and in 1941 Helen published her first novel, *Above Suspicion* under her maiden name. The plot was influenced by her travels with Gilbert and his intelligence work, and traces the journey of a newly-wed English couple, Frances and Richard Myles, who seek out an undercover spy living in Austria. The book was an immediate best-seller and adapted into a film in 1943. Her third book, *Assignment in Brittany* published in 1942, was reputed to be required reading for Allied agents being sent to work with the French Resistance. Over forty-five-years Helen wrote twenty-one espionage thrillers, four of which were later adapted as films, and her books sold more than twenty-three-million copies in the United States alone, and were translated into twenty-two languages. Helen won the Columbia Prize for Literature. Alongside his teaching, Gilbert aspired to popularise Greek and Roman civilisations, and culture generally, through a number of books, including his renowned, *The Classical Tradition*. He also hosted his own radio programme, which was broadcast on 300 stations in the US, and from 1954 to 1978 was a judge for the

Future Shock, No. 89, c.1980s.

Book-of-the-Month Club. He died in 1978, and Helen in 1985.

While there are many instances of novelists becoming rich, for a poet to become wealthy from their verses is almost unknown. One who did was Robert Service. When he lived in Paris in the 1920s he was reputed to be the wealthiest author living in the city. Service was born in Preston in 1874 but spent his teenage years living at 18 Roxburgh Street with his parents and seven siblings. He attended Hillhead High School and, after being expelled at the age of fifteen for giving cheek to the games master, went to work as a bank clerk, as his father had done. While working in the bank he attended a writing course at Glasgow University, but left after getting into a punch-up with the tutor who derided his work. In 1895 Robert decided to abandon his banking career and go to the Yukon in Canada as he had a hankering to be a cowboy:

> Having conceived myself in this character I prepared for the part. I bought a big knife whose blade shot out by a spring, and called it my scalping knife. I also purchased an air-pistol. Putting a match-box on my bed-post I practised being quick on the draw. Walking down the room I would swing round suddenly and plug the box with a lightning-like swing from the hip.

His aspiration to become a cowboy may have been inspired by being one of the thousands who saw Buffalo Bill's Wild West Show, which visited Glasgow in 1891. The extravaganza included a re-enactment of the Battle of Little Bighorn, and shooting displays by Buffalo Bill (William Cody) and noted sharpshooter Annie Oakley. That it was this show that triggered Robert's yearning could be the reason that his parents bought him a second-hand Buffalo Bill outfit as a leaving present. Service had been writing poems from a young age and in Canada a chance meeting led to a number being published. In 1906 his first book of poems, *Songs of a Sourdough*, was published and included his best-known poem, *The Shooting of Dan McGrew*:

> A bunch of the boys were whooping it up in the Malamute saloon;
> The kid that handles the music-box was hitting a jag-time tune;
> Back of the bar, in a solo game, sat Dangerous Dan McGrew,
> And watching his luck was his light-o'-love, the lady that's known as Lou.

The book was an instant success and it, and his later writings, made him a fortune. Many derided his poems as mere doggerel but Service was unfazed: 'I have no illusions about myself. I am not fool enough to think I am a poet, but I have a knack

Robert Service with Marlene Dietrich during the filming of *The Spoilers*, 1942

of rhyme and I love to make verse. Mine is a tootling, tin-whistle music.'

Stewart Conn's poems and other writing may not have brought him riches but they have gained him a reputation as one of Scotland's outstanding wordsmiths. Although for many years he has lived in Edinburgh – in 2002 he was honoured as the city's first Makar (poet laureate) – his early life was intertwined with Byres Road. In 1930, his father, Rev Dr John Conn was appointed minister of Kelvinside Church and in 1934 married Jessie Stewart. The couple lived in the top flat at No. 5 Cranworth Street and there Stewart, born in 1936, lived until the age of five, when the family moved to Kilmarnock. He returned to study at Glasgow University and later became BBC Scotland's Head of Radio Drama based at Queen Margaret Drive. Conn recounts that living in the West End area brought him and his wife, Judy into contact with, 'a stimulating cross-section of those in the arts and sciences, medicine and academe, with many a maverick among them. Friends' flats our milieu, life was a colourful caravanserai of writers, painters and composers.'

In 1961 the Citizen's Theatre premiered Conn's first play, *Break Down*, that was influenced by life in Byres Road; the contemporary take on the Orpheus and Eurydice tale takes place in a Glasgow café and the entrance to Hades is represented by an underground station and tunnel. Byres Road features in Conn's later writing. A poem in his 1987 collection, *In the Kibble Palace* begins:

> Hand in hand, the girls glide
> Along Great Western Road.
>   Outside
> The Silver Slipper the boys wait,
> Trousers flared, jacket-pockets
> Bulging with carry-outs.   [*Period Piece*]

And in his 2001 book, *Distances*, Conn recollects early Byres Road times:

> Those were the days of yellow pea-soupers: handkerchiefs folded in protective masks, and scarcely

In the Kibble Palace, new and selected poems by Stewart Conn, 1987.   *Courtesy of Stewart Conn*

seeing a hand at arm's length in front of you. The little red underground trundled round and round like a toy train, gusty stations with their distinctive tunnel-smell which could have been bottled for exiles. There were occasional dreaded visits to the Western Infirmary with its corridors and boiler-room décor. More often, as in another poem, to the Salon Cinema:

> The supporting programme always began
> At 5.30. But they didn't open till 5.28.
> So that by the time you'd got your ticket
>   And found your seat,
> You'd missed the first four minutes. [*The Salon*]

It might've been years before we realised there were such things as opening titles.

Apart from a few, such as Robert Service, artists always have had periods when they have struggled financially, and grants and bursaries can be beneficial. In 2011, two young men, a TV writing and directing duo, were informed that they were to be awarded an £8,000 writing scholarship from the British Association of Film and Television Academy (BAFTA) at a glittering BAFTA event at STV's Glasgow studios. The host for the evening read out their names to great applause and the former cabinet office minister, Lord Gus Macdonald stood ready to make the presentation. However, there was no traditional sprint to the stage by the winners to collect their award. After a hiatus, the applause died away as a bemused Macdonald looked round at the equally mystified organisers, all wondering where the two men were. It was only later that news reached the organisers that earlier that day, the pair had been arrested in a flat off Byres Road in a drugs bust, surely providing a great line in some future television comedy: 'And tonight's winners are… Under arrest.'

In his novel, *Old Men in Love*, Alasdair Gray's surrogate, writes: 'I believe a social history of Glasgow – of Britain! – could appear in a short description of how Hillhead shops have changed in the last sixty years.' There then follows an entertaining section describing the changes he has observed in the road, few for the better in his view. As this book relates, change has been a constant in Byres Road since the opening of Partick East United Presbyterian Church two hundred years ago, and throughout that time there always have been those who have lamented things lost and others who, in Stewart Conn's words, have recalled the road's past as 'part grimy sepia and part autumnal'. However, throughout those shifting decades, one constant has been that the vast majority of people who have known the neighbourhood have held a special affection for their Byres Road.

Index